Tuckwell Press Ltd

PUBLISHERS

Please accept this review copy with our compliments. We'd be delighted to receive a copy of any subsequent review.

THE MILL HOUSE, PHANTASSIE
EAST LINTON, EAST LOTHIAN EH40 3DG, SCOTLAND
Telephone/Fax 01620 860 164

W. B. FERRAND

W.B. Ferrand
(*Illustrated London News*, May 4, 1844)

John Ward
W. B. FERRAND

'The Working Man's Friend',
1809–1889

*Edited and with an Introduction
by Norman Gash*

TUCKWELL PRESS

First published in Great Britain in 2002 by
Tuckwell Press
The Mill House
Phantassie
East Linton
East Lothian EH40 3DG
Scotland

Copyright © Tuckwell Press, 2002

ISBN 1 89841 070 4

British Library Cataloguing in Publication Data

A catalogue record for this book is available
on request from the British Library

Typeset by Hewer Text Ltd, Edinburgh
Printed and bound by Bell and Bain Ltd, Glasgow

Contents

Frontispiece. W. B. Ferrand	ii
Preface	vii
John Towers Ward (1930–1987)	ix
Introduction	1
1. The Birth of a Crusade	11
2. Debut at Westminster	24
3. The Working Man's Friend	43
4. The Breach with Conservatism	59
5. Defeats and Victories	78
6. Wool and Cotton	92
7. St Ives and Devonport	108
8. Back at Westminster	124
9. Triumphs and Tragedies	141
10. The Last Elections	154
11. The End of Politics	170
12. The Close of an Era	185
Note on Sources	198
Index	201

Preface

When Professor John Ward died in 1987 he left a complete text of a biography of W.B. Ferrand (1809–1889), the Tory–Radical M.P. and social reformer. He had worked on the book for many years and clearly intended it to be one of his major works as an historian. Ferrand is frequently mentioned in histories of the factory hours movement, the Young England group, and the Protectionist Party. Surprisingly, however, no life of him had ever appeared and he was not even included in the *Dictionary of National Biography*. Ward, with his Yorkshire background, his Tory-Anglican sympathies, and his deep knowledge of the popular movements of the period, was ideally qualified to write his biography; and it is plain that he conceived a great, though not uncritical, affection for his subject.

When Mrs Kay Ward asked me to read her late husband's manuscript, two things became apparent. Firstly, that this was a work of great scholarship, based on much original material, which constituted a valuable contribution to the history of early Victorian England. Secondly, that for publication purposes it would need to be considerably shortened. The c. 570 pages of typescript ran to about 160,000 words, exclusive of footnotes; and the notes were very full. Ward himself realised the need to cut down his first draft, and had already started on this process. In editing the typescript I aimed at a total of about 100,000 words. This has been achieved in various ways: by leaving out the long account of the histories of the Busfeild and Ferrand families; by reducing (as we know Ward intended to do) the length and number of the quotations; by omitting details which, though of intrinsic interest, did not add anything significant to the main narrative, such as descriptions of continental holidays; and, finally, by compressing sections which seemed to have been given disproportionate length in the text as a whole. I have tried to retain all that Ward thought important in Ferrand's life; and it was satisfactory to find that, in those chapters which he extensively revised, only minimal changes had to be made. Where it was necessary to summarise or clarify parts of the text, or to bridge gaps between different sections, I have inserted (I hope not too obtrusively) words or phrases, on rare occasions brief passages, which are not in the original text. But essentially this is Ward's book, shorn only of those parts which were unnecessary for his central theme.

I am grateful to Dr Michael Hurst of St. John's College, Oxford, who with several other Oxford historians read the shortened text and wrote encouraging reports on it. Mrs Jean Fraser, formerly Secretary to the Department of History at Strathclyde University, devoted unstinted time and skill to the task of retyping both the original and the shortened versions of the book, and eventually put all the material on electronic record for greater ease of handling. Without this great practical assistance my work would have been immensely more difficult. Dr John Butt, a colleague of John Ward and former Head of the History Department at Strathclyde, read, checked and corrected the original typescript, and made valuable suggestions on how best to reduce its length. He has throughout acted virtually as co-editor, and the book's debt to him is very great. Though as editor I bear responsibility for any errors or defects that remain, the credits largely belong elsewhere.

Norman Gash

JOHN TOWERS WARD (1930–1987)

Born at Horsforth, Yorkshire, he was educated at Leeds Grammar School and Magdalene College, Cambridge, where he obtained a double first in the History Tripos in 1953 and graduated M.A. and Ph.D. in 1957. He was successively Lecturer in Modern History at Queen's College, Dundee; Senior Lecturer in Economic History, and subsequently Professor of Modern History, at Strathclyde University.

Principal publications: *The Factory Movement 1830–1855* (1962); *Sir James Graham* (1967); *Popular Movements c. 1830–1850* (1970). Editor: *The Factory System*, 2 vols. (1970, 1974); *Land and Industry: the Landed Estate and the Industrial Revolution* (1971). Joint editor with R.G. Wilson: *Chartism* (1973).

Introduction

I

It is a commonplace that the period from 1828 to 1852 was one of fundamental change in British society. The great legislative landmarks of the time – the Repeal of the Test and Corporations Act in 1828, Catholic Emancipation in 1829, the Reform Act of 1832, the Poor Law Amendment Act of 1834, the Municipal Corporations Act of 1835, the Repeal of the Corn Laws in 1846, the Ten Hours Act of 1847, the Public Health Act of 1848, the repeal of the Navigation Laws in 1849 – were outward signs of deep shifts which had taken place in the balance of political power, the structure of the economy, and the climate of ideas. The diffusion of wealth and education, rapid urban and population growth, the technical revolution in manufacturing and transport, the emergence of a vigorous and independent newspaper press, were all undermining the supremacy of the old aristocratic, rural, Anglican state. In effect a steady revolution was taking place; though it assumed many forms and moved at an uneven speed. Much was attempted, though not everything succeeded. Some issues were fiercely fought out; on others, perhaps equally important, there was more agreement, or perhaps more indifference. There were political compromises and sometimes political deadlock. Despite difficulties and controversies, however, there was an underlying atmosphere of optimism and energy in which large reforms seemed desirable and radical remedies worth attempting.

It was in this age that W.B.Ferrand passed the greater part of his public career. A member of the squirearchy who becomes a champion of the working classes offers a certain paradox; and there is much that is unusual about his life. Born into a needy professional family on the fringe of the gentry class, he achieved the status of a substantial landowner through an accident of genealogy. He attended neither public school nor university. In ordinary circumstances he would have ended his days as an obscure provincial solicitor. But like converts, parvenus are often more zealous defenders of their position than those who possess it from birth. It was also of importance that he happened to be a big man with a strident voice and a notably combative temperament. The final accident which helped to shape his public career was that his property lay on the geographical frontier between the old world of rural Yorkshire and the expanding industrial towns of the West Riding. From the great family mansion he inherited at Harden Grange it was only half a dozen miles to the centre of Bradford. North and west were the open moors where he rode and shot; east and south the advancing urban agglomerations created by the Yorkshire textile industry where tall factory chimneys belched smoke and small children went to work at the bidding of the factory bell. That Ferrand became involved locally in the campaign to protect women and children in factories was therefore not unnatural. But it was an event which led him into a series of public controversies and eventually made him a minor national celebrity.

The intervention of the state in the relations between employers and employed was at that time a sensitive and difficult issue. Conventional economic teaching held that labour was a commodity and its value best realised in a free market where the workman was able to sell it to the highest bidder. Women and children, however, were excepted from this rule by the classical economists on the grounds that they could not be regarded as free agents. As far as the cotton industry was concerned, and it was the only one in which the factory system was prevalent, there were already laws on the statute book, starting with the elder Peel's Act of 1819, which regulated hours and ages of child-workers. It was becoming apparent, however, that the hours of women and children could not easily be separated from those of the men they worked alongside: a fact well appreciated by the cotton unions and their members. There was a growing fear that an increase in the scope of the Factory Acts would shorten the working day for the whole textile industry, and that this in turn would lead to a lowering of profits and consequently of wages. Even among sympathetic economists the humanitarian principle had to struggle with considerations of wealth production; and when the issue descended into the public arena, the arguments on both sides became heated and dogmatic.

The Whig Factory Act of 1833, while forbidding the employment in textile mills of children under the age of nine and limiting the hours of those under eighteen, had maintained the standard working day of twelve hours recognised by a succession of factory laws since 1802. Oastler and Sadler, however, had asked for a ten-hour day and, with the support of cotton-spinners' unions and Short Time Committees set up in many industrial areas, they continued the campaign. The Whigs rejected ten-hour amendments in 1833 and 1838 but the real crisis came in 1844 with Graham's factory bill. He reduced still further the hours for children, brought women into a new category of protected adult, and strengthened the powers of the factory inspectors; but the twelve-hour day remained. Indeed, in negotiations with the manufacturers for their agreement to the new restrictions, they had been given a general assurance to that effect. In March, however, Lord Ashley, the parliamentary leader of the Ten Hours movement, carried an amendment in committee reducing the hours to ten. It was only by using its authority to the limit and making the issue one of confidence that the government eventually carried the original bill.

What made Peel so uncompromising was that he feared the effects of Ashley's amendment on the economy as a whole. It was accepted on all sides that the legal maximum day for women and children would in practice be the normal day for men also. All experts, including the factory inspectors, were agreed that a reduction of hours to ten would result in loss of production, lower profits and in due course lower wages for the workpeople themselves. The supporters of the amendment did not disagree with this; the argument was merely on the extent of the loss. For Peel, slowly nursing the economy back to health after the great depression of 1837–41, this was a threat to everything he had been working for since he gained office.

Cotton goods constituted 80% of British exports and he thought it wrong to single out one industry for special treatment when there were many others, including agriculture, where women and children worked as long and as hard as in the cotton mills, and completely unprotected by law. He felt also that some at least of the Conservative support for Ashley's amendment had been prompted by dislike of manufacturers and the Anti-Corn Law League.

The controversies over the Factory Acts in the 1830s and 1840s were part of an even wider debate. Taught, not so much by the writings of the classical economists as by the simplified versions of their doctrines expounded by popular writers like Harriet Martineau and by influential periodicals like the *Edinburgh Review*, the educated public had come to accept the general proposition that the less the government interfered with industry, the better. Most professional economic writers, from Adam Smith to McCulloch and Senior, distrusted state intervention because they thought (and had good historical reasons for thinking) that it was usually inefficient, corrupt, and self-seeking. But they did not make *laisser-faire* an end in itself. Their main concern was for the well-being of society as a whole and they accepted, not only that it was the duty of the state to provide the framework of law and order necessary for the success of a free economy, but that it should also undertake those functions which were to the benefit of the public but not in the interests of private individuals to carry out. The argument therefore was not about the principle of state intervention but about its nature and extent; and this, they thought, was best decided on the basis of contemporary needs. Their views on what in fact was proper and expedient tended in practice to change with the passage of time. With these reservations, however, it remained true that economic orthodoxy pointed generally to non-interference, free trade, and individual liberty as the guiding principles of economic and social life.

The concept of 'Free Trade' had much wider implications than the words themselves might suggest. By many publicists it was elevated to the status of a universal prescription applicable to a whole range of social activities. It was possible, for example, to talk about free trade in religion or free trade in education, as well as in economics. For its more fervent adherents these were all different but interdependent aspects of one great truth. From that point of view free trade furnished the guiding principle for a complete programme of social action. The Anti-Corn Law League founded in 1839 set out to achieve one single objective, the repeal of the Corn Laws; but in the hands of Cobden and Bright it became a vehicle for a general attack on aristocratic institutions such as primogeniture, the game laws, the Established Church, the armed forces, and the diplomatic service. Free trade, in short, was the solution to social inequality and institutional privilege.

Even in the purely economic sphere the Manchester School of Cobden, Bright and their adherents was synonymous with an unqualified *laisser-faire* doctrine going far beyond what most professional economists were ready to advocate or politicians to enforce. A simplistic philosophy, it naturally appealed to those individuals and classes who in their own sphere stood to gain most from private enterprise and unrestricted liberty of action. For other sections of the community it was a less attractive doctrine. It did not sit comfortably on those classes which were the guardians and beneficiaries of the older, more ordered and deferential society; and it elicited increasing criticism from those whose humanitarian feelings or Christian consciences were disturbed by much that was going on in contemporary society. By the start of Victoria's reign there was a growing feeling that those members of the community whose lives were inevitably stunted by ignorance and poverty demanded more charity and compassion than the arid prescriptions of Bentham's atomistic society seemed likely to afford.

To Oastler and Ferrand, as indeed to Cobbett and Carlyle, the enemy was not only the manufacturer, the capitalist, the financier, and the bureaucrat but the whole school of theorists whose writings seemed to underpin the social and economic outlook of society against which they were protesting. A special odium was incurred by Malthus whose warnings of the dangers of over-population and emphasis on 'preventive checks' were interpreted as a deliberate attempt to restrict the families of the poor; and by Bentham whose theories were thought to be behind the new Poor Law of 1834, with its proclaimed intention of making the lot of the pauper in the workhouse even harsher than that of the poor outside. It is unlikely that many leaders of the working-class movements ever read the works of the classical economists; they spoke from the heart rather than the mind. For them the question was a simple one. The poor man had a right to look to society to assist him in his penury; the state had a duty to protect its weakest members. For government, trying to find a way through rival pressure groups, complex and contradictory arguments, untested administrative schemes, and a perennial shortage of money, the issues were not so clear cut.

A case in point was the Poor Law Amendment Act of 1834. When it passed, it seemed relatively uncontroversial. There was wide agreement that the old structure of poor relief was unsystematic, full of abuses, extremely expensive, and socially damaging. The Act of 1834 was designed to make poor relief more uniform, more efficient, and less costly. In the southern counties it was generally approved by landowners, the more so since they were given a large share in its local administration. The difficulties started when the commissioners charged with setting up the new system moved into the industrial areas of the north and midlands. It was a misfortune for them that their arrival coincided with the great industrial depression of 1837-41. The problem of pauperism in the south was created by low agricultural wages, chronic under-employment, and surplus population. In the north, where wages were generally higher, there was no need for large-scale poor relief except in time of industrial slump and wide unemployment; and then the numbers requiring assistance were too great for any workhouse system to sustain. The principle, enjoined but not always adhered to even in the south, of no relief for able-bodied men except in the workhouse, was patently unworkable in the industrial districts. In the end this was recognised even by the Poor Law Commissioners in London, though not before a violent campaign of resistance had been launched against their local officials.

For those opponents of the new Poor Law who tried to carry their campaign into parliament, it was both an obstacle and an irritant that the leaders of the two main political parties were substantially agreed on the necessity for the 1834 Act and the principles of its administration. After 1841 anti-Poor Law Tories found themselves having to criticise their own ministers, while those with other grievances against their front bench were provided with a popular issue on which to vent their discontents. It was in this way that Ferrand was brought into contact with the Young England movement started by Lord John Manners and George Smythe and soon joined by Disraeli. The romantic Young England vision of a new Toryism, based on an alliance of aristocracy and working classes against mill-owners, shopkeepers, and the Manchester School, was given literary immortality by Disraeli's novel *Sybil*, published in 1845. But Manners and Ferrand had been talking that language many years earlier. It was an attitude which inevitably separated them from Conservative ministers like Peel and Graham, the Home Secretary, who were trying to make the system work.

This was not the only issue on which divisions opened up in the Conservative Party as soon as it gained power in 1841. The most pressing concerns of the last years of Whig rule had been finance and trade; and they were clearly uppermost in Peel's mind when he became prime minister. For him, as indeed for the Whig leader Lord John Russell and nearly all economic experts, free or at least greater freedom of trade was the right policy for the British economy. The difference was that, when at last in office, he put his beliefs into practice rather more courageously and effectively than the Whigs had done in their period of power from 1830 to 1841. Free Trade as an active government policy, however, was bound sooner or later to raise awkward questions about protection for agriculture. Was there a special case for treating it differently from the rest of industry? If so, how high should the level of agricultural protection be? How long could British farmers continue to feed Britain's ever-expanding population? Might not competition actually promote more scientific and therefore more efficient farming methods?

The Whigs, with little to lose electorally in the counties, had in the late 1830s allowed their party a free vote on the matter of the corn laws though they did not put forward a distinct party policy until 1841; and even then it was only for an alternative form of protective duty (a fixed tariff in place of the existing sliding scale). Peel, while defending the case for protection of some sort, had never committed himself to the system established in 1828 and one of his first measures was a new corn law in 1842 substantially reducing the rate of duty on foreign cereals. This was accepted with equanimity if not enthusiasm by the majority of landowners and agriculturists of his party. But other measures, such as lower duties on imported meat and cattle, followed in 1843 by preferential treatment for Canadian corn, created distinct unease. By securing parliament's consent in 1842 for the re-introduction of the income tax, Peel had given himself the financial freedom to experiment still further with tariff reductions; and his second great free-trade budget in 1845 was a clear signal that the process of liberalising the British economy was not yet over.

There were other aspects of Peel's policy as prime minister which disturbed his party. The most contentious was religion. The country gentry, the Duke of Wellington once observed, cared for nothing except their rents and, possibly, the Church of England. This was not entirely due to a disinterested zeal for true religion. Many material links bound the gentry and the Establishment together, both legal, financial and social. Historically the tenderness of the Tories for the Church was as old a tradition as the partiality of the Whigs for the Dissenters. The radical doctrine of free trade in religion taught that all religious establishments were objectionable; all churches should compete on equal terms for congregations and revenues. No Whig ministry would ever go to that extreme. Nevertheless, the state of the Church of England in the early nineteenth century (that of the Church of Ireland was immeasurably worse) prompted both main political parties to use pressure on church leaders to reform its antiquated structure of administration and finances. In addition the Whigs did much in the 1830s to remove the inequalities which affected Dissenters even after the repeal of the Test and Corporations Act in 1828. There was still continuing Anglican dislike of Dissent and Dissenting jealousy of the Establishment; and bitter disputes opened up over the issue of state assistance to education. In 1839 Anglicans were able to prevent Whig plans for a secular system of state-directed national education; and Dissenters in 1843 were able to prevent the Established Church from securing a dominant influence in schools designed for factory and pauper children. By the mid-forties both sides were forced to recognise the limits of their power; and parliament in turn the impossibility of devising any system of national education acceptable to all the churches. At local level, however, wrangling over school education and the payment of church-rates continued intermittently, often with great rancour, for another generation.

The question of the Roman Catholic Church offered an equally formidable array of difficulties. Historic anti-Popish prejudices were still engrained in the British people at large but had little hold on the educated classes. Had Catholic Emancipation been a purely English matter, it would have been settled long before 1829. What turned the issue into a great contemporary controversy was the connection with Ireland. The grant of full political and legal equality to Roman Catholics by the Act of 1829 had been the culmination of a violent agitation in Ireland led by Daniel O'Connell in which the Catholic parish priests had played a conspicuous part. Liberals, who hoped that the concession would put an end to the discontent and disorder that had strained Anglo-Irish relations since the Union of 1801, were soon disillusioned. Having secured his foothold in parliament, O'Connell promptly started a new campaign for a repeal of the Union. Although the Whig ministry could not endorse O'Connell's larger aims, liberal principles and political expediency alike induced them to take up the question of reforming the Anglican Church of Ireland, the state-endowed church of a small minority of the Irish population. That it needed reform was not seriously in dispute between Whig and Conservative leaders. Melbourne and Russell were prepared in the last resort to compromise; Peel and Wellington to accept almost anything short of disestablishment and confiscation of revenues. Even so, the series of Irish administrative and ecclesiastical reforms of the late 1830s no more brought about peace in Ireland than Emancipation in 1829. Peel's accession to power in 1841 was merely the signal for renewed agitation by O'Connell for the repeal of the 1801 Act and the return of an independent Irish parliament sitting in Dublin.

Peel's response to the growing threat of popular disorder in Ireland was to devise in 1844 a new approach to the Irish problem. His aim was to conciliate the Roman Catholic Church, restore the confidence of the Irish Catholic middle classes in the goodwill of the British government, and detach both from O'Connell's more proletarian Repeal movement. It was a policy which (as so often happens to well-intentioned proposals for Ireland emanating from London) elicited a fainter response across the Channel than he had hoped and a more vociferous opposition in England than he had feared. The most controversial of his measures was a bill in 1845 to increase substantially the existing Treasury grant to the Roman Catholic ecclesiastical training college at Maynooth. The principle of endowment dated back to 1795. What was new was the increased anti-Catholic feeling in England in the 1840s compared with fifty years earlier. The bill passed through parliament with the aid of Whig and Liberal support; but half the Conservative party in the Commons voted against it and in the country at large Evangelical Anglicans joined with Methodists, Congregationalists, Baptists, and Presbyterians to denounce the measure.

Two factors had brought old historic animosities to life again. The first was the personality and actions of O'Connell who seemed to be using the weapon of popular violence once again to secure his political objectives. The other was the emergence of what appeared to be a conspiratorial Roman Catholic party in the Church of England itself. The so-called Oxford or Tractarian movement of the 1830s had originally been part of a wider Anglican protest against the Church reforms of the Whig government after 1832. But an influential school of theologians who emphasised both the independent spiritual authority and the Catholic tradition of the Anglican Church, and among whom there were a few but spectacular conversions to Rome in 1845, appeared to indicate that there was a serious danger to the whole Protestant national tradition. As it was, Roman Catholicism was clearly on the increase in England and Scotland; though the impetus for that did not come from the Oxford Movement or the conservative English Catholics under their traditionally aristocratic leaders. It came from the post-1815 Irish immigration into Lancashire, London and the West of Scotland. This was a new form of Catholicism – proletarian, impoverished, impervious to Protestant culture, and not much liked by the English and Scottish working classes.

II

These were the issues which formed the background to Ferrand's public life and coloured his career. What gave a special character to that career, however, was the fact that he moved on the borderline, so to speak, between gentry politics as played out at the parliamentary level, and popular politics as practised by the demagogues of the period such as the Chartist leader, Feargus O'Connor, or the greatest agitator of them all, Daniel O'Connell. With both of them incidentally Ferrand had certain things in common. The two worlds overlapped, particularly at election time; but the natural sphere of one was the House of Commons, the Pall Mall clubs, and the great country houses; of the other the mass meeting, the torchlight procession, and the open-air rhetoric of the platform. Ferrand moved easily in both worlds. That he could do so accounts for much of his success and most of his notoriety. It also explains why he never had a secure parliamentary career. He raised too many misgivings in his own class and his own party. Despite his many election contests he was only in the House of Commons a total of eight years. At no time did he seem likely to achieve the dignity of a county M.P; not because he lacked broad acres and a family lineage, but because he lacked 'respectability'. He was virtually turned out of Knaresborough by Lord Harewood in 1847 and after that he was never able to find a secure borough in his own county of Yorkshire. He had to take his chances elsewhere with a succession of unpromising constituencies which either came his way fortuitously or were tossed to him by his party managers.

Nevertheless, the nine further elections he fought after 1847 offer a fascinating study of mid-Victorian borough politics. In their rowdy, abusive partisanship and Hogarthian atmosphere of drunkenness, bribery and violence, with lawyers, bankers and brewers discreetly pulling the strings behind the scenes, it seemed that little had changed from pre-Reform days. The natural strength of the Protectionist, later the Conservative Party of Derby and Disraeli was of course in the rural shires. It is clear, however, from Ferrand's experiences that even in the boroughs there was a persistent Conservative element in the electorate. If it was not always able to get its candidates into parliament, it was able to sustain the grind of party warfare at constituency level, whatever happened at Westminster. It is clear also that the 'Conservative working man' was not a myth; and his existence, along with a Conservative leaven among the urban, professional classes, helps to explain why the Conservative Party, though never securing a majority in the House of Commons between 1847 and 1874, was always a substantial opposition. It is not surprising that, with the larger urban electorate created by the Reform Act of 1867, the Conservatives were easily converted into a party of government under Disraeli and Salisbury in the last quarter of the century. Palmerston's success in securing a degree of party consensus in the middle of Victoria's reign tends to obscure the extent to which the continuity of local politics, local issues, and local personalities kept party feeling alive in the provinces.

Ferrand, with his old-fashioned Crown and Altar, Church and King brand of Toryism, may perhaps be dismissed, as he was by critics in his own day, as a prehistoric creature from a vanished age; a relic of the obsolete Toryism of the early eighteenth century. Yet it was out of this traditional soil of historic Toryism that came his interest in contemporary issues, especially the plight of the poor, the defence of the Established Church, the dangers of central government, and the defects of a society based on the profit motive. He was fighting some of the powerful forces of his time; much of what he advocated was wrong-headed, muddled, or plainly impractical; and his failures make a longer list than his successes. Yet along with tenacity of purpose and indomitable courage, there is a rough unsentimental humanity about Ferrand which lifts his career above the commonplace.

It can hardly be doubted that a personal and class hostility towards the Liberal oligarchies of urban, industrial society also played a part in shaping his outlook. He was not a democrat or an egalitarian or even perhaps a popular agitator in the true sense. Though he welcomed Chartist cooperation in his campaigns, he did not subscribe to their political demands for manhood suffrage or secret ballot and he strongly disapproved of the 'physical force' aspect of their movement. In 1848, the year of the last great national Chartist demonstrations, he was almost excessively active in swearing-in special constables and making arrests in his own district. His role as the Working Man's Friend did not prevent him from being a strict defender of the rights of property and a firm believer in the sanctity of law and order. As a magistrate he came down severely on poachers, a species of offender which like many landowners he regarded with peculiar distaste.

Moreover, some of his economic views were not fundamentally different from those of the Manchester School he so often castigated. He condemned all strikes against employers, and though he could see the need for trade unions, he deplored any attempt on their part to deny to an individual workman the right to sell his labour where and how he chose. He observed the same principle himself as an employer. During the agricultural depression of 1851 he revealed that his own labourers, who formerly had been paid 15/- a week, were now getting only 12/- and that he was even employing sixteen Irishmen at 9/-, though he claimed credit for having rejected offers from some 200 others to work for even less.

It is characteristic that we learn of this from one of Ferrand's own public speeches. Though attacked by opponents for hypocrisy, as for example in his attitude towards the Chartists, he never troubled to hide his actions or conceal his opinions from the world. He saw no need to justify himself to anyone. What he did was simply the product of his temperament and instincts. It is doubtful whether he had ever consciously worked out a coherent set of political views, and there is little evidence in his speeches and writings of wide reading or profound thinking. He was an active rather than a reflective creature. Such programmes as he did produce, like the Farmers' Wool League, were eccentric rather than original. Like many persons whose feelings are stronger than their reasoning, he easily persuaded himself of the feasibility of anything that fitted into his emotions and prejudices.

It is worth remembering also that what filled his public career did not represent his whole life. There were other matters to occupy his time and energies besides factory laws, workhouses, Whig scandals, protectionism, and Popery. It is one of the many virtues of Ward's book that, thanks to the wealth of family papers he uncovered, he was able to give an account of Ferrand's life in all its varied aspects. The biographies of politicians and social reformers frequently concentrate on their subject's public career to the exclusion, or at least the neglect, of much that is socially and personally significant. In real life few people, not even moral reformers, live a totally dedicated existence; Ferrand certainly did not. He was a landowner and practical farmer who sowed turnips, reared sheep, and planted trees; a keen sportsman who hunted, coursed, shot, and fished; a sociable man who joined London clubs, went the rounds of great country houses, and entertained lavishly himself; a magistrate who sat in judgement on drunkards, wife-beaters, and prostitutes; a captain in the Volunteer Rifle Corps who did his best to inculcate discipline and improve the shooting of his more casual rank and file; a litigious man who threw himself into lawsuits and wrote argumentative letters to the press; a traveller who went all over Britain and occasionally penetrated into Europe; a monied man who bought shares in banking and insurance and invested in canals and railways; a man finally who had a tragic family history, with his first wife dying in childbed after less than two years of married life, a bitterly estranged daughter, an heir who died prematurely, and a second son who proved to be mentally incapable. Whatever else may be said of Victorian squires, it would be unsafe to assume that they lived either narrow or carefree lives.

Norman Gash

CHAPTER ONE

The Birth of a Crusade

In January 1852 William Busfeild Ferrand related in a public letter to the Peelite Duke of Newcastle how he had become a social reformer and champion of the factory child-workers. The episode he so emotionally described had taken place some nineteen years earlier.

> It was soon after Sadler and Oastler unfurled the banner of protection that I became a public man. At the hour of five on a winter's morning, I left my home to shoot wild fowl. On my road, I had to pass along a deep and narrow lane which led from a rural village to a distant factory. The wind howled furiously, the snow fell heavily and drifted before the icy blast. I indistinctly traced three children's footsteps. Soon, I heard a piteous cry of distress. Hurrying on, again I listened, but all was silent except the distant tolling of the factory bell. Again I tracked their footmarks, and saw that one had lagged behind; I returned and found the little factory slave half-buried in a snow-draft fast asleep. I dragged it from its winding sheet; the icy hand of death had congealed its blood and paralysed its limbs. In a few minutes it would have been 'where the wicked cease from troubling and the weary are at rest'. I aroused it from his stupor and saved its life. From that hour I became a 'Ten Hours Bill' man and the unflinching advocate of 'protection to native industry!'

It was a conversion to a new cause almost Pauline in its suddenness and dramatic quality.

The plight of children in the expanding textile industries of early nineteenth-century Britain had over many years attracted the interest of humanitarians. Acts of parliament had been passed in 1802, 1819, 1820, 1825, 1829 and 1831, though they exerted little control over the cotton mills, the chief employer of child labour. Indeed the very number of the statutes testified to their ineffectiveness. In September 1830 a new era in the history of factory reform opened when the leading Bradford worsted-master John Wood urged his fellow Tory churchman Richard Oastler, agent for the Thornhill estates near Huddersfield and Leeds, to demand greater protection for the children employed in Yorkshire's woollen and worsted industries. Oastler opened his famous campaign with letters to the great Liberal newspaper the *Leeds Mercury* but the controversy which followed soon produced an alignment of Tories and Radicals against the predominantly Whig-Liberal factory owners.

Undeterred, Oastler, with Trade Union support, organised 'Short Time Committees' in the textile towns and villages of the West Riding to agitate for a maximum working day of ten hours. Since this new and peremptory demand was found too extreme even by the radical Whig J.C. Hobhouse, who had sponsored the Acts of 1825 and 1829, the campaigners turned to Oastler's close friend Michael Sadler M.P., an evangelical Leeds Tory noted for his opposition to Catholic Emancipation and parliamentary reform. In 1832, during the Reform Bill excitement, Sadler proposed a ten-hour bill but under government pressure found himself instead chairing a parliamentary committee of enquiry into factory conditions. By the late summer, when parliament was prorogued, he had amassed a terrifying though indiscriminate and not altogether unbiassed indictment of northern industry, based mainly on workers' evidence. The *Report* of the 1832 Commission was to arouse humanitarian and religious feeling in the country and open the way for the first time to decisive state intervention. The government Factory Act which eventually took its place on the statute book in 1833 was a landmark in the history of industrial legislation. Sadler's defeat at Leeds in the general election of 1832 ended his parliamentary career; but the young Lord Ashley, heir to the earldom of Shaftesbury, was persuaded to take his place as parliamentary spokesman for the movement. Sadler himself died three years later at the early age of 55. Oastler continued for a few more years as the great orator and propagandist for this and other working-class causes until dismissal from his employment and imprisonment for debt in 1840–44 virtually brought his meteoric career also to a close. Lord Ashley went on to become the best-known philanthropist and social reformer of the century. W. B. Ferrand, who in many respects deserves to be regarded as the fourth member of this oddly disparate group, was not on the face of it a natural recruit to social reform. A young, needy Yorkshire squireen, with rugged good looks and a stentorian voice, he was known as an ardent sportsman who shot, fished and galloped his horse over the bleak moors soon to be made famous by the Brontë sisters. He was accustomed to hard manual work on the land, drank heavily round the mahogany tables of neighbouring country houses or with no less enjoyment with his rustic inferiors in the more primitive rooms of local taverns, and had a probably deserved reputation for amorous affairs with the girls of the neighbourhood. He seemed poles apart from the pious, methodical Sadler or the morbidly conscientious evangelical Ashley. It was characteristic that it was his own impulsive nature and determined character that took him into the factory movement.

The two families which contributed to his name were both well established. Traditionally the Ferrands were Church and King Tories, proud of their lineage and their land, supporters of the old hierarchic and benevolent order now threatened by the Industrial Revolution. The Busfeilds were more sophisticated, liberal and intellectual people, who spent their money on classical mansions, landscaped parks, libraries, portraits and Cambridge degrees. Important as these two families were in his life, William oddly enough was only a Busfeild and a Ferrand on the female side. His paternal grandfather was a Dr Atkinson M.D. of Leeds who had married a wealthy heiress, Elizabeth Busfeild, and took the name and arms of his wife's family when she succeeded to their estates in 1772. One of his three sons, Currer Fothergill Busfeild, married a Sarah Ferrand in 1805. Thirty-two years later she inherited the property of her brother Edward and reverted to the surname and arms of her own family once more. By that time she was a widow, her husband having died in 1832.

In 1839 her eldest son William Busfeild followed her example and assumed the additional surname of Ferrand. It was thus by a double shift of family nomenclature in the space of some 65 years that the grandson of Dr Atkinson became the W.B. Ferrand of early-Victorian political history. As in many other instances of family genealogy, the pull of landed property was more powerful than the continuity of a mere patronymic.

The eighteenth-century Busfeilds had been landed gentry of some wealth and many business connections in the West Riding. But Dr Atkinson had allowed his wife's fortune to infect him with an enthusiasm for spending unchecked by business caution. At his death in 1817 he left a greatly diminished estate and a trail of debts which led to the selling-off of even more of the original estate. Currer Busfeild did not even have the much reduced family property to support him since he was only a third son. He owned a little land but it was not enough to provide him with a living and he had to supplement his income with a succession of small salaried posts. He obtained a clerkship which brought him £60 per annum; he managed the Castlefields cotton-mill for a time, procured election as High Constable of the Morley Division in 1824, and became land-agent to Mr Field, squire of Heaton, in 1825. He also received assistance from his wife's family who provided the house at Cottingley Bridge near Bingley in which he lived for twenty years after his marriage.

His permanently straitened circumstances were made worse by the growing size of his family. In all Sarah Ferrand presented him with thirteen children, five sons and eight daughters, though not all the girls survived infancy. It was a mark of his comparative poverty that he was unable to send his sons to Cambridge where he had gone himself. A kind-hearted, easygoing man, Currer Busfeild did the best he could for his boys by having them educated locally and putting three of them in a lawyer's office when they reached a suitable age. When he died in 1832 he left little for his family except a few souvenirs of the miscellaneous public offices he had held.

The Busfeilds of Cottingley Bridge were thus only in the lower fringes of the gentry class. It was a socially precarious position and their limited means were in mortifying contrast to the dominant position in the Bingley neighbourhood of their mother's relations, the Ferrands of St Ives and Harden Grange. With a pedigree which harked back to the Norman Conquest and the Crusades, and intermarriage with many of the leading families in the north of England, various branches of the Ferrands had long been established in the West Riding and at Barnard Castle and Stockton in Co. Durham, with extensive landed and commercial interests. Early in the nineteenth century Edward Ferrand, the head of the Stockton branch, inherited the Ferrand property at St Ives near Bingley. He took up permanent residence there and his brother Walker Ferrand at Harden Grange nearby. While the Ferrands towered above their Busfeild relatives in material wealth, however, they lacked what Currer Busfeild had in abundance – children to inherit their name and property. Walker, despite two marriages, was childless; Edward had an only child, a girl. Of his two sisters the elder, Jane, died in 1798 leaving a son who died unmarried in 1817. As the years passed, therefore, his younger sister Sarah, Currer's wife, and her five sons appeared the likely ultimate heirs to the great Ferrand fortune.

Reared in the cheerful, indulgent and slightly rackety household at Cottingley

Bridge, the Busfeild boys were not conspicuous either for their industry or self-discipline. William, the eldest, went with his brothers to the local grammar school at Bingley, and briefly to Giggleswick School as a boarder. Known as an unruly scholar at Bingley, he fared even worse at Giggleswick, being sent home after only a few months. He was then sixteen and it proved the end of his formal schooling. Before the end of the year he entered a solicitor's office in Bradford, where his father had rented a house. He proved difficult and quarrelsome as an office junior and eventually his long-suffering father installed him in another solicitor's office at Keighley in lodgings of his own. Here he was able to lead a lively social life free from parental supervision. This greater personal freedom had one important consequence. In the spring of 1831 a marriage with Sarah Priestley, daughter of a retired army officer, had to be hastily arranged in anticipation of the birth of a baby boy at the beginning of July.

At the age of 22, therefore, without a settled profession but a married man and a father, William was hardly a model elder son. Some of his other brothers were little better. The seventeen-year old Johnson Busfeild, who had been courting another daughter of Captain Priestley, tried to elope with her to Gretna Green, a plan foiled at the last moment but followed by a more orthodox wedding the same year. Anxieties over his wayward and hot-blooded sons perhaps aggravated the ill-health of Currer Busfeild who died in the summer of that year followed three months later by Captain Prestley. Yet if his eldest-born did not have a very creditable record to look back on, his expectations of a brighter future were ever-present. How long he would have to wait before they were realised was another matter. At the close of 1832 his uncle Edward was still only 55 and though his father and grandfather had neither of them been long-lived, the quiet retired life he followed at St Ives was as good a recipe as any for reasonable longevity. Though he could hardly have approved of his unruly nephew, he continued to show generosity towards his sister's family. On Currer's death he gave her a pension and moved her to a house called Myrtle Grove, a luxurious villa built by old Dr Atkinson; while her eldest son William took up residence at a house called Milner Field, an old manor-house at Gilstead belonging to a friend of the family. Then, in December, William's wife died giving birth to a daughter. With his succession to the Ferrand fortune still in doubt, William Busfeild had lost his father, father-in-law, and wife in the space of six months. Once more his two rich uncles came to the rescue, Edward giving him an annuity and Walker taking charge of his motherless children.

It was at this unsettled if not unpromising stage in his life that he threw himself with characteristic impulsiveness and energy into the factory movement. When the workers' short-time committees in Yorkshire protested at what seemed the government's procrastination in implementing the original Sadler-Ashley bill, he presided over an open-air rally of some 2,000 people in April 1833 to petition parliament. He was well received and when the Yorkshire committee resolved to hold a mammoth meeting on Wibsey Moor on 1 July to protest against the new Royal Commission set up by the Whigs, the young squire with the resonant voice was invited to address the expected 100,000 audience. It is clear that with Oastler's example before him he was already mastering the technique of assembling and addressing large crowds in the open air. He hired a band to parade through Bingley at dawn and provided transport and food for those who turned out to support him. At the rally he seconded the first motion (proposed by the Leeds radical John Ayrey) against any compromise. The speech – 'eloquent and well-delivered' according to the radical *Leeds Times* – was loudly cheered. It presaged much similar oratory. Busfeild saw the vast crowd as 'witnesses, jury and judges upon the factory system ... which sanctioned child murder'. He gave his audience the cry of 'the Ten Hours Bill and no concessions for ever'.

But while he achieved local success, the national campaign failed. The Commissioners reported quickly and Government reacted likewise, passing the first effective Factory Act in the late summer. Children under 9 were banned from working, those under 13 were gradually restricted to 8 hours' labour (with 2 hours' schooling) and those under 18 were limited to 12 hours. Seemingly more generous than Ashley's Bill, providing for education and inspection, the Ministerial measure actually made possible child relays to maintain long adult hours.

There was little that reformers could do; they were themselves divided. Oastler's Factory Reformation Society of October soon lost support to the rash 'Society for the Promotion of National Regeneration' founded in November by the eccentric socialist industrialist Robert Owen to promote a universal 8-hour day by strike action. 'Regeneration' fell with the rest of Owen's impractical schemes during 1834, amid strikes, lockouts and the transportation of the 'Tolpuddle Martyrs'.

As a Tory, Busfeild could not support the 'godless' Owen. But he became a disciple of the handsome Oastler, whose Right-wing Toryism and immense appeal to workers created a new political force among 'Church and King' groups and radicals alike. This alliance of Right and Left was renewed in opposition to the Poor Law of 1834, with its centralised executive, 'unionisation' of old parochial authorities and bleak negation of Christian and local paternalistic charity. Once more Tories and radicals – generally 'ultras' in both camps – could combine against Benthamite-Malthusian doctrine.

II

During January 1835 Busfeild enjoyed 'capital sport', hunting almost daily. He killed his first fox on New Year's Day, recalling 43 years later that 'he weighed 28 lbs – too fat and big to run much'. Six days later he ran a fox from Airedale into Wharfedale for almost four hours, earning local renown for his stamina. But politics exerted a growing attraction and he chose the traditional Tory stance of the Ferrands, rather than the Whiggish posture of current Busfeilds.

In the spring Morpeth – heir to the vast Howard estates of the Earls of Carlisle – fought a West Riding by-election (on being appointed Irish Secretary) against the first Tory candidate, John Stuart-Wortley. In April he visited Bingley, where Busfeild challenged him over petitions against the appropriation of Church of Ireland funds. Angered by Morpeth's superciliously facetious reply, the 'Protestant Elector' told his fellows that

I do not hesitate to declare that every Elector who gives his vote to the Noble Lord adds one link to that Chain which Daniel O'Connell is forging to bind down the Protestant Religion at the Shrine of Popery.

Support for Irish Churchmen henceforth formed another strand in Busfeild's politics.

With growing reputation he now devoted much of the energy hitherto reserved for sports to Tory politics. In June he was a guest of the Bradford Conservative Association at a 'sumptuous dinner' in Shipley, under the benevolent worsted master Matthew Thompson. In a long speech he proposed 'the immortal memory of the late William Pitt', detailing the achievements of 'that unrivalled statesman'.

Toryism received a further access of strength in the worsted capital of Bradford with the defection of the Liberal MP John Hardy, to whom Thompson's Association gave a dinner in November. Busfeild was present and spoke strongly, lambasting the *Mercury*, Daniel O'Connell, 'the two-legged hog Lord Mulgrave and the sucking pig Lord Morpeth', praising the Church and House of Lords ('the finest ornaments of Britain and the first men in society') and demanding better conditions for tenant farmers. He was now firmly established in local politics. On 29 January he presided over a Bingley Tory dinner, for which Sir Charles Ibbetson of Denton Park and the Ferrands provided venison, game and wine. He delivered familiar onslaughts on 'that bullying demagogue O'Connell', radicals from Cromwell onwards and American slavery. Next day he formed a Bingley Operative Conservative Association, a branch of a growing Tory working-class movement which had started in Leeds in March 1835.

In 1836 the Factory Movement revived to oppose the Whig Minister Poulett Thomson's proposal to weaken the 1833 Act, and an angry campaign developed. On 9 April Busfeild chaired Bingley's meeting in the Brown Cow Inn to plead that 'the factory child had a greater right to protection than the master had to profits or the man to wages' and that 'ten hours a day for children to work in mills was sufficient, and a due regard to their health and strength would not allow of more'. He was determined to

> treat the question as one of humanity, and to keep it apart from every political taint or bias; he could work in such a cause with Radicals as well as Tories; he had pleaded, and always would plead, the cause of the weak against the strong, and in his conscience he believed that a Ten Hours Bill regulation for factories would be equally beneficial to masters and workpeople.

When Thomson's motion only narrowly succeeded in May, it was withdrawn.

In the summer, as Oastler condemned evasions of the Act, eventually splitting his Movement by threatening sabotage, Busfeild devoted himself to local affairs at Bingley, entering on a violent controversy over Church rates to maintain the fabric of ancient All Saints. When, in July, he moved the levy, a dissenting amendment to adjourn for a year was carried by 123 votes to 85. A week later many parishioners were barred from the church, and while non-conformists again favoured postponement, the church wardens resolved to collect the rate. One of England's most bitter controversies thus reached Bingley, with the Liberal *Bradford Observer* and the Anglican *Leeds Intelligencer* heatedly supporting the rival factions.

Busfeild claimed that more inhabitants would have to pay only 1d. to aid the Church, their only protection against Popish persecution:

> he called upon them . . . to cheerfully and with a Christian feeling pay a small sum towards supporting in all its grandeur that holy building, which was emphatically styled the Poor-man's Church, at whose font they had been baptised and Christened, at whose altar they had been married, and within whose sacred ground, at their deaths, they would rest by the side of their relatives and friends.

But he was hotly opposed by the Baptist Stephen Skirrow, the hereditary leader of local dissenters, and – to his horror – by 'uncle Busfeild', now seeking 'Radical' support by advocating voluntary Church rates. It was all very painful, though typical of many parochial battles. William later told the *Intelligencer* that 'one of the most disgraceful and outrageous scenes that ever was witnessed in a place of worship' had occurred when 'the greatest blackguards of the district' were mobilised by dissenting millowners.

On 2 December William sealed his association with Bradford Tories (and his breach with his uncle) at a Constitutional Association dinner. After his brother Johnson toasted 'Protestant principles, and may they ever have the ascendancy', William replied in praise of county Conservatives: in 1832

> the West Riding Destructives . . . had excited the people to that pitch of desperation that no Conservative durst show his colour without the certainty of being murdered . . . They had to thank Mr. Wortley for being the first to hoist the lion standard of their party . . .

To great cheers, he advised fellow-diners 'that if ever they returned a Busfeild, he should be of the right colour'.

III

While William Busfeild senior continued to address Liberal rallies, his nephew turned to an increasingly popular Tory-Radical cause. Oastler and his friends had bitterly opposed the Poor Law of 1834 and were now mobilised to prevent the implementation of the Act by the assistant commissioners in the North. Busfeild threw himself into the militant campaign. 'If you do not show a firm and determined opposition', he told Bingley operatives in February, urging them to oppose a Keighley meeting to establish a Poor Law Union,

> the Poor Law commissioners will tell their masters that you are perfectly regardless of its consequences, and they may put it into effect as soon as they think proper.

The commissioners had ordered the formation of a Union in January, but riotous opposition hindered their officials in such towns as Huddersfield, Bradford, Keighley and Todmorden, and in Keighley and Huddersfield hostile majorities dominated the ultimately-elected boards of guardians. Busfeild, like Oastler, condemned the separation of families in the bleak workhouse 'bastiles' and the refusal of outdoor relief. He wrote to Lord Wharncliffe (father of Stuart-Wortley and a leader of West Riding Toryism) against implementing the Act. The 'denial of Christian charity' and centralised usurpation of traditional local benevolence implicit in the measure seemed basic matters of principle, and a torrent of (often exaggerated) tracts poured out against the 'inhuman' system.

In the spring young William also involved himself in Bradford Toryism, a staunchly Anglican but remarkable body which included some of the greatest worsted princes and ironmasters, local squires and Evangelical parsons and working men. This classless form of Conservatism inevitably attracted Busfeild. The Tories hoped that the seats might be divided at the next election between their new convert Hardy and Cunliffe-Lister (who had won in 1835 by 611 and 589 votes to the Radical George Hadfield's 392). But Liberals could not forgive Hardy's secession and proposed Busfeild of Upwood to take the second seat. Younger Busfeilds were appalled.

Meanwhile William's prospects dramatically improved on 21 March, with the death of Edward Ferrand. Currer's widow Sarah now entered into her inheritance, under a complicated series of family testaments, faculties and codicils, as life tenant of the estates, lady of St. Ives and *grande dame* of the neighbourhood. William was her heir. He was already living in squirearchic style, maintaining his own pack of harriers and running a fox for nearly forty miles in February. Now, from being a member of a junior Busfeild line, he was heir apparent to the proudly-held acres of the Ferrands.

This changed fortune probably determined him to enter politics. Bradford's campaign for the general election following the death of William IV on 20 June had actually already begun. But on the 22nd Busfeild informed 'the Free and Independent Electors' that he would oppose his uncle, as

> an unflinching Advocate of the just Prerogatives of the Crown, and [one] resolved to maintain the independence and Authority of the House of Lords, as one of the best and surest safeguards to the Rights and Liberties of the People. I am also a determined supporter of the Established Church, whilst I am ready to reform all proved Abuses and anxious to redress every practical Grievance of which the Dissenters can justly complain.
>
> I need scarcely add that I am resolutely opposed to the principle and provisions of the New Poor Law Act and that I will never cease from my exertions till it has been blotted from the Statute Book and Poverty shall no longer be treated as a Crime . . . I have studied to promote through life the Interests of my poorer Fellow-Countrymen and shall ever anxiously and strenuously support all Measures which are conducive to their Welfare . . .

Such sentiments honestly reflected Busfeild's heartfelt beliefs, but were scarcely calculated to attract Bradford's bourgeois voters.

The battle began instantly, as partisans assembled nightly at the Liberal headquarters in the Bowling Green Inn and the Tory White Lion. The Liberal *Bradford Observer* alleged that Tories hoped to place the unpopular Orangeman Duke of Cumberland on the Throne in place of his 'youthful and gracious' niece Victoria. Whigs claimed that the 18-year-old Queen 'had already proclaimed herself a Reformer' and advocated continuing change, Irish equality and the abolition of Church rates.

Tory appeals had some similarities. Electors were urged to 'rally around their young Queen . . . and show their Determination to support the Throne, the Altar and the Cottage' – Oastler's beloved motto. On the 24th Busfeild told 5000 people that (although the family division was embarrassing) he was opposing his uncle 'to prevent Mr. Hardy being ousted by an unfair coalition'. As elsewhere, both sides claimed to be supporting Her Majesty. But while Busfeild senior promised 'Safe and Progressive Reform', William talked of traditional institutions and social change. When the Liberal Charles Harris stressed the new Whiggish monarchist enthusiasm, Tories retorted by pointing to Hardy's support of the unemployed and claiming that

> YOUNG BUSFEILD stood forward in defence of the poor Factory Child, at a time when he did not anticipate the honour of representing you in Parliament, and he has since opposed with all his power and influence that monstrous tyrant the Poor Law Amendment Act.

As the campaign developed, other less seemly controversies appeared. Both sides reportedly hired 500 strong-arm men, the Tories probably getting the better bargain by retaining the notorious 'Brassy' Leachman. Pugilists were followed by poets and publicans. A local poet Storey urged electors to vote

> Not for Lister the Rad, but for Hardy the True,
> Not for Busfeild the Yellow, but Busfeild the Blue.

Liberals retorted with counsel to vote

> Not for Hardy the Cantwell – but Lister the Rad,
> And Busfeild the Elder – not Busfeild the Lad.

Gallons of alcohol sustained thirsty supporters. Johnson Busfeild, vigorously aiding William, noted that ward committees met each night

> in various public houses, when the district canvass books were revised and speeches made, besides a good supply of punch to keep up the good feeling and do justice to the toasts of the evening.

'Good feeling' did not last for long. The booze and the bullies – John Leachman's gang cost 5s. each – and even rival poets, Storey and Reuben Holder, were costly. Hardy's third son, Gathorne, recalled that

> I had a busy time at Bradford, where we were forced into a coalition with Busfeild Ferrand, which was fatal. I had to go about with him on his speaking excursions, and cannot say I liked my company much! At the same time he was

> admirable for the mob, as I noted then and remember now. If the committee had worked as hard as they drank, the result might have been different!

The future Oxonian barrister, Minister and peer, fastidiously 'liberal' and only belatedly Disraelian, could scarcely understand rough and sometimes violent Bradford politics. Equally characteristically, William enjoyed the hurly-burly of his first election.

Amidst all the controversies in bustling, dirty Bradford's third election, at the heart of the Liberal-dominated worsted industry, the younger Busfeild proclaimed an uncompromising Tory-Radicalism. On 23 June he announced his first speech next day and, noted Johnson, 'a good deal of interest was excited, between five and six thousand persons having assembled' at the Court House. Busfeild was

> the advocate of Conservative principles and yet the poor man's friend. Since he came to manhood he had always made it his endeavour to promote the welfare of the working classes.

He was a Tory

> first, because he was a member of the Established Church . . . which had nurtured the Dissenters in its bosom and which they now turned round and basely tried to sting to the heart – but which he would ever support . . . [secondly] because he lived under a monarchical government and [thirdly] because he was a determined opponent of the New Poor Law Act, which parted those whom God had united, gave a premium to murder and made poverty a crime . . .

He 'was for the total repeal of this measure'. When Radical hecklers recalled that Peel and Wellington had supported the Act (in the latter case, despite Oastler's admonitions), Busfeild retorted:

> What had it to do with them? He stood there to support no man's opinions but to avow his own. Let them support the men who cared for the wants of the poor; let them look at the names to charitable institutions, and they would see that nine-tenths of the contributions were made by Conservatives.

He asked local operatives

> who had oppressed them since 1830? – was it not the Whigs? Did not Whigs transport the Dorchester unionists? Did not the Whigs give them the New Poor Law Bill?

He supported the Corn Laws of 1815 and 1828, the Ten Hours Bill and the abolition of Army flogging but condemned O'Connell's Irish campaigns, the Ballot, universal suffrage and shorter parliaments. And he disarmingly supported a revision of the pension list – particularly of the sizeable portion of it notoriously devoted to relatives of the previous Whig Prime Minister, Earl Grey.

During July the four candidates toured the districts. 'It is needless to add', commented Johnson, the Liberals gave the most satisfaction . . . [their] audiences usually comprising a mass of violent Radicals thirsting after organic changes; still . . . all passed with comparative quiet, with the exception of a skirmish now and then, when perhaps a banner was destroyed or a few stones thrown.

New posters were designed nightly over convivial punch. Liberals particularly assailed Hardy's 'apostasy and impudence' and the benevolent ironmaster Joshua Pollard's 'intimidation'. The ultra-Radical (later Tory) publican Peter Bussey supported them.

Bradford's politics had undoubtedly changed since 1832, when Cunliffe-Lister and Hardy had trounced the Tory-supported George Banks by 650 and 471 votes to 402. Conservatives were undoubtedly heartened by the accession of the Hardy ironowners of Low Moor. But Liberal textile magnates favoured the great Cunliffe-Lister, squire of Manningham and creator of a major worsted complex. Dissenting entrepreneurs who opposed factory reform – Ackroyds, Ellises, Milligans and Salts – followed the princely lead, urged on by the *Mercury* and *Observer* against the 'violent but not very discreet' William and his personal bodyguard of 200 Tory roughs (paid 4s. daily).

Toryism, however, was not supported merely by decaying mercantile groups, as sometimes supposed. There was John Rand, 'father of the worsted industry' and pioneer factory reformer. And there were men like the socially-concerned curate John Boddington, Oastler's friend, and John Wood's partner William Walker and workers such as Squire Auty (a factory boy at 6 and later an Orange leader), the 'Short-Time' leader Matthew Balme and another John Wood – 'a plodding working man', latterly a pauper. Such disparate characters were linked by Anglican beliefs and 'Ten Hours' sympathies. Stuart–Wortley invariably supported them; as did his brother James.

On 25 July bands, banners and bullies paraded through crowded streets to the hustings. 'Several Gentlemen' told Johnson that

> as the Blues marched up with their music and lofty Banners [the scene] had the appearance of two Armies about to engage in Battle, which he could easily believe, for it was a noble and thrilling scene, which would never be forgotten by those who witnessed it.

Local gentry, led by that cold beauty Mrs. Walker Ferrand, watched from their emblazoned carriages, as the rowdy heckling began.

Amidst an almost deafening din, William roared out his beliefs:

> Give me fair play, Lads . . . as the poor man's friend for this last seven years. Neither of my opponents alluded to the New Poor Law Act . . . Will my opponents give you universal suffrage? – if they won't, I stand upon level with them. ('Will *you?*'). No, I will not . . . (*disapprobation*). You are called upon to support these men because they are supporters of the present Ministry, whose last act was to refuse inquiry into the case of the handloom weavers.

He attacked the Radical 'military-flogging General Evans' and promised to use 'his youthful energies to support the constitution'. And he told noisy opponents that he could speak until midnight. He was probably right.

Almost inevitably, all was in vain. At the show of hands the Liberals were said to have 15–20,000 supporters to the Tories' 1000. Johnson consoled himself by thinking that two or three thousand Tory hands were raised, including 'considerably above two-thirds of the Rank, Wealth and Intelligence of the Borough'. Hardy tested this view by demanding a poll of qualified electors next day. By 10 a.m. Cunliffe-Lister and Busfeild senior clearly led, by 465 and 456 votes to Hardy's 263 and 'young Busfeild's' 246. As the totals rose hourly the parties sent urgent messages to known or supposed supporters. But by 4 p.m. all was over (except the payment of candidates' debts, largely to tavern-keepers). Cunliffe-Lister had added 170 votes in six hours and Busfeild 165, while the losers, Hardy and young William Busfeild, reached totals of only 443 and 383 respectively. Defeat was 'mortifying' to Johnson and expensive to William. While the Liberal Press exulted over a double victory and Upwood tenants hauled uncle William's triumphal coach, the *Intelligencer* could only allege Liberal intimidation.

Election excitement did not subside with the Bradford contest. Even during the borough campaign William took time off to aid Stuart-Wortley in the Riding. After an unpleasant mauling at Halifax, Stuart-Wortley reached Bingley in mid-July. His coach was dragged into town by supporters, followed by the carriages of such gentry as Ibbetson, Dr. Busfeild, Mrs. Busfeild of St. Ives and Pollard. William introduced the candidate at a rowdy meeting, and later a Tory reception was held at Harden Grange. While Ibbetson escorted Stuart-Wortley to the Whig Duke of Devonshire's Keighley, William addressed the dour Radicals of Haworth and later spoke at Skipton.

On 31 July 'the rank and wealth' of both parties assembled at Wakefield with over 30,000 supporters. Trouble began almost immediately, as a drunken Whiggish group fought Oastler's equally violent Tory Radical bodyguard. Stones, slates and cudgels flew, as the dignitaries on the platform fled for cover. Before troops arrived two men were dead and scores lay injured. Arguments over responsibility for the riot raged for some time. Francis Fawkes of Farnley, the Whig chairman, blamed Oastler, who censured Morpeth's louts. At the Tories' afternoon dinner Busfeild and Oastler indignantly denied Fawkes's charge – though both had joined the battle, instead of running. Next day Morpeth and Strickland narrowly defeated Stuart-Wortley, by 12,576 and 11,892 to 11,489. Morpeth soon left to shoot with uncle Busfeild at Upwood.

Doubtless, Busfeild found it difficult to settle down again to a reasonably quiet rural life. The elections had gone badly for the Tories. Oastler was narrowly defeated (by 22 votes) in the Whig Ramsdens' tightly-controlled Huddersfield. James Stuart-Wortley lost his seat at Halifax and the factory-reform supporter Sir John Beckett lost his at Leeds. And the Bradford contest had cost William dearly. By October he owed £1196 to his aunt Margaret of Harden alone. As security for his debt, he mortgaged his interest as tenant in tail to St. Ives, in return for an annuity from Mrs. Ferrand. In 1838 Dr. Busfeild, James Milnes Gaskell of Thorne House (a

Protectionist family friend), Mrs. Margaret Ferrand and others joined in a similar arrangement – a very odd one, to William's brother Currer, as 'property worth 200,000£ [was] demised to secure such an absurd sum!!!!!' William, however, merely followed normal procedure in giving the security demanded by trustees' lawyers when he borrowed on expectations. He also had to arrange for the succession of the estates after himself and his heirs.

During these negotiations Busfield fell 'alarmingly ill' and it was only a few days before Christmas that his recovery was announced. Almost simultaneously, he was appointed a magistrate. The *Bradford Observer* was scandalised when Tory flags were raised on the tower of the old parish church of St. Peter and bells rang all day to welcome Busfeild's improvement:

> How far this display was likely to advance the dignity and usefulness of the Church, they must leave others to decide: to them it appeared highly unseemly.

To have provoked such wrath in liberal, dissenting editor Byles probably cheered the recuperating invalid.

CHAPTER TWO

Debut at Westminster

In the years which followed the general election of 1837 the Busfeild-Ferrands displayed increasing signs of their new affluence and higher social status. Busfeild's youngest brother Benjamin was sent to board at Shrewsbury School and then, in a revival of an old family tradition, to Cambridge as an undergraduate in 1841. His own boy William started a new and even grander family tradition by being entered for Eton. His proud father, who had at first moved to the luxurious villa at Myrtle Grove, when old Mrs. Busfeild went to live at St Ives, eventually took up a more permanent residence in the seigneurial mansion of Harden Grange.

Aided by his younger brother Johnson (one of three professional lawyers in the family), he was now virtually in charge of his mother's great St Ives estate which stretched from Keighley and Haworth to the outskirts of Bradford. It was as part of a complicated plan of family inheritance in case of the failure of his immediate heirs that in October 1839 he assumed by Sign Manual the additional surname of Ferrand. Despite his Tory and rural outlook much of the profit of the estate was prudently put into industrial and commercial undertakings calculated to yield a higher return than agricultural rents. By 1841 the Ferrands had invested over £36,000 in canal shares, almost £14,000 in six different railway companies, some £8,000 in four gas companies, over £19,000 in banking and insurance firms, and another £55,000 in a miscellany of other ventures ranging from real estate to docks and mining enterprises. King Corn might quarrel in public with King Coal, but Ferrand (as he must now be styled) had a large stake in Britain's industrial future. In this, however, he was no different from many other wealthy Tory landowners who ran their financial affairs with at least half an eye to maximising their income without allowing that economic factor to dictate their political behaviour.

But for Ferrand prosperity without controversy was an egg without salt. Placed on the board of trustees of Bingley Grammar School, he immediately fell foul of the majority of trustees who included two Whig M.P.s (one was his uncle William Busfeild), and seemed under Dissenting influence bent on weakening Anglican control of the school and altering the traditional classical curriculum. The resulting quarrel received much press publicity. This was not surprising in view of Ferrand's high-handed methods of carrying on an argument. When a meeting was called to oppose his activities, he used his powers as J.P. to ban it as likely to cause a breach of the peace. At a later parish assembly summoned to condemn Ferrand's intemperate attacks on the Board, he led in a force of operatives, spoke for two hours, and succeeded in winning both the popular vote and the subsequent plaudits of the Anglican party in the parish. This was only one of a number of incursions into local politics. He fought running battles with both the Bingley charitable trustees and the Keighley Poor Law Guardians (where he was the sole Tory member), and was successful in an appeal to a House of Commons committee to prevent the new Bradford Waterworks Company from taking without compensation the waters of a trout stream which fed the St Ives estate. The company eventually got their bill through parliament but had to pay compensation and allow the estate to continue to draw water form the stream.

Besides these local squabbles he made characteristic contributions to more national controversies. When the Home Secretary Lord John Russell endeavoured both to widen the class from which J.P.s were drawn and ingratiate himself with radical opinion by inviting recommendation for the magistracy from town councils (in industrial districts almost invariably radical-liberal in complexion), Ferrand published an anonymous pamphlet (his first) attacking both Russell and 'the class of uneducated, illiterate, coarse, underbred, vulgar-minded, low-lived and bankrupt men with whom his Lordship had deluged the country'. In 1841 he turned his attention to the Bingley factory-masters who had organised a meeting in favour of the Anti-Corn Law League. 'Do not these mill owners examine your carcases with the same eye that a dealer views a horse?' he stridently asked the operatives; and went on to remind the employers 'in the language of Mr O'Connell, that there are *Eleven Millions of us*' whom they would have to face if they persisted with their policy. He himself was becoming increasingly associated with the agricultural interest and opposition to the campaign for the repeal of the Corn Laws. Earlier that year he had presided over the annual dinner of the Wharfedale Agricultural Society. It was one of the many ironies of family politics that his uncle William, mindful of the opinions of his industrial allies in the West Riding, spoke the same month at a Bradford tea-party organised by the Manchester Anti-Corn Law League.

Old causes and old friends were not forgotten. In January 1839 he addressed the Bradford Operatives Conservative dinner and used the occasion to air a number of his political views. He criticised the Whigs for their equivocal attitude to the Corn Laws, announced his decided opposition to their repeal, and went on to launch attacks on the new Poor Law and Pope Gregory XVI. Such a potent mixture of protectionism, social concern and Protestant fervour went down well with the Tory workers and henceforth Ferrand was one of their heroes. Two years later he joined a small group of Bradford Tory factory reformers in forming a new Bingley Short-Time Committee. By that date their original champion was in the Fleet Prison, incarcerated for debt by his employer, Thomas Thornhill of Fixby Hall, who had been enraged by Oastler's opposition to the new Poor Law. A fund was opened locally to relieve Oastler, and Ferrand was determined to give him all the support he could.

In all these diverse controversies, national and parochial, there was a consistent philosophy behind Ferrand's apparently indiscriminate vendettas. In his own passionate way he was only reflecting the beliefs, fears and prejudices of many members of his class. The clash between industrial and rural interests was one of the growing-pains of Victorian society. Ferrand, a Tory landowner embedded in one of the great expanding industrial districts of England, was peculiarly affected by the strains it imposed. He saw things, as he always did, in black and white.

His was a simplistic view of the gathering struggle. The old order of the countryside, hierarchic, deferential and bound together by bonds of mutual trust, obligation and loyalty, was being challenged by brash industrial *nouveaux riches*, who cared nothing for either tradition or their overworked employees in their immoral pursuit of profit. All the battles between Church and dissent, between bucolic streams and foully-polluted urban rivers, between anciently-endowed classical free grammar schools which had trained many a humble leader of Church, State and Empire and the technological-commercial training centres desired by industrialists, between the benevolence of parochial and squirearchic paternalism and harshness of the new, centralised, intentionally cost-saving Poor Law, between the slow-moving, predestined rhythm of the countryside and the urgently-pulsating vibrations of urban industry with its cycles of slump and boom were part of the same conflict.

II

In May Melbourne's ever-weakening Government was defeated in the Budget debate and on 4 June a 'no confidence' motion was carried by one vote in a tense Commons. Preparations had already begun for a general election, and when Sir Gregory Lewin declined a Tory nomination at Bradford, the *Mercury* supposed that Ferrand would rejoin Hardy to fight the seat. Uncle Busfeild announced his own candidature, favouring

> Safe and Progressive Reform, the radical Removal of all Grievances and the immediate Destruction of all impolitic Restrictions on our Trade.

The other Liberal, Cunliffe-Lister, advocated 'Total Repeal of the Corn Laws' (which 'had produced the most unexampled Distress, lowered Wages and . . . Dear Bread'), tax reductions, suffrage extension, Poor Law reform and 'Total Abolition of Church Rates' ('a payment as obnoxious as it was unjust'). Hardy's determination to regain his seat was well-known but no hint of action came from Harden Grange.

Of course Ferrand was interested in the contest in the worsted metropolis, but he was more heavily involved in the Riding battle. Viscounts Morpeth and Milton, heirs to the Whig earldoms of Carlisle and Fitzwilliam, with their vast estates and palatial houses, shared impeccable genealogies and free-trade views. The Tories challenged them, under John Stuart-Wortley and Edmund Beckett-Denison, a member of the Leeds banking family and a prominent railway promoter. Both supported agricultural Protection, Poor Law Reform, wider education and Oastler's factory campaigns. In their support, the *Intelligencer* published regular attacks on workhouse cruelties, a particular concern of the editor, Robert Perring. These were candidates whom Ferrand could warmly support, as representatives of the Toryism which appealed alike to Oastlerite traditionalists, sturdily defending 'Altar, Throne and Cottage', and the Radical readers of the megalomaniac Feargus O'Connor's

Chartist *Northern Star*, printed and eventually edited by the Oastlerite Radical Joshua Hobson. O'Connor's popularity enabled him to fill the gap left by the imprisoned Northern Tory demagogues Oastler and the 'revolutionary' Joseph Rayner Stephens.

Ferrand threw himself into the Riding campaign, speaking at Keighley, Morton, Skipton and elsewhere. His biting attacks provoked Liberal retaliation, the *Observer* alleging that he was angry at not being nominated at Bradford, but in fact his hopes had moved elsewhere. On 3 June he agreed to contest Knaresborough.

This ancient borough had returned two MPs ever since 1553. After many years under the Tory influence of the Slingsby family in the late eighteenth century it fell to the lords of the manor, the Whig Dukes of Devonshire. In 1832 it had loyally returned two Whigs, John Richards and Benjamin Rotch, but in 1835 it turned from London carpetbaggers to the Tory squire Andrew Lawson of Boroughbridge Hall with Richards as junior Member. The Tory incursion was crushed in 1837, when Henry Rich (unsuccessful in 1832 and 1835) and Charles Langdale (son of the local magnate, Lord Stourton of Allerton Park) triumphed by 172 and 124 votes to Lawson's 118. A minority of only six votes encouraged local Tories to bid now for both seats, despite past experience.

On his first visit Ferrand explained his beliefs to a large crowd: he was

> A Tory, or . . . a determined supporter of our Glorious Constitution in Church and State, fully resolved to resist any attempt . . . to benefit one part of her Majesty's subjects at the expense of another, determined to give equal protection to all classes, from her Majesty on the throne to the peasant in his cottage, a conserver of all that is good in our institutions and a destroyer of all that is bad.

Such Oastlerite (and later Disraelian) sentiments delighted the *Intelligencer*, though the Liberal *Mercury* sourly noted Ferrand's rudeness to hecklers and asserted that he

> feigned to be very homely and familiar, by addressing his audience as 'Lads', beginning his sentences 'Na Lads' and occasionally 'Na then Lads'.

Events proceeded rapidly. On the 4th, as Ferrand's address appeared, the Liberal Hutchinson retired. Next day Lawson, Langdale and the Hon. Robert Colborne published their messages. On the 8th, as Ferrand issued his riposte, Colborne and Langdale resigned. 'Mr. Ferrand', claimed the *Intelligencer*, 'has the right to say *Veni, Vidi, Vici*'. The mortified *Mercury* could only allege that he had bought up local taverns and urged Rich to keep out the obnoxious Ferrand,

> a red-hot Tory . . . arrogant, blustering and quarrelsome, who had the indecency to offer himself . . . in express opposition to his own uncle. He has no claim on any constituency possessing a spark of liberality or desirous of maintaining courtesy and peace.

Ferrand for his part continued to lash 'degraded and corrupt' Whigs, and their

Treason and Rebellion . . . Wilful Waste . . . disgraceful jobbing . . . destruction of the Rights of the Poor . . . and insane cry of the Repeal of the Corn Laws.

Knaresborough had rarely heard such stuff since its riotous election of July 1804. But Ferrand was also a constitutionalist reformer and Churchman, who would always defend the 'Protestant Faith against the Errors of Popery and the deadly sin of Socialism' and could not forgive Melbourne for introducing 'Robert Owen, the Founder of Socialism' to the Queen.

In addition to exciting Knaresborough, Ferrand energetically participated in the Riding battle. Despite Whig condemnations of the 'Bull Dog' he was given a hero's welcome at Keighley, where local Chartists supported Denison and Wortley, who stayed at St. Ives. Whigs had less happy experiences. At Otley Milton was assailed by the left-wing Chartist organiser Julian Harney and (with 'unmanly abuse') by Ferrand. It was later alleged that Ferrand threw money to the crowd, enjoining it to 'drink like hell and fight like devils'.

He also visited Leeds, where the Tory candidates were Denison's brother, the banker William Beckett, and Viscount Jocelyn (Ashley's brother-in-law) – both inevitably factory reformers and anti-Poor Law campaigners. The imprisoned O'Connor (despite opposition from such socialistic Chartists as Bronterre O'Brien) urged his followers to support the Tories. Everywhere, Oastler's call for an alliance between workers and Tories seemed to be bearing fruit. In Bradford, for instance, it was claimed that Chartists were 'chiefly instrumental in throwing out Mr. Busfield': Hardy and William Cunliffe-Lister headed the poll. Oastler delighted to quote the Whig *Morning Chronicle*'s view that 'the Chartists, such as are voters, have almost to a man supported the Tories'.

Knaresborough's nomination occurred on 29 June, when Ferrand proudly declared that his qualifications were 'Yorkshire coal, Yorkshire houses, Yorkshire stone and Yorkshire corn'. On the hustings he reviewed his family's history, condemned the 'un-English and detestable' Ballot and told hecklers that 'the Whigs had never had such a thorn in their sides as he was to them'. The Liberal London barrister Charles Sturgeon confessed that he had only arrived at the prompting of the raffish Radical dandy Thomas Slingsby Duncombe (MP. for Finsbury) to keep Ferrand out. The show of hands favoured Lawson and Ferrand and next day Sturgeon fell at the poll by 85 votes to 150 and 122. The victors were chaired and cheered through the little town.

Still better news came on 12 July, when Stuart-Wortley and Beckett Denison won the Riding by 13,165 and 12,780 votes to Milton's 12,080 and Morpeth's 12,031. Here was cause for great Tory rejoicing. Written off as a doomed irrelevance in 1832, Conservatism was now making striking gains in the manufacturing districts. 'Yorkshiremen were not Fitzwilliam's serfs!', wrote the delighted Oastler. 'This is indeed a marvellous work', recorded Lord Ashley, in something akin to excitement. After an enthusiastic chairing of the new MPs 1500 Tories boozily dined in Leeds Corn Exchange under Harewood's son, Edwin Lascelles. Ferrand joined the delirious assembly, with such friends as Milnes Gaskell, Beckett and Lord Pollington. Amidst the numerous toasts he thundered against Whiggery. The despondent *Mercury* could only comment that

> Judging from the shouting outside, the company seemed intoxicated with joy, as, indeed, many of them were in reality. We have heard of one rabid Tory from Leeds, who proposed as a toast 'The Whigs – a speedy passage of them to Botany Bay, and may they sink in the middle of their passage!!!' As a specimen of the speakers at this meeting, we may mention the hot-headed member for Knaresborough, Mr. Busfeild Ferrand, during whose ranting effusion the band stationed outside played the appropriate air from Jack Sheppard of 'Nix my Dolly'.

After the election Ferrand presented a silver tankard to his Knaresborough agent and, with Sarah, added to the estate by buying the manor of Harden and Marley Hall for £17,300, with a reversionary interest for Walker Busfeild; thus the fine Stuart yeoman's house of the Currers returned to their descendants.

After a few days' shooting at St. Ives, Ferrand arranged lodgings in London. His first visit was to Oastler's cell – already a fashionable calling-place. On 22 August, Oastler recorded,

> W. Busfeild Ferrand, Esq., MP, did me the honour to dine with me, and gave me 5£. Upon my word, I was delighted to see that man!

Since his imprisonment Oastler had published a weekly journal, *The Fleet Papers*, to propound those causes – Protection, Anglicanism, industrial and Poor Law reform and socially-concerned Toryism – beloved by his disciple. Constantly during the future months Oastler was cheered by Ferrand's company and generosity, while Ferrand benefited from the master's valuable advice.

III

The new parliament assembled in the latter half of August and the Member for Knaresborough experienced no coy qualms about his maiden speech. On 23 August he informed the Commons that

> he was himself sent to Parliament by a constituency strongly opposed to [the Poor Laws]; and he came there to oppose them to the utmost of his power.

When he went on to accuse Lord John Russell of 'enormous lying', the Speaker gently called him to order. He next gave an Oastlerite warning to Peel:

> anxious as he was to see [him] continue long at the head of the Administration, . . . he would still fearlessly assert that [he must] repeal the more obnoxious clauses of this Bill . . .

'Such supporters', mused the *Mercury*, 'would soon make Sir Robert Peel quake'. But Ferrand achieved instant fame. His phrases were 'more valuable for their blunt honesty than for their polished elegance', commented *The Times*, adding that

We like plain speaking like this; it is honourable to the member who uses it, and may be profitable to the Minister to whom it is addressed.

A month later Ferrand enhanced his reputation by seconding the Radical Sharman Crawford's motion against establishing further Poor Law unions. To him the Poor Law remained unconstitutional and immoral:

it deprived the poor of that adequate relief and protection to which they were entitled by the constitution of the country [and gave Liberals an excuse] to button up their pockets, and not to relieve the poor to that extent which feelings of humanity prescribed and the duties of property demanded.

He told of aged Keighley paupers tramping miles to solicit a 'miserable pittance' from a board dominated by masters. Indeed, he 'identified the Poor Law with the present disgraceful factory system': it was designed to aid wealthy employers, who so often blamed landowners for all distress. The wretched inhabitants of Manchester, of whose plight the Opposition complained, were

their own worn-out, cast-off machinery, out of whose sinews they had extracted their wealth, and then flung them away to die in misery and want.

Such Yorkshire bluntness was new to Parliament, and the chamber filled as Ferrand thundered on. Amid Tory enthusiasm, he championed the agriculturalists against Mancunian industrialists:

I tell those boasting cotton-spinners that their immense wealth has its duties, as well as its rights, and that it is their bounden duty, instead of constantly preaching of the misfortunes and distresses of the poor, to disgorge some part of the enormous fortunes they have amassed out of their labour and sinews, and to relieve their present distresses. How different is their conduct from that of the landed nobleman! . . .

Where is the hon. member for Stockport, who the other night declared that the Corn Laws were baptised in blood? ('Here', from Mr. Cobden). I tell [him] that every farthing he has obtained by the cotton trade is sprinkled with the blood of the poor infant factory children . . .

Sir, I am convinced that food is sufficiently cheap in this country, if the operatives received a just requital for their labour; and I tell the manufacturers who come here to lay the blame upon the shoulders of the landed proprietors, that they themselves are the most avaricious and selfish class of all the holders of property. The landlords are very well contented if their rents pay them $3\frac{1}{2}$%, but I doubt if these millowners are satisfied with a profit of 1000%. Sir, if I don't speak within bounds, what did they mean by boasting at the Manchester dinner that they could buy up the nobility of England?

Ferrand went on to praise Oastler's brave fight against the factory and Poor Law systems. He underlined his conviction that the two were connected by quoting letters from Edmund Ashworth and Robert Hyde Greg – two prominent Lancashire Liberal masters and opponents of factory reform – requesting the Commissioners' aid in recruiting cheap pauper labour for their mills. England was 'a land of slavery', for men, women and children were 'regularly picked, bought, sold and invoiced by the Poor Law Commissioners to the cotton-spinners in Lancashire, there to be worked to death'. Ferrand bluntly passed responsibility to the Home Secretary, Sir James Graham, and demanded wide social reforms.

Tory squires from the shires were not expected to make knowledgeable speeches about industrial matters, but the silent majority on the back benches rejoiced in their new champion, who could voice their long-felt beliefs and employed biting invective against the 'millocracy'. Ferrand thus became a celebrity, whose speeches were widely published and discussed. The *Bolton Chronicle* praised the 'sterling, stirring, staunch and noble address'. Ferrand's speech, declared the *Intelligencer*, 'excited unusual attention and interest':

> His manner was earnest, his language severe, his reflections somewhat discriminate; but the valuable truths that he told more than compensated.

'The poor of England ought to feel deeply indebted' to him, asserted the *Yorkshire Gazette*. The *Manchester Guardian*, the voice of the cotton magnates, condemned Ferrand's 'unscrupulous dealing with facts'.

The London Press was equally interested. The *Morning Chronicle* noted the 'somewhat juvenile Boanerges, whose voice was no bad echo of the honest and manly spirit of the orator'. *The Standard* and *St. James Chronicle* rejoiced at his 'extremely eloquent and just denunciation' – which *The Courier* thought 'most impressive and unanswerable'. Ferrand had 'exposed the whole truth', rejoiced the agricultural *John Bull*. And *The Age* commented that he had 'redeemed the mean monotony of the general dullness' and told Parliament 'something like the truth – a commodity of not very frequent occurrence in the walls of St. Stephens': Ferrand had

> nobly pleaded the cause of the landowners – the truest friends of the people of England, against the griping and grinding millowners and sweltering manufacturers.

The Parliamentary reaction was intense. Ferrand 'appeared amongst his friends on his own side of the House', commented the *Chronicle*, 'as if a shell with the fuse burning was lying ready to explode'. His 'thundering vehemence' had electrified the Commons:

> But it is not enough to read [his] speech. It must have been heard in order to convey an idea of its richness. His ideas wriggled in his brain like eels in a frying pan. Logic, law and authority all jumped together . . .

The *Weekly Chronicle* percipiently considered that Ferrand's speech – 'the most remarkable in the recent 'Debates' – was based on 'the extraordinary stories [of] Mr. Oastler and Dr. Holland's *Millocrat*, with an occasional spice of the *Northern Star*'. Such a Tory-Chartist alliance appalled defenders of Liberal capitalism. 'War on the Factories is the cry of the Squires', asserted the *Globe*, to meet the watchword of war on the Corn Laws. Mr. Ferrand put himself forward last night as their boisterous and boiling representative . . .

But to Tories the hirsute young squire was the man who could effectively deal with the masters.

Although Crawford's motion was easily defeated by 131 votes to 49, Ferrand was now the cynosure of the dinner parties. Oastler delightedly shared his views. He was suspicious of Peel:

> Somehow, I do not like the casting of this new Conservative administration. I fear there is something rotten, out of joint, and ricketty about it. I am always jealous of those cotton lords.

And gradually he came particularly to distrust Graham, a former Whig Minister: 'the people were sick of Whiggery; they would not endure it even under the name of Conservatism'. Ferrand continued to please and help him, arriving with a brace of moor game on 27 September. 'Did not FERRAND do his duty manfully?', Oastler wrote:

> I thought that he made a breach in the Towers of Oppression, by which my gallant Ten Hours Bill men will enter the citadel!

Nearly half a century later the impression made by Ferrand was vividly recalled by Alexander Baillie-Cochrane in his reminiscences:

> The effect . . . in the House when he made his first attack on the manufacturers will live long in the parliamentary memory. He had only recently taken his seat, and had not attracted much attention except for his strenuous, bold and burly appearance; but as soon as he rose the House was taken by surprise by his Dantonesque appearance and stentorian voice. The great denunciator of all manufacturing wrongs, of tyranny and fraud, had at last appeared. It was a Danton, a Mirabeau, addressing the Convention – not a simple member of Parliament fresh from the hustings. When he spoke of the truck system and tore in shreds a piece of cloth, full of what he styled 'devil's dust', the effect was electrical. 'Who', each one asked, 'was this man come to judgment, to strike the manufacturer root and branch with his terrible invective?' – a Yorkshireman, who was master of his subject and clearly well acquainted with all the secrets of the factory system. It was a new revelation . . .

Parliament was prorogued in October, and after his remarkable Westminster debut Ferrand departed home to pick a quarrel with local Whig magistrates for granting inn licences to their own tenants, shoot on the moors with his son, and prepare for the new session.

IV

Early in 1842 factory and Poor Law reformers anxiously awaited information on Peel's policies. During the previous autumn, aided by William Beckett, Yorkshire

Debut at Westminster

Short-Time delegates canvassed the Ministry, gaining nothing from Peel, Edward Stanley, Graham and Gladstone, while Wharncliffe and Buckingham pledged full support. Wharncliffe's son, Stuart-Wortley, praised the workers' report and also promised help. Ashley himself could obtain no clear answers and came to regard this non-committal stance as hostile. Peel's decision to lower the corn duties hinted at a liberal approach and provoked the resignation of 'the farmer's friend', the rash Buckingham, in February.

A deputation of Bradford operatives who called at Harden Grange in early January received a warmer reception. Ferrand

> assured them that his whole time and attention was devoted to the welfare of the labouring classes, nor should any man be found more zealous and willing than himself to alleviate the sufferings and distresses under which they laboured.

The delegates were 'highly satisfied' with his views on 'Ten Hours' and the Poor Law.

When Parliament met, Peel's Corn Law announcement of 3 February dominated interest. Oastler condemned the move as a sop to the League:

> it was simply 15% in favour of long black chimneys, with clouds of thick smoke, and 15% against our cornfields and country breezes.

These were entirely Ferrand's sentiments, and henceforth nothing restrained his expression of growing doubts about the policies of his nominal leader.

On the evening of 14 February Ferrand delivered a long speech to a crowded House, 'on behalf of the Working Classes' against the League. He claimed that many Free Trade petitions were fraudulent:

> the Manufacturers had exacted the signatures of their workpeople to them by a Tyranny and Oppression which destroyed the Liberty of the Subject.

Again he assailed League propaganda and wealthy employers – particularly Cobden (who 'was . . . running his mill both night and day') – and supporters like John Bowring, the amply-pensioned Member for Bolton – who

> had made such exertions to carry out his free-trade principles against the public purpose as to have fairly entitled himself to the character of a free-booter.

And again he attacked 'that infamous conspiracy . . . between the Poor Law conspirators and the cotton spinners, for the purpose of reducing the amount of wages'.

Ferrand reserved his maximum venom for O'Connell – who had declared that

> the Manchester cotton spinners were possessed of sufficient wealth to buy up all the landed estates of England, that the landowner's venison was moistened with the widows' tears and his claret dyed with their infants' blood – rather a

cool assertion of [him] to make, when he himself had subsisted for many years out of the pence of the poor.

To Ferrand, the Leaguers' sole aim was 'to increase their profits by lowering the price of labour'. He exposed the 'tyranny, oppression and plunder' of the truck system of payment in (often inferior) goods instead of cash. Leaguers, indeed,

> lived and moved and had their whole being for money alone; money was the sole object of their lives; they cared not how they got it, even by the ruin and oppression of the operative, so long as they amassed wealth. They looked for nothing but enormous profits. They declared that there was no religion in trade; nay, they were, to use the language of Burke, a set of men 'who had made their ledgers their Bibles, their counting-houses their churches and their money their God'.

Ferrand appealed to landowners to rescue workers from industrialists' 'tyranny, oppression and wicked designs'.

'The Friend of the Working Classes' achieved immense publicity. To Leaguers he might be 'the buffoon of the House', but to Northern Tory-Chartists he appeared brilliantly charismatic and to squirearchical MPs he was a providential scourge of the hated League. *The Times* considered that his speech 'ought to be a lesson to the . . . League' against oratorical violence, and the *Bradford Herald* welcomed 'the most humorous, straightforward, manly speech'. Other Tory journals commented similarly, though the *Manchester Chronicle* thought him 'indiscriminate, and therefore unjust', while confessing that 'his language towards the manufacturers was far from equally unjust, extravagant and mischievous with that directed against the landowners by the Leaguers'.

Liberal reaction developed quickly. On 24 February, during the debate on Charles Villiers' annual anti-Corn Law motion, Cobden, the 37-year-old Stockport master, was put up to reply. Fervent, confident and (thought Disraeli) 'saucy', he opposed industrial reform and agricultural Protection alike and particularly hated 'booby' squires. He denied every allegation:

> The people may not be crying out exclusively for the repeal of the Corn Laws, because they have looked beyond that question, and have seen greater evils even than this, which they wish to have remedied at the same time; and, now that the cries for 'Universal Suffrage' and 'The Charter' are heard, let no hon. Gentlemen deceive themselves by supposing that, because members of the Anti-Corn Law League have sometimes found themselves getting into collision with the Chartists, that therefore the Chartists, or the working men generally, were favourable to the Corn Laws.

Cobden was, to say the least, ambiguous and ambivalent: Northern Oastlerites had long recognised leading Leaguers as their principal opponents in the factory and Poor Law campaigns, and more honest Liberals than Cobden recognised the fact.

Inevitably, Ferrand instantly counter-attacked, amidst Tory enthusiasm. He answered recent attacks upon himself and bluntly told Peel that he would never have his support, unless he thought it his duty to give it; and he would seek no other reward than an approving conscience.

He roared out attacks on his detractors, as 'vociferous and long-continued cheering from the ministerial side' greeted his exposure of the word-chopping, semantic casuistry of the radical Joseph Brotherton, who had denied the charge that Cobden's mill worked through the night on the grounds that it was really a printworks. If Leaguers persisted in provoking Chartists to revolt, the workers 'would first bury their bayonets in the bosoms of those whom they knew to be their oppressors'.

Ferrand aroused intense party passions and wide comment. The League's first historian recalled, eleven years later, that he

> kept the house in a continual state of excitement, alternate cheers from the protectionists and laughter from the free traders following every libellous and abusive sentence.

High Tories were overjoyed:

> The terrible denunciation of [Leaguers'] falsehoods, frauds, cruelties and hypocrisy delivered by Mr. Ferrand in a style of indignant eloquence such as has rarely shaken the House of Commons or any other public assembly in modern times . . . which struck them almost dumb, and, as they confessed, made them tremble at the time, has sealed their doom for ever . . . a more effective or more crushing speech was never delivered in the House of Commons, or a speech that produced its effect more promptly or unequivocally . . . Mr. Ferrand has dealt a death-blow to the League, and, therefore, we owe to him every line that we can spare.

His 'stinging but truthful delineations' delighted the Right. 'Few could have commanded so attentive an audience – none could have elicited more rapturous cheers' than that pre-eminent champion of the working classes, and especially the poor', asserted Northern allies. Even *The Times* wrote of 'the signal and utter rout of the Jacobin . . . League'; Ferrand had 'held up them and their practices to the contempt of the population . . . [by] unanswerable facts . . . fearlessly and ably stated'.

Oastler delightedly hoped that 'everybody would read the speeches' of his friend, to whom 'thanks of the Christian people of England were due'. One Northern worker, in a 16-page printed letter to Ferrand, confirmed his allegations from 25 years' experience. He wrote of masters' wealth based on such practices as deceptive starching, mixing of 'Devil's Dust' and truck – together with the replacement of males by women and children, fines, industrial injuries and children's nightwork (as practised by Cobden). He hoped that Ferrand would 'go on exposing this cruel system, which he considered equal to slavery'. John Almack, 'a backbone Tory' from Beverley, later declared that Ferrand's 'general charges were strictly true'; his 'defect was that he was too sparing' of the League!

Liberals inevitably felt very differently. 'One of the worst features in the conduct of the Tory members', insisted the Whig *Chronicle*, was the mode in which they received the calumnious charges brought by Mr. Ferrand against the master manufacturers of England. They were absolutely frantic with joy . . . The exhibition reflected a disgrace on the House . . . Our sole motive for bestowing this attention on Mr. Ferrand is the manner in which the Tory majority identify themselves with his statements. For this reason we do not think the knowledge which he claims of the views of the Chartists is altogether to be neglected. The late disclosures at Leicester have proved the intimate connections between Tory gold and Chartist movements. Mr. Ferrand may know more of the uses to which the contents of the Tory purse have been applied than he chooses to disclose to the House of Commons.

One reader complained of Ferrand's 'plagiarisms' from Oastler's *Fleet Papers*: he was 'led to infer that, beyond all doubt, Mr. Oastler was Mr. Ferrand's monitor and correspondent'. A *Times* reader instantly 'wished many more [MPs], as well as members of the community, would improve both their minds and their hearts by a regular perusal of these genuine English Fleeters'.

Cobden was particularly bitter. 'The way in which [Ferrand's] speech had been received showed that . . . the great Ministerial majority had declared open war against the manufacturers', he claimed:

> The grosser the insult . . . the louder were their cheers, the fouler the calumny the more rapturous was the applause, and the intensity of the Ministerial exultation was only equalled by the malignity of the libel.

He told his brother that he had heard at his club that 'Master Ferrand' was 'planted' to follow him:

> Away he went with the attitudes of a prize fighter and the voice of a bull . . . Colonel S[ibthorp] plied the fellow with oranges to suck, in an affectionate way that resembled a monkey fondling a bear.

Cobden himself caught the excitement of Ferrand's midnight oration, as late-dining Members crowded into the House:

> You never witnessed such a scene . . . The Tories were literally frantic with delight. Every sentence he uttered was caught up and cheered by a large majority, far more vehemently than anything that ever fell from Peel or Macaulay. It was not ironical cheering, but downright hearty approbation. I have not the least doubt that [he] spoke the honest convictions of a majority of the members present.

With such acclamations and warnings Ferrand was content. He was in action again, on 7 March, replying to opponents. He quoted from his vast correspondence from Northern masters and workers and Birmingham operatives' resolution of support. 'In the name of the working classes of England, he challenged the hon. Members opposite – he implored them – to ask for a Select Committee to investigate his statements'. A week later he moved for a copy of all convictions for truck payments (which were technically illegal under an Act of 1831). Operative friends had sent him a League circular to Lancashire employers, suggesting that 'it might be well to direct the foremen of works to obtain declarations signed by a few of the men', to 'complete the exposure of Mr. Ferrand's charges'. No such papers had appeared, 'because', declared Ferrand,

> the working men had at last shown a proper spirit . . . [and] rebelled against the attempt to make them sign what they knew to be false.

He promised to move for a committee on the truck system after the Easter recess.

V

On 19 April Ferrand proposed his motion for a Select Committee on industrial frauds. He frankly admitted that

> when he first brought forward the charges . . . he was induced to do so in self-defence – he was driven into it by the accusations brought against the Landed Interest . . .

He quoted examples of frauds which were now reducing exports: 'There was, indeed, one law for the rich and another for the poor, so long as such a system was allowed to go on'. On truck he could present a large volume of evidence, but

> the responsibility rested on the House and on the Government dealing with the claims for justice and redress of honest manufacturers and distressed workmen . . . Ardently did he hope that the Government would discharge the duty they owed to the public as the guardians of the country's honour and of the sovereign's dignity . . . by agreeing to the motion, which he urged on the unassailable principle that the labourer was worthy of his hire.

The motion was not adopted, but an amendment moved by Graham for an inquiry into truck was eventually accepted by Ferrand.

Eleven days later Ferrand and his latest opponent, William Hutt (the Liberal husband of the Dowager Countess of Strathmore), were both rebuked by the Speaker for violent speeches during a discussion of a petition on the Southampton election. Ferrand thereafter developed a long (and often justified) suspicion of the way in which such matters were handled. But he was now clearly a figure of some renown. In early May he was invited by Dr. Howley, the last 'Prince Archbishop', to a public dinner at Lambeth Palace, which was graced by Chevalier Bunsen, the Russian ambassador, a score of peers and many MPs. The doors of High Society were now open.

Fame was, however, balanced by unpopularity. In June Ferrand was the second in a series of 'Popular Portraits' published by Herbert Ingram's new *Illustrated London News*, as 'just now one of the men whose names float on the stream of political conversation'. But it was considered that 'his reputation . . . was the growth of a single night, and would be but of a short duration'. His first speech earned notoriety, the others contempt:

> He certainly surprised the House in his first essay; no one could imagine that such recklessness of assertion could exist with such inability to support it by proof; and his coarseness of manner was, in the excitement of the moment, mistaken for strength . . . For three days or more the lately obscure member . . . was a parliamentary lion, with a mane and tail of the first magnitude; his name stood printed in letters of great length and height; it was heard at the clubs, repeated at Bellamy's, and re-echoed in the lobbies. Party thought it had found a new weapon . . . Party, however, was deceived.

Ferrand was 'an extinguished politician' to the *News* for failing to answer Leaguers. Though sincere and energetic, he had spoiled 'a good cause'. And to the fastidious editor, Frederick ('Omnibus') Bayley, he was not even personally prepossessing:

> his figure and face, though not bulky, have something coarse about them; there seems to be a continual and unamiable scowl upon his countenance, as if he were pondering the possibility of condemning the poor-law commissioners to three months of their own dietary, or of grinding the leaders of the corn-law league to 'devil's dust' in the machinery of their own mills.

The *News* was to amend its views (and its original atrocious portrait); but its early attitude typified hostile Liberal defamation of the Northern prodigy.

Before the summer recess Ferrand spent several busy weeks at Westminster. As an inheritor of the traditions of the squirearchic 'Country Party' which had so opposed Roman Catholic Emancipation in 1829 that it favoured suffrage extension in 1831 and which remained wedded to notions of bucolic paternalism and local control, he could scarcely support Peel's moves towards economic liberalism. But, like most Tories, he did not yet directly attack Peel, Graham and other front-benchers while expressing the doubts of already-disturbed country gentlemen. Ferrand's *forté* was to delight the mute gentry, with their ancient estates and rural interests, by his vitriolic charges against their cocksure industrial slanderers.

Such activities did not endear Ferrand to Peel and Graham. But an agricultural Protectionist standing up to the party establishments and to Liberal tormentors immensely cheered the knights from the shires. One by one, Ferrand noisily argued with prominent Whigs and Radicals. In June, during a debate on a reduction of cotton duties, he reached Bowring and Joseph Hume. His charge that Bowring had hidden evidence on Swiss attitudes towards free trade caused 'a scene of great confusion', as Liberals angrily turned on Ferrand. The accusation was probably correct.

Nine days later, on 16 June, Ferrand proposed a new motion in a small house. He asked for a grant of £1,000,000 to relieve growing misery, 'on the broad ground that it was [workers'] right; the legislature . . . had reduced them to their present distress' by passing the Poor Law. In the debate Peel typically condemned the proposal, as it would necessitate extra taxation. The Whig Fox Maule 'strongly deprecated [Ferrand's] dangerous language', and Villiers earned the Speaker's rebuke by alleging that Ferrand 'had done everything in his power to excite disaffection'.

The Peelite Bickham Éscott attacked the 'most dangerous motion' and 'dangerous speech'. Cobden oddly 'abstained from personalities', as

> he thought that to bandy words with [Ferrand], in the present state of the country, was like playing with fire while sitting on a barrel of gunpowder.

Only Slingsby Duncombe supported the motion; and he wanted a larger sum, believing that only a Chartist march on London would provoke real action. Ferrand would not agree, maintaining that 'the people put more confidence in his assertions than in those of the whole party opposite'. But he was defeated by 106 to 6 (Radical) votes.

Defeats never deterred Ferrand. On 17 June he opposed Graham's plan to continue the Poor Law for five years. He appealed for a return to the Elizabethan system: 'the people of England had a right . . . to the soil of the country . . . and to be protected from oppression'. He quoted local examples of harsh injustice, and Graham devoted much of his reply to countering Ferrand. The Home Secretary quoted reports from Assistant Commissioner Charles Mott criticising the decisions of the reforming Keighley Union under Ferrand: there, the paupers actually 'claimed relief as their right'!

Mott's report had never been seen by anyone but the author and Graham, and Ferrand angrily denounced it as 'grossly unfounded' and resented Graham's sneer that he had obtained 'an easy character for great humanity' and had caused trouble in the Union. Graham succeeded by 260 votes to 61 at the Second Reading, but on the 20th Ferrand demanded a copy of Mott's Keighley report, and in Committee Sibthorp and Thomas Wakley (a London Radical coroner given to announcing verdicts of murder on pauper deaths) proposed a postponement of Graham's proposal. They lost by 219 votes to 48. Ferrand again assailed Mott's 'tissue of falsehoods', maintaining that the devious investigator had been sent 'expressly for the purpose of setting up a case in favour of the Bill and against the Keighley Union'.

Thus began the controversy which became known as 'the great Mott Case'. Mott had initially tried, from 1838, to modify the hostility aroused in the North by the tactless Assistant Commissioner Alfred Power since 1836. But his courtesy achieved nothing with the Tory-Radicals and he gradually adopted a firmer policy and by 1841 was trying to enforce the Act in recalcitrant, depressed textile Unions. In 1842, with his colleagues Sir John Walsham and Charles Clements, he rigorously acted in the hard-hit boroughs. From April he attempted to implement the full rigours of the Act against the opposition of Keighley's newly-elected and largely-hostile Board, in particular trying to enforce the hated Labour Test Order. As chairman, Ferrand bitterly opposed Mott, obtained the withdrawal of the order and had the satisfaction of seeing Mott dismissed in strange circumstances in 1843.

Ferrand's opposition to the Poor Law was shared by many Tory members, including such Yorkshire friends as Beckett, Denison, Hardy, Lawson, Pollington and Stuart-Wortley, along with such Radicals as Crawford, John Fielden and Oastler's untrustworthy friend Charles Hindley. But when Ferrand resumed his denunciation of Graham on 24 June, Peel himself assailed Bingley's leader, authorities and abominable workhouse. And so Ferrand was unfairly crushed by unpublished evidence. But on the 27th he bounced back, to claim that Peel's information (based on Walsham's notes) was entirely false and especially concocted. He did not fear the premier's disapproval. 'The country [was] betrayed when it placed confidence in the government', he roared, amidst mounting disapproval.

The traumatic moment for a break with Peelite Conservatism seemed to have arrived, after these bitter rows. But Ferrand 'cared not for friend or foe', bluntly asserting that

> the government had been raised to power by the deep-rooted hatred which the people bore to the New Poor Law. It was the detestation of that law which placed the Conservative candidates at the head of the poll. It was to raise their voices against that law that they were returned to that House, and he stood there to perform the duty for which he had been sent.

The Poor Law was 'arbitrary, unconstitutional, monstrous, inhuman, unChristian and unEnglish'; but Ferrand's opposition had always been strictly proper: he had never adopted Whiggish methods. Peel ostentatiously walked out and, though the rural Press warmly supported 'the fear-nothing Member for Knaresborough', Graham tried to underline Ferrand's rejection by accepting a Select Committee. Subsequently, the Commons found Mott's allegations unfortunately phrased but 'substantially correct', although on 2 August the Commissioners themselves confessed that they had no evidence of irregularities at Keighley, while local officials vigorously denied all charges.

VI

After the violent speeches, with Leaguers threatening lockouts, redundancies and wage cuts and Chartists talking of general strikes and violence, the hot summer saw a climax. Wage reductions in the Midland colliery districts provoked fierce strikes, which soon escalated. Chartists, whose second National Petition had been rejected in the Commons by 287 votes to 49 on 3 May, did not cause the subsequent violence but gladly used it for their own ends. Lancashire wage cuts (made, thought suspicious Tories, by Liberals determined to embarrass a Conservative ministry) led to widespread 'plug plots', as touring bands of workers forcibly removed mills' boiler plugs throughout the textile districts.

The harassed Graham complained to the Queen of magisterial inactivity and many millowners' 'want of proper spirit in defending their property'. Gloomily observing 'a state of social disorder', he privately acknowledged that 'sullen and discontented' operatives had 'just cause of complaint against their masters'. He 'was by no means prepared to use Military force to compel a reduction of wages or to uphold a grinding system of Truck. But Government must act to preserve peace, to put down plunder and to prevent the forced cessation of labour by intimidation' – although it could not act everywhere, especially 'if men of substance would not furnish means for defending their own property'. Meanwhile, John Wilson Croker, encouraged by Peel and Graham, explored evidence of League complicity: 'the more we hunt out these Leaguers the viler vermin we shall find them . . .', he told Graham.

Oastler, Ferrand and other Northern Tories unknowingly shared Ministers' suspicions, as voiced in the *Quarterly Review*. Certainly, Leaguers had often discussed bringing down the Government by lock-outs or provoked strikes; and Bailey had openly talked of plans to shoot Peel (as Croker recalled in January 1843, when the crazed Daniel MacNaughten murdered Peel's secretary, Edward Drummond). Oastler had presciently warned operatives in the spring, 'if the Leaguers urge you to violence, leave that work to them'. Once the strike wave began, however, the Chartists naturally took advantage of it, advocating its continuation until the Charter was granted. As the militant mobs toured the factory towns, the forces of law and order were inevitably mobilised, and many Radical Tories faced difficult personal decisions over their sympathies.

The Busfeilds and Ferrands reacted in line with family tradition. Johnson was enrolled as a special constable by Matthew Thompson at Bradford. And William, despite his deep feelings for the operatives, could never condone virtual revolution. With 500 others, he left the harvest fields to serve with the Hussar Yeomanry, which helped to defend the mills and disperse the mob.

Liberals sneered at the apparent breach between Tories and Radicals. In Bradford, asserted the *Observer*, Ferrand appeared 'very fierce and very terrible' – like Cromwell, 'who, in his ruthless days, kicked up rows in ale-houses and kissed the girls on the highway'. Despite Ferrand's efforts, in the end Chartists rather than Leaguers were punished for the episode. And while Croker blamed the League, Liberals contrived to blame the Tory reformers. 'The cause was with Peel and the Aristocracy and their Corn Laws', Bright unctuously claimed at Rochdale. And at Leeds the *Mercury* bitterly commented:

> The Tories want to throw the blame on the Corn Law repealers, and appear anxious to shake off their connexion with the Chartists. Do they wilfully forget they gave open encouragement to Oastler, Holland Campbell, Ferrand and other declaimers against machinery?

In the autumn Ferrand went shooting at Bingley and with Sir George Armytage at Kirklees Park, near Brighouse, sending several parcels of game to Oastler. In October he attended a Derbyshire public dinner at Ashbourne, with local MPs, Walter and other dignitaries, to support the old 'Gilbert' Poor Law Unions. Here Ferrand was among friends: the Derbyshire squires had for long supported the Protectionist, 'Protestant', traditionalist stance of the old 'Country Party'. Whatever the dynasts – the ubiquitous Devonshire, in particular – might say, the southern squires, removed from the domination of Chatsworth, had secured Tory victories since 1835. The platform included such prominent landowners as Sir George Crewe of Caulke Abbey, Edward Mundy of Shipley Hall, Charles Colville of Lullington Hall (a future Peelite), John Harrison of Snelston Hall, Sir Henry Fitzherbert of Tissington Hall and the Chandos-Poles of Radbourne Hall. Such men were of Ferrand's kind – moderately prosperous squires, deeply embedded in the traditions and ethos of their country, men who served as magistrates, deputy (and occasionally Lord) lieutenants, Yeomanry officers, agriculturalists, Poor Law Union chairmen, Church patrons, sportsmen, charity organisers and considerable (and generally considerate) employers. Ferrand again attacked Peel, asserting that personally

> he knew no party in politics but his country . . . no political principle but the general weal.

Meditating over a stormy year in parliament, Ferrand could recall rows with Cobden, Bowring, Hume, Henry Ward ('that mincing, minikin Cicero' to *The Times*), Villiers, Hutt, Lord Howick, Maule, Escott, William Williams and their kind, and the support of Sibthorp, Crawford, Johnson, the Tory Thomas Grimsditch, Stuart-Wortley, Beckett, Denison, Hardy, Pollington, Sir Walter James, Sir John Hanmer, Henry Yorke, Mathias Attwood (Tory brother of the semi-Chartist Thomas) and Hindley – a pleasing political mix.

CHAPTER THREE

The Working Man's Friend

The year 1843 was a busy one for Ferrand. In January he enjoyed a row in Bingley court over an assault case. He dined with Knaresborough supporters and, dogged by the *Mercury*'s sarcastic reporter, paid some election debts demanded by local innkeepers, while declining to make further contributions. Several days were spent on estate legal documents, particularly arrangements with his mother over Marley property. And Ferrand also prepared new cases for Parliament before returning to his rooms in the St. James Hotel in Jermyn Street. He certainly noted the murder of Peel's secretary, Edward Drummond, on the 21st.

I

On 9 February he presented a petition from over 1,000 Lancashire colliers, asking for efficient weighing of coals at the pit-bottom rather than the surface. It was a demand to be made with increasing vehemence until the checkweighman system was adopted in 1860. Ferrand next opposed Villiers' annual 'free trade' motion, announcing an amendment of great length against repeal of the Corn Law, emigration, industrial cruelties, low wages, Truck and the misuse of machinery. Roebuck sardonically 'begged to ask whether it was in accord with the rules of the House, under the guise of giving notice of a motion, to print a political pamphlet', and the Speaker ordered Ferrand to withdraw his proposal.

Nothing daunted, four days later Ferrand lengthily contributed to the debate on Lord Howick's motion on 'the distress of the country'. The 'steady and remunerative' wages of hand-weavers 'under the rule of the old Tory party', he asserted, had been halved 'under Whig misrule' and continued to fall. He condemned this social tragedy and demanded Protection of both labour and land. He berated Government's rejection of old socially-concerned Toryism, urging colleagues 'to resist the destructive policy of the Government'. Certainly,

> he would not, to support any party or any government, adhere to those who would not stand by the principles which had placed them in power.

Almost inevitably, Greg and Ashworth were again assailed. For Ferrand was concerned with the plight not only of old craftsmen and rural workers but also that of women and children in Northern mills, where

> the husbands and fathers lived in a state of idleness, being unable to obtain work – living, he might say, by the murder of their own offspring . . .

He inveighed against uncontrolled, ever-speedier 'labour-destroying' machinery and the erosion of protective tariffs: not 'one nation . . . was prepared to enter into the reciprocity principles of free trade'. He quoted Peel's father and 'the immortal Pitt' on the need for social protection and blamed the 1842 riots on League machinations.

On the 17th both Cobden and Mark Philips angrily replied and Ferrand's requests for official enquiries were rejected. Oastler, however, rejoiced at the 24-page report:

> The voice of the suffering millions is echoed in the House of Commons – with what delight will Mr. Ferrand's speech be read by them! If those who wish to keep their property (the small portion that is left, I mean) are wise, they will distribute this speech by thousands. Yes, Mr. Ferrand has hit the right nail on the head – protection and regulation. He has dared to attack the giant evil – the misdirection of the power of machinery.

When his friend John Walter assailed the Poor Law – giving it a 'death blow' and exposing 'the foulest conspiracy ever entered into in the dark against the rights, liberties and privileges of the poor' – Ferrand spoke again. On the 19th he had angrily demanded copies of the Ashworth and Greg correspondence on moving rural paupers to the mills, details of this Poor Law migration 'service', the dietaries of Belper and Derby workhouses and reports on strike-breaking at Addingham by overworked Skipton paupers. Bowring and Thomas Milner Gibson protested, but when Ferrand modified his language Graham agreed to provide the information. When it was announced that only 4228 persons had been moved and even Factory Inspectors' reports were denied, Oastler and Ferrand were enraged. On the 23rd Ferrand supported Walter's demand to see the secret reports of the recently dismissed Mott, substantiated his Addingham charges, denounced Graham for using false evidence to put him down in Committee, complained of the lack of educational provisions at Ashton, Dukinfield and Stalybridge and quoted the Radical trade unionist John Doherty on Poor Law migration. He assailed several masters, Assistant Commissioner Charles Clements and the untruths used by the Commission and Ministry alike to protect Mott, and ended by arguing with Peel. It was a long, detailed, vigorous but rambling and ill-planned speech which pleased the Radical Crawford and Tory Thomas Grimsditch but not the Government. The 'great Mott case' was a storm in a teacup, but Ferrand was obsessed by the need to prove that he had been unfairly denounced; his credibility depended upon it, and Grimsditch's support was valuable.

II

February had been an energetic time, but Ferrand maintained his pace. He was now a marked man for Leaguers, whose agents stirred up Knaresborough opposition. When Richard Dewes, a Liberal solicitor, told him that most local electors now supported Villiers, Ferrand saw further evidence of League corruption:

> My constituents are aware that BEFORE they elected me their Representative, I distinctly declared my intention to oppose a repeal of the Corn Laws, and I

beg explicitly to inform them that I neither intend to forget the pledges I gave upon the hustings, nor to betray the interests of those who then reposed their confidence in me: if therefore this my firm determination to act in conformity with the assurances I gave them meets with their disapprobation, they will, at the next election, have the opportunity of placing their confidence in some person whose principles may be more congenial with their own; and if so, it will cause me no regret to bid farewell to a constituency who consider that deception and dishonour ought to be the chief qualifications of their representative.

The Junior Member for Knaresborough, who thus risked his political career, would never yield to bullying blackmail. As if to demonstrate his anti-free trade convictions he joined the new 'Society for the Protection of British Industry', formed in February under Oastler's eccentric friend and fellow anti-Poor Law campaigner, the 4th Earl Stanhope. The Society hoped to

> obtain full and effectual Protection to British Industry, whether employed in Agriculture, in Manufactures, in Handicraft Trades, in Mines, or in Fisheries, securing it from the Competition of Foreigners in the Home Market and in the Colonies by adequate Duties, or by Prohibition; and full and effectual Protection to the Working Classes in the remuneration of their Industry, and to those whose Labour is superseded by Machinery.

Such aims represented the views of such Tory-Radicals as Ferrand, Oastler, Dr. William Sleigh, Dr. George Holland, Stephens and Northern proletarian Tories. But most Conservatives still trusted Peel.

The thunderous assaults on the Poor Law continued. Ferrand presented a petition against the Act together with Income Tax assessments by the Oastlerite George Wythen Baxter, author of the *Book of Bastilles*. He condemned the Halifax Guardians' treatment of paupers and, while losing his motion against Peel by 11 votes to 53, after a bitter argument secured Graham's promise to prohibit treadmills in their workhouse: Clements had been infuriated by the failure of both Bradford and Halifax Guardians properly to implement the hated 'labour test'. Yet Ferrand could not rely upon local Guardians' support. At Keighley George Pollard and William Briggs supported Clements. The Knaresborough electors were unreliable. Ferrand was let down by bourgeois elements, but could draw sustenance from wide proletarian support.

Concern with the Poor Law led to wider interests, and Ferrand had a new scheme in mind. On 30 March he moved to bring in a long-planned Bill for the allotment of waste lands. He shared some beliefs with the long line of reformers who thought that industrial society's problems might be solved by 're-settling' allegedly dispossessed peasants on the land. 'The working classes', he told the Commons, '. . . were suffering misery, want and privation unparalleled in the history of England.' He quoted local examples. In Keighley immorality and typhus ('no respecter of persons: like the cholera, it attacked both rich and poor') were rife. Ferrand's remedy for industrial overcrowding was not emigration or an abdication of responsibility, but 'a general system of allotment of the waste lands',

> as an act of justice to the poor . . . admitted by the law of England, as a right acknowledged for centuries by the greatest writers on our laws and constitution . . .

Sharing Oastler's belief that Protection must be all-embracing, Ferrand fervently held that handworkers, miners, factory operatives, labourers and artisans should share its benefits. Government sat 'on the verge of a volcano, which might burst forth with mischievous and destructive effect, unless precautionary measures were immediately taken'. For

> Thousands are in want and suffering, and have borne their distress and privation with a patience and humility that have been praised by almost every member of Her Majesty's Government; but praise will not fill their empty bodies.

Allotments would alleviate the situation, and Ferrand instanced many thriving schemes; there must be replacements of the 'wretched hovels, in which fevers were generated' and wider improvements. Almost four million acres of cultivable waste should be enclosed by their legal owners, with a permanent reservation of 5 per cent for the poor. Five acres in every parish should be laid out as drying grounds; laughing Liberals 'probably did not know the miseries of wet and tattered clothing'. Five further acres should be used as recreation grounds, to revive 'our old national and healthful sports'. The remainder should be divided into gardens, for which, after initial assistance, the poor might pay rents. Such a scheme would end the 'heart-rending sight' of men 'who through life had been honest, industrious, sober, loyal subjects, sinking into the depths of misery when on the brink of the grave'. Ferrand asked Parliament to 'restore' dignity to the poor,

> as a matter of right, as a matter of justice, of which they have for centuries been plundered; and whilst they obey the command of Heaven, they will – believe me – not forget the gratitude they owe to those who, under Heaven, shall have thus rescued them from the horrors which now surround them.

Natural allies like Charles Wyndham – a Conservative mocker – and Lord Worsley – a Protectionist Whig who believed the Bill to be impracticable – were hostile, but Graham agreed to the introduction, by Ferrand and his friend, the romantic Lord John Manners. The Bill was drawn up by the 'Oastlerite' Leeds lawyer Robert Hall, who refused any fee.

The measure was destined to fail. After the First Reading on 12 May, debate was postponed on 19 and 24 May, 9, 17, 21 and 29 June and 6 July, and the Bill was ordered to be withdrawn on 12 July. Seventeen petitions were presented in its favour and one (from Llandudno fishermen) against. Government was hostile, and eventually a weary Ferrand resolved to support a measure proposed by Worsley. A biographer of Manners later recalled that Ferrand had united throughout his political career (as should ever be the case) the most ardent devotion to Constitutional principles with the most earnest desire for the material welfare of the people . . .

and that he and Manners had shown

> their sympathy for the suffering people and [given] a practical refutation of the ingenerous charge so often brought against them, of supporting measures militating against the supremacy of capital, whilst, at the same time, they opposed those which in any way trenched upon the exclusive privileges of the landed interest.

Whatever 'official' Conservatism thought of Ferrand, he remained a heroic figure to Northern Tory operatives. Such workers were now widely organised in pioneer constituency societies. The first Operative Conservative group had been formed at Leeds, under Oastler's motto of 'Altar, Throne and Cottage', in March 1835. Within a year similar bodies had sprouted in Ashton, Blackburn, Bolton, Liverpool, Manchester, Oldham, Preston, Sheffield, Wakefield and Warrington. During 1836 societies developed in such towns as Barnsley, Birstal, Bradford, Dudley, Huddersfield, Hull, Pudsey, Ripon, Salford, Stockport, Tamworth, Walsall, West Bromwich, Wigan and Wolverhampton; and the movement spread to Dublin, Edinburgh and Glasgow – and even to Knaresborough. The members were predominantly 'Oastlerites' – Protectionists, factory reformers and anti-Poor Law men; and they naturally supported Ferrand.

The Bradford association, meeting under the self-made printer Squire Auty in the New Inn in March, was typical. It praised Ferrand's 'bold, unflinching and persevering conduct' in opposing Poor Law treadmills and exposing the Addingham case: his work had been 'manly and straightforward . . . in support of the Working Classes of the community'. Similarly, the Leeds men expressed gratitude for Ferrand's

> manly, persevering and unflinching conduct in exposing . . . the evils of the Truck System, the Tyranny . . . of the Poor Law Amendment Act, and for his truly disinterested Spirit evinced in the cause of the Suffering labouring Classes.

They condemned the abuse of 'a vile, corrupted Whig radical Press, aided by Millocracy, Steamocracy and Machinocracy'. Pudsey operatives praised Ferrand's determined and persevering efforts in Parliament to respect the Rights and promote the welfare of the labouring Classes', especially by opposing the Poor Law, manufacturers' 'trickeries' and Truck. Their president movingly added:

> As an Individual Operative I beg to thank you and may God bless you with health and long life and may you never tire of the noble exertions which you have hitherto made in the cause of the suffering and oppressed.

And Birstal parish association sent 'sincere and grateful acknowledgements' for his advocacy of 'the rights and privileges of the humbler classes of the community', particularly his 'endeavours to ameliorate the harsh and oppressive portions of the New Poor Law' and his Allotment Bill. Such messages, carefully penned by working men, were treasured at Harden.

On 4 April a family tragedy occurred when Ferrand's brother, young Benjamin Busfeild, was accidentally drowned in the Thames in London. It was over three weeks before his body was found. Before the news arrived, Ferrand had been in Nottingham, where Walter had been unseated on petition and his son lost the by-election. On 5 April he was at the West Riding Spring Sessions at Pontefract, under Edwin Lascelles, where (on the nomination of John Plumbe Tempest and Arthur Lascelles) Johnson beat two rivals for the treasurership of the Bradford, Batley and Keighley court of requests. He then retired wearily to Harden, where the news of Benjamin arrived. His normally terse diary entries then ended for three weeks. Certainly, there were local matters requiring attention. The precise details of the qualifications of the Grammar School headmaster had to be considered. The estate's little coal pits had to be surveyed. And poachers must be deterred. As messages of condolence arrived, the *Bradford Observer* reported on 'Mr Busfeild Ferrand At Home: A Village In An Uproar', asserting that Ferrand had set his hounds on poachers' terriers or shot and hanged them and closed paths across Harden which the surveyor Robert Milligan had re-opened. The last part was certainly true; by May this old enemy was actively breaking Ferrand's gates, and Ferrand prepared to sue him at the Bradford Sessions. Even at a time of sorrow and personal illness, Ferrand was never far from controversy.

On his birthday, 26 April, Ferrand returned to 'Town', living quietly through recurring bouts of influenza, dining out once with his Tory friends Hugh Lindsay and Richard Benyon. As Ferrands and Busfeilds buried Benjamin at Bingley, Milligan smashed their gates and stiles. Ferrand morosely attended an Aylesbury dinner on 8 May, making close contacts with Buckinghamshire Tories under the eccentric Duke, hurrying back to London next day for Villiers' motion, 'very poorly in influenza'. Quickly recovering, he dined at Greenwich with Frederick Knight and Henry Easton and with the Yorkshire Society and met a deputation of Leicester workmen. He returned home for Whitsunday and attended Bradford Sessions, where a true bill was found against Milligan.

III

Ferrand never forgot old friends and on returning to London anxiously investigated conditions in Oastler's new home, the Queen's Prison. His circle was extending. Arthur and Octavius Duncombe, Protectionist politician brothers of Oastler's friend the 2nd Lord Feversham, were close associates in Yorkshire and kindly hosts at Grosvenor Street and Eaton Square. Charles Colvile, a Derbyshire landowner, was a pleasant companion on trips to Greenwich and dispensed hospitality in Eccleston Square. Indeed, Ferrand was invited to many Tory houses, including the St. James Place home of the lavish old radical Sir Francis Burdett. These evening visits were supplemented by days at Richmond with Mrs Walker Ferrand and Sarah – the 'Lilla' of his diaries.

Among friends made in this period were some of Ferrand's closest and dearest companions. There was young William Rashleigh, returned for East Cornwall (where his family had often sat since Elizabethan times) in 1841, at the age of 24, and scion of an ancient local line at Menabilly. He had married, in March, Catherine Stuart, eldest daughter of the 11th Lord Blantyre, and their house in Cumberl and Terrace and later in Stratford Place was ever-open to Ferrand. Equally close was the 25-year-old Lord John Manners.

At Eton and Cambridge the gentle and generous Manners and his more cynical and worldly friend George Smythe had become romantic Jacobites. Their Toryism had a Cavalier, Laudian, Staffordian, Catholic colouring. But with this traditionalism were consciences shocked by the horrors of industrial life. Manners turned to a fanciful medievalism, visualising a society in which Church and aristocracy tended to the needs of the poor. Under the influence of the Tractarian Father Frederick Faber, Manners had combined his notions of colourful chivalry with a mystical devotion to the grandeur of the undivided Church, though halting at the step which Faber took (in 1845) of turning to Rome. The young Cavalier, nurtured at gently-decaying Haddon and newly-Gothicised Belvoir, felt impelled to support the Legitimist Pretender Don Carlos in Spain and the victims of Liberalism in Britain.

It was with this background, and under the influence of Kenelm Digby, that Manners and Smythe had toured industrial Lancashire during their first Parliamentary recess. Lord John was appalled by much of what he saw and produced his verses on *England's Trust*, including two notorious lines which, dragged from their context by mocking Liberals, were to bedevil him throughout his life:

> Let wealth and commerce, laws and learning die,
> But leave us still our old nobility.

Smythe, however, was amazed by industrial energy and romanticised a new nobility among 'the Merchants of Old England, the Seigneurs of the Seas'. Ferrand generally shared Manners' views. Both nostalgically admired the now-passing rural ways; both detested what they saw as a Mancunian war for profit; both sincerely pitied the poor; and both distrusted Peel.

From 1842 Smythe and Manners acted together in the Commons, as they had in the old days at Cambridge. They gradually attracted other allies, largely Etonians and Cantabrigians. There was 'Kok' Baillie-Cochrane, a 26-year-old Lanarkshire laird. From Shropshire came 24-year-old Viscount Newport. 'Feudal' Ireland in Clare, Limerick and Tipperary was represented by Augustus Stafford O'Brien of Blatherwycke, and the 'feudal' Highlands by Henry Baillie of Redcastle and Tarradale, Smyth's brother-in-law. Henry Hope of Deepdene, Trenant and Castle Blayney was a sympathiser. With such actual and potential support the young politicians planned joint action at Geneva in the summer of 1842. In October they and 'Kok' allied with Benjamin d'Israeli, the flamboyant 37-year-old novelist who already disliked Peel for (quite reasonably) refusing him office. Here was a 'shady', suspect, semitic associate, and Rutland and Strangford feared for their sons. But 'Dizzy's' charm, talent and avowed hostility to the social consequences of the Reformation and Revolution endeared him to the little coterie. 'Young England' was born.

Men like Peter Borthwick and the millionaire Quintin Dick announced their sympathy, while Hope and the two John Walters were generous hosts to the group at Deepdene and Bearwood. From his cell Oastler praised their 'honest ardour', hoping that they would do more than write poetry. Ferrand could play an important role: to his friends' social sympathies he could add detailed knowledge of industrial conditions. Lord John's little *Plea for National Holydays* and the restoration of national sports fired his imagination; together they had planned the allotment scheme and supported Worsley's more successful Bill; and on 12 July they voted, with 'Kok' and Smythe, against Peel, on O'Brien's much debated motion on Irish grievances. Only one major issue separated the two men. Far from sharing Lord John's Tractarian views, Ferrand was a spokesman for Irish Loyalism, earning 'thanks, hearty and true, for his generous and able defence' of Colonel Verner's Armagh Orangemen against Hume. But on other matters they thoroughly agreed, and a lifelong friendship was sealed when Manners visited Harden for the August shooting.

The early summer had been pleasantly spent in London, with numerous social events – including dinner with the clan chief William Mackinnon – and visits to Aylesbury and Colchester. But on 13 July Ferrand left for Harden and a round of squirearchical duties and pleasures.

IV

At home Ferrand went fishing with Johnson, attended Keighley court, hired a new housekeeper, visited the farms and prepared to receive a succession of house guests. The old-style Tory sportsman George Lane Fox of Bramham Park, squire, farmer and lord of the manor of Bingley, led the guest-list. He was followed by Dr. Busfeild and other neighbours, Manners, Milnes Gaskell and Colvile. Shooting was interspersed with jaunts to Bradford, Bolton Bridge, Malham and Doncaster races. And Ferrand busied himself with estate matters, the burial of poor Mary Wood ('bedridden for 43 years'), and the licensing meeting. Next he stayed with young George Lane Fox – struggling to save a heavily-indebted estate and the almost-destroyed mansion – at Bramham, to shoot hare, rabbit and partridge, visiting Wetherby show and York. There followed visits to the Misses Gascoigne, the heiresses of Parlington Park, and a shooting visit to Welbury. Parcels of game, including a hamper for Oastler, were sent to friends. At Harden the slaughter continued, land was bought at Gilstead and Margaret Ferrand made her will.

In October Ferrand went to York for the races, a hunt dinner and a week with the Hussars. At home there was frost and a snowstorm, but shooting continued, with Dr. Busfeild, Sir George Armytage, Donald Cameron of Lochiel, Thomas Staveley of Old Sleningford and others; and Ferrand also went out with Bradford Coursing Club. Next he visited Ireland, staying with Charles O'Hara of O'Hara Brook, for more shooting and visits to the Falls of the Bann and the Giant's Causeway. There was further sport at Widgeon's Lodge and Shane's Castle with Viscount O'Neill, before the late November return to Yorkshire for some final shooting at Kirklees and to hear of Johnson's and Walker's joyful revival of the Harden Court Baron. Then more serious work began.

During the autumn Oastler's friends became increasingly concerned about the plight of their hero, whose health had deteriorated after almost three years' imprisonment. *The Times* considered that it was 'high time to do justice to him', and many Tories, Radicals and Chartists agreed; Northern Chartism was, indeed, dominated by Oastler's old allies. Ferrand generously offered to speak at an extensive series of meetings to raise money to pay off Oastler's debts. While he was in Ireland a new Yorkshire 'Liberation Committee' had been founded, including himself and John Fielden (the millowning Radical MP for Oldham since 1832), with William Beckett, the Leeds Tory banker-MP, as treasurer. Ferrand also joined the London committee, with Rashleigh, Colvile, Walter and Sir George Sinclair, under Feversham's chairmanship. He thus began one of his most energetic campaigns.

The 'Oastler Liberation' movement began on 22 November, when Ferrand joined Fielden, Walter and various factory reformers before an enthusiastic audience in the Huddersfield Philosophical Hall. 'Received with loud cheers, which at length merged into several tremendous huzzas', Ferrand set the pattern of the campaign in its Tory-Radical context. He had entered politics 'under the wing of Michael Thomas Sadler and Richard Oastler': he was 'one of the oldest of [Oastler's] disciples'. If 'Oastlerite' views were not adopted 'a revolution would be near at hand', for

> Labour ought to be protected. Labour is the source of all wealth; and unless the working classes are fully employed, and their employ amply remunerated, the nation will be ruined. What I mean by being amply paid is 'a fair day's wages for a fair day's work'. The people seek no more, and they have no right to receive any less.

Northern editors thought that 'the prime mover' had 'faithfully discharged the obligations of friendship'.

Three days later Ferrand left Kirklees to address a rally in Bradford Temperance Hall, backed by local factory-reforming Anglican clergymen and Tory manufacturers. His first knowledge of 'the state of the working classes', he declared, 'was occasioned by reading [Oastler's] public writings' – which had horrified him. The Poor Law was 'a great blow levelled at the working classes'. But he looked hopefully to the future:

> He belonged to a small party in the House of Commons, which was pledged never to cease agitating for the rights of industry . . . until the working classes of England obtained that protection for their labour which was awarded to every other description of property . . . He would not be a party in the attempt to get anything but on sound and constitutional principles . . . If men sought from their rulers that which they had a right to claim, they would not long have to agitate, if they asked for what they wanted in a legal and constitutional manner . . .

This authentic Tory-Radical message was repeated next day in the little Ferrand Arms tavern in Bingley, before Ferrand moved to the magistrates' room in Dewsbury, on the 29th. He then hoped that a freed Oastler would enter Parliament (to which he had twice aspired at Huddersfield during 1837) – '*then* there would be no thimble-rigging, no quailing before the minister of the day'.

At each meeting Ferrand was received with immense enthusiasm by predominantly working-class audiences. 'It was impossible to notice [his] ardent devotion without admiration', commented *The Times*: his labour 'did honour to his heart'. Money flowed in, from operatives and noblemen, Anglican priests and agnostic Radicals, from factory masters, Walter, Fielden, Stuart-Wortley, the Chartist O'Connor, the Lancashire Tory factory reformer Lord Kenyon and even the Liberal Edward Baines.

On 4 December Ferrand addressed an all-party meeting in Leeds Court House, 'He coincided in almost every political sentiment' with Oastler, instancing the Poor Law: 'scarcely a day passed that the public prints did not record the cruelties, the oppression, the hardships, nay, the murders, committed by that Act'. He had just attended the inquest on an old Harden woman who had died of starvation and 'declared emphatically . . . that the New Poor Law had been guilty of [her] manslaughter'. Government's duty was to provide

> equal protection to all classes of persons and of property. The property of the poor man was as much entitled to protection as that of the rich man. It was to the property of the poor man that they owed the wealth and grandeur of the land.

But improvement was impossible until work was found for men 'drones against their will', for 'unrestrained machinery had deprived them of doing that duty which God himself decided they should do'.

Under Ferrand's impassioned oratory, the campaign became a crusade for paternalist social reform. His 'conduct was beyond all praise' to the *Wakefield Journal*. On the 5th he spoke in Keighley Working Men's Hall and next day in Barnsley Oddfellows' Hall. The message was constant. He 'would never rest satisfied' until the Poor Law was repealed. And unrestricted machinery was

> unscriptural and at variance with the Divine Word of God, for that blessed Book told them that man should earn his bread by the sweat of his brow; but unregulated machinery prevented him from doing that. Was it not a disgrace and a stain upon the English character that their wives and . . . female . . . children should be compelled to go to the factories to labour and do that which was destined to be the lot of man? . . . They *must* have a Ten Hours Bill for their protection.

He continued to attack the Leaguers:

> Their end is to bring down your wages, and make you more wretched . . . They go up and down, deceiving the working classes by crying out 'free and cheap bread', when at the same time they mean more slavery and less remuneration.

'Ten hours a day', he told cheering workers in Wakefield Court House on the 7th, 'was sufficient for any human being to labour'.

Such widely-reported speeches firmly established Ferrand as the 'lion-hearted' hero of Northern Tories. And a wide spectrum of friends sent donations. Such 'Whigs' as the 2nd Duke of Cleveland, Edward Cayley (Protectionist MP for the North Riding) and John Maxwell of Pollock (son of the weavers' champion) joined Tories like Manners, Richard Fountayne Wilson, Matthias Attwood, Ashley, Hardy, John Spencer-Stanhope of Cannon Hall, Charles Newdegate, Sir Charles Burrell, the 2nd Earl of Eldon, Earl Stanhope and John Hornby. Other supporters included the 2nd Lord Northwick, Lady Carr, Sir Alexander Hood, Lady Caroline Cape, Sir George Beaumont, the 12th Lord Blantyre, Sir Henry Fitzherbert, Colonel Charles Wyndham, Alderman William Copeland, Sir Walter Farquhar and Sir John Trevelyan. But while such prominent people – and many workers – welcomed Ferrand's speeches, Liberal commentators were naturally less happy. The *Liverpool Mercury* condemned Oastler's own 'violent and seditious speeches' and *The Globe* attacked 'unworthy and grossly incorrect statements' on his 'very large defalcations'. Tory journals, however, took up the cause, the *Morning Post* sagely doubting

> whether there was any other public man in England in whose behalf – save on political or religious grounds – the labouring classes would make the slightest effort.

Ferrand addressed his last Yorkshire rally in Halifax Oddfellows' Hall on 11 December. Here he was praised before a great audience by Oastler's old Chartist friend Joshua Hobson, for 'having prevented the introduction of a mill into their bastille to grind devil's dust'. To 'most deafening applause' Ferrand claimed to have prevented the abolition of outdoor relief at Keighley and that League machinations to unseat him would fail. He also promised to challenge Graham with Lord Chief Justice Denman's ruling that separation of families was illegal. Now he prepared to move over the Pennines to face his most bitter opponents.

V

The Lancashire campaign opened on 14 December, at a vast rally in Manchester Corn Exchange, when Ferrand was supported by such Tory-Radical leaders as John and Richard Cobbett, Robert Sowler, John and Thomas Fielden, the Protectionist workman James Leach and the vitriolic Ashton minister Joseph Rayner Stephens. 'Ignominy and disgrace' had been forecast if he dared to visit the cotton capital, but Ferrand made no compromise. 'Are the masses of England to be destroyed for the benefit of the few?', he roared:

> To whom is England indebted for its great pre-eminence? To the working classes: their hands have raised the monuments of its glory; their hands have fought their country's battles by sea and land. Ever foremost against their foes abroad, it is too bad that they should be crushed by foes at home.

From this Cobbettite theme he turned to a particular 'foe at home'. Alderman John Brooks, cotton master and Leaguer, was a convinced free trader – but, having speculated in coffee, had urged Ferrand to oppose a reduction in the duty. The League, declared Ferrand,

> might well proclaim to the world that, to give capital its due reward, the price of labour must come down. But I appear before you tonight to say that, to give capital its due reward, the price of labour must be maintained, for capital is produced by you, and you alone.

He explained his own philosophy in Disraelian terms:

> We are now divided, as nearly as possible, into two classes – the very rich and the very poor. Search history, and you will learn that no country can long exist in which society is broken into such widely distant divisions. We must have the intermediate links, amalgamating into each other, descending with a regular and even gradation, in order that the monarch on the throne and the peasant in the cottage may alike enjoy the privileges and blessings of our free and glorious Constitution.

The close of the meeting was enlivened by the arrival of a perspiring Brooks, angrily alleging misrepresentation; but his explanations only confirmed the charge.

Next day Ferrand moved to Oldham Town Hall and then to Bolton Temperance Hall. He was 'received everywhere with the most heartfelt welcome', noted *The Times*:

> his truly English sentiments are universally applauded, and his devotion to the cause of his imprisoned friend wins for him the admiration of all.

'Surely', commented the *Stockport Advertiser*, 'since the world began, no prisoner ever had a friend like Ferrand!' Typically, he introduced himself to Bolton operatives as 'a Tory of the old school', who

> believed that when a man went to Parliament he ought to legislate for every class of society, and especially for the working classes. It was this policy that actuated him when he entered the House of Commons. He had acted up to it ever since and, in consequence, had obtained the honour of being characterised as the representative of the working classes of the country – and he fervently prayed that he might never do one single act that might deprive him of such an honour.

His Protectionist policy for labour consisted of Ten Hours, Poor Law repeal and arbitration boards.

On 18 December Ferrand announced the same policy in Stockport Hall of Science, backed as usual by local Tories and Chartists. He alleged that George Wilson, the League chairman, had prevented a reduction of starch duties, to protect his own interests. A tipsy suspected 'Leaguer' got short shrift. 'You little know your man, if you think of putting me down by your interruptions', bellowed Ferrand. 'Go on, give it him – he's sent here and he's drunk', roared the delighted crowd. It transpired that the wretched interrupter was the factory reformer Edward Nuttall, who thought that Ferrand was a League lecturer! He was consoled with a platform seat, as Ferrand assailed the Poor Law, child labour, industrial frauds, the migration scheme and Free Trade.

Next day Ferrand gave 'an excellent speech . . . in high spirits' (according to *The Times*) to a large Charlestown rally. On the 20th he spoke in the Theatre Royal at Preston. 'The labouring classes are the life blood of the country's existence, and if they shall be crushed, its greatness will be gone for ever', he repeated. The hateful Poor Law was the work of both parties:

> there is not a pin to choose between [them]! I may say, however, it originated from the greatest mountebank that ever performed. And I may also say that the measure has to claim its original supporters from the two great parties – Whigs and Conservatives – but not from among the Tories of the good old school. This law, I say, will destroy the institutions of the country, unless it be repealed.

His message was the same at Stalybridge on the 21st and in Fielden's Todmorden next night. On Saturday the 23rd Ferrand wearily returned home for Christmas. His tour had been courageous, immensely popular, very successful and, no doubt, tiring, even for a man of Ferrand's stamina.

At Harden Ferrand found evidence of the fury which he had raised among Leaguers. Thursday's *Times* had contained a letter from Brooks, denying some of the charges over coffee. In reply Ferrand insisted on the truth of his account, recalling that Cobden had denied selling milk to his workers and subsequently sat silent when proof was provided to a Parliamentary Committee. For good measure, he blamed the League for the Plug Plot and asserted that one member had talked of murdering Peel shortly before Drummond was killed. There was nothing new in the second charge. Croker had told Graham in January:

> See in the *Quarterly Review* on the League what the Revd. Mr. Bailey says about *shooting* Sir Robert Peel. He says '*a gentleman*' told him that he would willingly do so if it fell to his lot . . .

But a considerable controversy developed. One Manchester Leaguer, Abel Heywood, confirmed some of Ferrand's observations in *The Times*; and Cobden claimed that his employees welcomed his milk.

On Boxing Day Ferrand returned to Lancashire to speak at Rochdale, where he was heckled by a score of Leaguers under two of John Bright's brothers. He was attacked for supporting a Parliamentary grant to Princess Augusta of Cambridge on her marriage to the Grand Duke of Mecklenberg-Strelitz in July. There were shouts of 'we want no Royal family', and Ferrand henceforth characterised the League as republican. He moved on to Bury and Liverpool, where he told a Commercial Hall audience that Leaguers were traitors and that Cobden had collected £1500 to unseat him. On the 29th he spoke in Sheffield Town Hall against noisy heckling, led by a dissenting minister, R. S. Bailey. Ferrand asked whether he was the Bailey who had talked of killing Peel. 'I have them in the frying pan, and I will fry them', he shouted, before finally standing on a chair to bellow to the interrupters:

> I will give Mr. Bailey to the Free Traders with all my heart. I trust he will not subscribe to the fund, for one farthing of his money would pollute the whole lump.

As Ferrand returned home for New Year shooting, he meticulously recorded his total expenses as £16.19s.8d.

Throughout the energetic campaign, asserted *The Times*, 'all parties, all grades, cheered [Ferrand] in his course'. But one group certainly disagreed. The League's organ commented on the Manchester rally that

> There was the Rev. Mr. Stephens of Ashton notoriety, side by side with the editor of the High Church organ. There were ex-Chartist leaders, the worn-out tools of O'Connor, cheek by jowl with Tories of the ancient Jacobite school; there were, in a word, Eldonites, Cobbettites, O'Connorites, Stephensites, Oastlerites, in fact there were men of every kind, excepting the rational men of free trade.

It attacked Hobson, who shared Protectionist platforms with the redoubtable Dr. William Sleigh, for speaking 'in the true Ferrand style . . . a mixture of Chartism and Toryism, and a compound of heterogeneous absurdities'. Ferrand's 'career of personal slander received a wholesome check at Rochdale', it claimed. And Wilson insisted that the League had triumphed over every Tory stratagem 'from the bluster of Ferrand to the foul slanders of Peel', who accused it of condoning murder.

The fact was that Ferrand's wide spectrum of supporters annoyed middle-class Leaguers. His Tory support was natural, though its social range – from Lords Feversham and Kenyon, MPs like Beckett, Colvile and Rashleigh and industrialists like William and Charles Walker, Joshua Pollard and Henry Edwards to journalists such as James Walker, Thomas Micklethwaite of Wakefield, Sowler of Manchester and John Beckwith of Leeds, from lawyers to workmen was surprising. Clerical help was also impressive, from such Anglican priests as the renowned Walter Hook, Cecil Wray and Thomas Allbutt. But what most dismayed Leaguers was the extent of Radical and Chartist support for Ferrand, whose 'Left-wing' aides included the Fieldens, William Stocks, Isaac Ironside Philip Grant, Abraham Wildman, Lawrence Pitkeithley, John Leech, James Mills, William Hill, Thomas Pitt, David Weatherhead, and John Hanson. The Tory-Radical alliance created by Oastler and Ferrand was as infuriating to contemporary Liberals as it was perplexing to many subsequent historians.

Two free traders launched particularly violent attacks on Ferrand early in 1844. James Mitchell, a Preston supporter of Joseph Sturge's Complete Suffrage Union (a watered-down bourgeois version of Chartism) and enemy of factory reform, bitterly condemned the 'vile calumnies' on Brooks. Ferrand was 'worthless . . . the Yorkshire of . . . the vile fellow . . . the monstrous thing without a memory . . . a truly pitiable creature . . . a recorded calumniator'. For 32 pages Ferrand was assailed for his 'most wanton, wicked and false attacks' and because he was 'quite willing to make a noise about the Ten Hours Bill and about the 'accursed poor law', he was 'as silent as a mouse in cheese about the real starvation and slavery law, the Corn Law!'

One Nicholas Smith next attacked Ferrand's allegations over Drummond's death. Protectionists, 'like vermin retreating to a corner', were hiding their defeats by wild attacks. *The Times, Standard,* Oastler, Ferrand, Stephens, Hobson and their kind uttered 'stupid falsehoods', but 'the personal worthlessness of some of the, professional dishonesty of others and political recklessness of all rendered them harmless . . .' Nevertheless, MacNaughten was 'schooled in murder' not by Leaguers but, probably, by 'the Tory-Chartist correspondents of the *Standard* and *Times* . . . the school for teaching how to war against master manufacturers'. Smith recalled the murderous tradition of the Glasgow spinners' union. 'The instigators of such outrages' were Stephens, Oastler, Hobson, Ferrand and O'Connor – who 'in hypocrisy the most disgusting and most criminal that ever dishonoured the name of man, professed to be the conservators of our institutions'. In reality, such men were 'the very Alpha and Omega of revolution, spoliation of property, levelling of ranks and destruction of all existing institutions'.

During a very busy year Ferrand had actually spent little time on the factory reform cause itself. Yet the Government, shocked by the violence of 1842, had moved from its earlier reluctance to legislate. After intensive discussions, Graham responded to Ashley's call of 28 February for 'a moral and religious education among the working classes' and on 8 March introduced a new Factory Bill. Children were not to work under the age of 8 and until the age of 13 were to be restricted to a 6-hour 'half-time' system of labour. A further three hours were to be spent in decently-organised schools, in place of the often wretched system provided under the 1833 Act. Both proposals were anathema to Liberals and nonconformists. Restriction was inevitably opposed, while compulsion was detested by 'voluntaryists':

> . . . all should tell the State
> She has no right to educate.

Indeed,

> It was a tyrannical stretch of power to compel parents to send their children to any school at all, much more to do so without leaving them any choice as to the school, and, most of all, to compel attendance and exact the provision of a school-fee.

Furthermore, since the Church of England, as by far the largest provider of education, was to exercise much influence in the new scheme, there were bitter suspicions of 'a Bill for establishing a compulsory Church Education at the public expense'. The spread of Oxford Catholicism particularly incensed Protestants: 'if not actually drawn up, as some have supposed, in the College of Jesuits at Rome, it has at least been revised, though not improved, by the College of Jesuits at Oxford'. Dissenters demanded 'that we shall be free; in labour, free; in trade, free; in action, free; in thought, free; in speech, free; in religion, free – perfectly free'. The concentrated venom of the nonconformists forced Graham to withdraw the proposal on 15 June. As Peel sadly commented to Ashley, Dissent had won 'a sorry and lamentable triumph'.

Government intended to re-introduce its proposal, shorn of the education clauses, in 1844, and Ferrand, with his allies, had to prepare for a struggle to engraft a 'ten hours' clause on any Bill. But the immediate priority remained Oastler's release from his cell.

CHAPTER FOUR

The Breach with Conservatism

While Ferrand was being branded as a dangerous revolutionary by Leaguers early in 1844, he indulged in the eminently unrevolutionary life of a sporting squire. One Rawson threatened a slander action over recent speeches and League agents stepped up activity in Knaresborough. Ferrand prepared to counter both attacks. And he busied himself over local matters, especially the gift of land for a new church and school at Oakworth, in the parish of his cousin William (son of the Bradford MP), since 1840 Rector of Keighley. But on 22 January he addressed a huge 'Oastler' meeting in the Dublin Rotunda, together with Auty, Dr. Stanley Gifford (editor of *The Standard*) and Tresham Gregg and other Church of Ireland clergymen, delivering a 'Protestant' speech, with customary attacks on Liberalism and the Poor Law. His campaign ended only on 6 February, with a small but noisy meeting in Nottingham Assembly Rooms.

The meetings and appeals had raised £2053, but Oastler's debt (originally agreed at £2600, with a counter-claim of £500) now amounted, with interest and expenses, to £3243. This had certainly never been envisaged by the dying Thornhill's counsel, Fitzroy Kelly, but the trustees of the family heiresses were adamant. Ferrand had hoped not only to pay off the debt but also to buy an annuity. Certainly, he had toiled hard for the cause; and family tradition avers that he sold pictures to aid the fund. Now, the total collected fell short even of the accumulated debt. However, the 'old King's' declining health led his friends to borrow the difference from Beckett's Bank, in order to obtain an early release. Ferrand was one of the twelve guarantors, and on the 12th he and Rashleigh led the much-moved 'ransomed patriot' to meet Feversham's London committee in the British Coffee House in Cockspur Street.

At a celebratory luncheon Ferrand was thanked for his labours and declared that 'Mr Oastler would add dignity to the House of Commons when he obtained a seat in it, as he would do in a very short time' – a hope sadly dashed. 'There can be no doubt', declared *The Times*,

> Mr Oastler would never have been shut up in a prison – and once there, would not have been kept a single day – but for his persevering advocacy of the Ten Hours Factory Bill and resistance to the New Poor Law. Mr. Oastler's liberation, therefore, is a popular triumph . . . [He] is the providential organ of the oppressed and suffering poor; and it is no wonder that his language and his measures are sometimes too close and lively an expression of what, after all, is the actual truth of the case . . .

Ferrand was one of five trustees of Feversham's fund to provide for Oastler; but after his 'liberation' subscriptions virtually ceased. Oastler himself travelled to Yorkshire, for a tumultuous reception and a period of recuperation.

I

Ferrand had earned golden opinions among Tories – though not with Conservative Ministers and Members – by his campaigns. On Oastler's liberation day he asked his promised question in the House about Government's reaction to Denman's widely-reported ruling that mothers and children should not be separated in workhouses. Graham insisted that Denman had been misrepresented and that the Commissioners had already prohibited such family divisions. He would not alter the Act, so Ferrand gave notice of a motion specifically banning separation. Two days later Ferrand quoted *Times*, *Chronicle* and *Herald* reports supporting his case, but Graham maintained that the Lord Chief Justice 'had said the very converse'. It was after midnight, and the Commons was in no mood for a debate. But Ferrand, always suspicious of Ministerial references to unpublished papers, demanded the production of the Commissioners' order, as family separation was still widely practised. After some argument, he agreed to resume next day.

A considerable controversy ensued. *The Times* supported Ferrand: Graham had selected only part of Denman's speech, perhaps because he 'would prefer some other and gentler confessor' to hear his 'recantation'. Others confirmed that separation was still enforced: at Fulham, wrote John Perceval, there were once '20 to 30 such cases, if not more'. But Denman himself denied the words ascribed to him for three months. This did not affect Ferrand's case, maintained *The Times*:

> It is a fact ... that quite recently, for half a dozen years or more, great numbers of children, 3 or 4 or 6 years of age, have been forcibly separated from their mothers, contrary to the laws of nature, and, as is now repeatedly declared by Lord Denman, and not denied by Sir J. Graham, contrary to the Common Law of England.

Yet, after years of 'painful and hurtful injury' to the poor – now revealed as illegal – Graham, without apology or regret, was concerned only 'to floor his questioner and get the laugh of the House'. As Guardians themselves were ignorant of an order, 'it was no small feather in Mr. Ferrand's cap that he had procured publicity and, perhaps, thereby, execution for [it] . . .' Ferrand had scored another popular victory.

The Irish leader Daniel O'Connell had been arrested in October 1843 and, after a mismanaged trial, found guilty on eleven counts of sedition by a Dublin jury in January. The Law Lords, under Denman, were later to reverse the decision. But when Russell proposed a Committee of the whole House on Ireland, Ferrand joined the debate. On 19 February he observed that he had supported the Ministry's effort to 'put down the disgraceful [Irish] agitation' and condemned 'a small republican party' for aiding the 'convicted conspirator'. 'Thank God', he told the Opposition, 'you are powerless in this House and in the country too!'. He lashed Lord Grey's Whig Government – which 'gave to the country the New Poor Law, out of which had sprung Socialism, Chartism and the Anti-Corn Law League' and O'Connell's 'Tail'. And he gleefully attacked Grey's son, Lord Howick, who had recently asked

> How could a British House of Commons listen without disgust to a proposal that they should legislate upon the assumption that a faith so held and honoured was false and idolatrous' (although the noble lord had almost immediately afterwards avowed his belief that the Roman Catholic faith was founded on error)? Why, it was the duty of the House to legislate on that very principle, that the Roman Catholic faith was false and idolatrous. The Government were bound by the most sacred oaths to support the Protestant religion and to prevent the extension of Popish idolatry. Did anyone deny the obligation of the oath? Did anyone say it was the duty of the Government to encourage Popery, and that it should be placed on an equality with Protestantism?

This sectarian outburst delighted the squires. Ferrand had spoken 'in his usual effective manner', and although 'the speech of the night' was given by the Solicitor-General, Sir William Follett, *The Standard* thought that Ferrand 'even excelled himself in manliness, vigour and perspicacity', while Milnes was typically 'a little contradictory and inconsistent, and somewhat absurd'. Among the still sizeable and influential Anglican and Protestant community in Ireland there was enthusiastic approbation. 'In their misery and confusion', Dr. Gregg told the Dublin Protestant Operative and Reformation Society,

> the manly speech of the noble-hearted Ferrand came upon them with healing on its wings (*great and prolonged cheering*). He spoke like a Protestant, and as a British senator ought to do (*loud cheers*). He made the words of truth reverberate through Parliament (*renewed cheers*)

To 'tremendous cheers, Kentish fire, and waving of hats and handkerchiefs', he proposed that, as the first group to invite Ferrand to speak in Ireland, they should send him an address in a gold box; and he forecast the imminent 'conversion of Ireland'. To loyalists, indeed, Ferrand was 'among the very few' MPs who remembered hustings pledges:

> His Protestantism is not worn like an electioneering cockade, pinned on and unpinned at pleasure; it is carried with him into his place in the national convention, and there not reserved timidly in abeyance for more favourable time and auditory, but boldly and impressively promulgated with the force and truth of an earnest and faithful witness . . .

Dublin's handsome presentation was made in Bradford Church Institute on 9 April. As chairman, L. Haworth (curate of Pudsey) called Ferrand 'the champion of the poor man and of truth' and Gregg declared that Ferrand's 'language . . . was as life from the dead to him and his Irish brothers'; Auty and Balme made supporting speeches. A few Irish Roman Catholic hecklers were physically thrown out: as Ferrand said, they 'had no right' to be present. 'Arrah, long life to you, Mr Ferrand!' shouted a remaining infiltrator. 'And long life to you, Sir', retorted Ferrand, 'and may you not die until you have been brought to discern the errors which cloud your understanding here and endanger your safety hereafter.' After this typical repartee, Ferrand proudly bore his casket – 'to . . . the Champion of truth and humanity, the zealous opponent of idolatry and oppression, in admiration and sympathy . . .' – to Harden, where it was long cherished: and that night he wrote a grateful message to 'Brother Protestants'. Again *The Illustrated London News* chose him, with Smythe and Manners, for examination in its series of political biographies.

II

After settling family and estate legal matters, Ferrand returned to Westminster in March, while Oastler praised him in Yorkshire. Both men now prepared for another 'Ten Hours' campaign, determined to carry an amendment to Graham's revised 'Twelve Hours' proposal. Oastler again revived the Northern agitation, supported by Anglican clergy and Chartists alike, while Ferrand in London backed the despondent Ashley – now unfairly blamed by counter-attacking Leaguers for bad social conditions – in Dorset.

Ashley proposed his amendment on 15 March, aided by such stalwarts as Lord Francis Egerton and Viscount Sandon – two old Oxford friends and relations – and opposed by Graham, Milner Gibson and (in 'a style perhaps the most vindictive towards the working classes ever made in the British Parliament') Bright. Three days later – now aided by such Whigs as Howick, Sir George Grey and Russell, Tories like Beckett and Hardy and the Radical Fielden, Charles Hindley and George Muntz – Ashley triumphed over a blustering Peel by 179 votes to 170 and (on a motion) by 161 to 153. But rejoicing was premature – as was the Liberal gloom. 'A large section of the Monopolists', moaned *The League*,

> have supported Lord Ashley's amendment . . . they have made an attack on the manufacturing interest, in the hope of injuring the League . . . For the first time in the annals of commerce, a British Parliament has asserted its right to restrict the profits of capital and the wages of labour . . .

But Ashley's proposal to restrict women and teenagers in the textile industries to a ten-hours day was anathema also to Government, and Peel 'could not and would not acquiesce'. Ministers were furious and, wrote Sydney Smith, 'were making great efforts to beat [Ashley] . . . but mankind are getting mad with humanity and Samaritanism . . .' That Whiggish observer Charles Greville mourned that 'we are just now overrun with philanthropy, and God knows where it will stop, or whither it will lead'.

Ferrand, inevitably, stood by the cause, undeterred by rumours of Ministerial resignations. And such loyalists as Manners and Sir Robert Inglis were aided by the Radicals Charles Buller and Joseph Brotherton. But on the 22nd Whig and 'Peelite' support proved untrustworthy, as several Members (notably William Aldam) preferred an 'eleven hours' compromise. Graham lost by 186 votes to 183, and Ashley by 188 to 181. Greville never remembered so much excitement . . . nor a more curious political state of things, such intermingling of parties, such a confusion of opposition . . .

And the Radical *Leeds Times* declared that

> The discussions and divisions on the Factory Bill have been of the most confused and almost ludicrous kind. Whigs, Tories and Radicals are jumbled together in inextricable disorder. Lord John Russell and Mr. O'Connell voted with Busfeild Ferrand, for, Hume and John Bright with Sir James Graham!

Opposition remained bitter, with Baines assailing Ashley's 'strange combination of Socialists, Chartists and ultra-Tories' and Graham his 'Jack Cade system of legislation' on the 25th. To facilitate a clear decision, Ashley agreed that Graham should introduce a new proposal on the 29th. It would limit children of 8 (not 9, as in 1833) to 13 (to 11 in silk mills) to a 6½hours 'half time' day and women and 'young persons' aged 13–18 to 12 hours – which Ashley would try to reduce to 10.

Ferrand moved North to aid Oastler (now subsidised by the Bradford Tory worsted master and Protectionist William Walker, old John Wood's partner and successor) in the wide, exciting campaign. On Easter Monday, 8th April, Oastler and Ferrand appeared together in Leeds Music Hall. Their support demonstrated the nature and extent of the Tory-Radical alliance. The chairman, Dr. Hook, who thought it 'his duty, as vicar of the parish, to defend the weak against the strong', was accompanied by seven other priests, including Thomas Nunns, who had campaigned for industrial reform in Birmingham. Medicine was represented by Samuel Smith and Francis Sharp from the Infirmary, perpetuating that medical social concern begun by their fellow-Tories Charles Thackrah and the Hey family; education by the Bradford Tory factory teacher Matthew Balme (Yorkshire factory reformers' secretary) and the Rev. Richard Wilson of Leeds Grammar School; trade and industry by Benjamin Jowett and William and Charles Walker; and Chartism by Councillor Hobson and Julian Harney. 'Let me ask you', roared Ferrand,

> who are the men that say you shall not have the Ten Hours Bill? They are those who have grown rich by the sweat of your brow, who know not what it is to have one day's want – while you know not what it is to have a day's peace and contentment.

In particular, only Graham's 'cold-blooded dogged stupidity' prevented success. He accused Graham of procuring a false report from Mott and his tool James Hogg of unfairly unseating Walter.

Now Ferrand finally broke with Conservatism, declaring that

> We may not have the cunning expediency of Sir Robert Peel or the cool effrontery of Sir James Graham amongst the honest Tories that sit in the House or live in the country, but there is a more earnest desire growing up amongst the party to see justice done between man and man, between master and servant, than any I can find in the present Government. Don't you despair. Recollect, though the British Army lost a Wolfe at Quebec, an Abercrombie in

Egypt and a Moore at Corunna, it had a Wellington to lead them at Waterloo. If Sir Robert Peel were to resign tomorrow, I for one should not shed a tear.

Certainly, Peel 'was not going to play the same game in 1844 that he did [over Roman Catholic Emancipation] in 1829'. *The Times* gave instant support: Ferrand and Oastler 'spoke with their usual decision and force' and were enthusiastically received. Ferrand, it observed,

> speaks his mind distinctly and fearlessly. He is apt to say what he and many others are convinced of, though few have the courage to lay the accusation before the world.

The two Tory-Radicals repeated their message to a huge open-air crowd at Bradford next day. Here the redoubtable Vicar, Dr. William Scoresby, was a strong sympathiser, and three priests joined the platform, with Pollard, Auty and William Walker. Ferrand was unable to accompany Oastler throughout his tour, but invited him to Harden and rejoiced to hear 'the old king' tell Bingley workers that 'it was particularly pleasing to him to meet his best friend surrounded by his neighbours, who, because they knew him best, loved him most'. Oastler went on to Huddersfield, Halifax, Keighley, Holmfirth, Preston, Bolton, Stockport, Oldham, Blackburn and Ashton: 'never before', asserted *The Times*, had it 'known such an extraordinary exhibition of versatility on one subject'. At the greatest Lancashire rally, in Manchester Corn Exchange on the 17th, Oastler was joined by Wray, Ferrand, Fielden and Walter. And when the Roman Catholic Temperance campaigner Fr. Daniel Hearne forecast that Ten Hours would end the Corn Laws, Ferrand bluntly said that, if so, 'let them fall this very night'. The sharply critical *Illustrated London News* noted that he had 'poured the most unmitigated abuse on the Government'.

III

Even in his stormy career, Ferrand never caused such a furore as with his Leeds speech. During the resumed discussion of Graham's Bill, on 22nd April John Roebuck stirred the controversy by asking about Ferrand's allegations – without, complained Ferrand, giving notice. Ferrand again recited his evidence against Mott's false report and Graham's use of it. Called to order by the Speaker for attacking Roebuck, Ferrand repeated his charge against Graham, who demanded substantiation. Hume and H.G. Ward delightedly stoked the fires by raising the charges against Hogg, who now entered the fray. Although unprepared, Ferrand stoutly defended himself:

> The object . . . which you have in view is to crush me, and I will not permit myself to be put down in this House, where I have as much right to state my political opinions as any other honourable Member . . .

He ascribed the rowdy outburst to envy of his popularity with Northern workers and told Graham that he wanted to know how he contrived to obtain the false report. Russell considered that the matter ought never to have been noticed but that

The Breach with Conservatism

now Ferrand must prove his case or appear 'most unjust and contumacious'. And Peel denied reports of his own speeches.

The trouble was, as *The Times* observed, that Ferrand 'was . . . assailed on all sides for what he had said, for what he had not said, for what others had said, and for what nobody had said'. It fairly summarised the case:

> The subject . . . is one the rights of which, it is evident, never can and never will be dragged from official obscurity. A false report, containing false charges against an opponent of the Government by an officer of that Government – the report unexpectedly and triumphantly used by a Minister of the Crown – inquiry long refused, and only by a sort of necessity granted – that officer long and almost indecently shielded – a fresh inquiry, in the shape of returns, with difficulty obtained – the charge proved false – the officer dismissed in time to prevent a thorough investigation – all this may not carry conviction of downright conspiracy to all minds, but may very well leave in the most candid an impression of some culpable, though indefinable, management.

The matter did not end there, however. Next day Ferrand announced that, having re-examined reports of his speeches, he would not 'retract one syllable . . . nor extenuate nor explain away a single sentence'. He had 'asserted his sacred prerogative as a free-born Englishman to express his opinions upon the public conduct of two public officers', and he 'defied the House to deprive him of that privilege'; he was backed by the Press and public opinion, and the Commons was 'the last tribunal . . . for him to appeal to'. He thereupon walked out of the crowded but suddenly hushed House. Opposition laughter and 'noise and confusion' followed. Borthwick tried to bring on the next business; Roebuck insisted on continuing; Disraeli objected; Hogg demanded protection; Graham talked of Ferrand 'running away'; Peel joked at the House's 'disappointment'; Russell thought the charges should be declared untrue; Stanley condemned the 'gross and libellous calumnies'; and the Tory William Blackstone complained that Russell had supported similar libels against himself. *The Times* thought that Ferrand was right and mused that

> A miscellaneous majority had supported Lord Ashley; perhaps the equally miscellaneous minority would hoot down his most active coadjutor . . . All the guns of the House, therefore, great and small, secretaries *in praesenti*, secretaries *in futuro* and secretaries *in paulo post futuro* were to have their flings . . .

But the *Standard* and *Post*, though sympathetic, were less convinced of Ferrand's case.

After rooting around for precedents, the Commons returned to the issue on the 24th, when Peel and Russell agreed that Ferrand should be called to the House. Fitzstephen French, though a Liberal, defended Hogg but opposed a Minister who had used a false report being allowed to condemn his accuser. The Radical Slingsby Duncombe mocked the whole proceeding. Disraeli, while disagreeing with Ferrand's abuse of manufacturers, condemned Roebuck and recalled that Peel had once accused Cobden of condoning murder:

> You did not attempt to cow him, you did not hoot [him] as you did [Ferrand] but you quailed under the accusation which he could not prove ... But [Ferrand] comes before you, obnoxious to many on account of the cause he advocates; he comes forward unsupported by a great and powerful party, and then an opportunity is taken of getting up a cry against him. He is baited and bullied ... the hon. Member did not in any way fly from the charge, but he did, clearly and distinctly, demur to the tribunal.

Ferrand's speeches, he thought, were more moderate than usual, and Graham was making too much of 'the great Mott case' (which Disraeli confessedly could not understand). Furthermore, by accusing Ferrand of knowingly uttering untruths, Stanley 'first destroyed his opponent, and then destroyed his own position': he was 'the Prince Rupert of Parliamentary discussion'. Disraeli almost succeeded in getting the issue laughed out.

Opponents remained viciously adamant, particularly Captain Grantley Berkeley, the bullying lecherous son of the reprobate 5th Earl of Berkeley, and Roebuck. In vain, Manners and Smythe tried to end the proceedings, backed by Howick. *The Times* still maintained that the House was 'excessively unfair ... and not less ridiculous'. Ferrand had certainly achieved fame, though scarcely of the sort he desired. However, Lord Ingestre thought that Ferrand would explain – though why he should *The Times* found it 'by no means easy to say', as 'he had not asserted anything sufficiently definite to be capable of proof'. *The Standard* agreed: 'what error was he to confess?'. The *Post* hoped that the matter would end and gave Ferrand some advice:

> Mr. Ferrand possesses many qualities that fit him to be eminently useful as a public man. He is honest. He is courageous. He is enthusiastic in the expression of his opinions; and in these days of trimming and treachery ... courage, honesty and enthusiasm are attributes of no mean value. Mr. Ferrand has, however, much yet to learn; he has also much to unlearn, before he can hope to give fitting effect to his assaults on men, who, in addition to considerable talents, possess unlimited resources of cunning and cant. Mr. Ferrand is frequently rash in his assertions. He is often violent in the language which he employs. He is, moreover, at times, illogical in the conduct of his arguments ...

Thus encouraged, Ferrand entered an expectant House on the 26th. Proceedings began by Roebuck revealing that Smythe had challenged him to a duel. A far from contrite Ferrand apologised for wasting time, particularly for postponing the vital factory debate. But then he assailed 'that common informer ... that public accuser' Roebuck, Stanley's 'most unjustifiable' language and Peel's facetiousness. Such men were not proper judges, as they 'yelled for revenge'. Consequently,

> As a member of this House, I solemnly protest against these proceedings. In the name of the people of England, I deny your right to try me on this charge ... I pronounce this self-constituted court of honour to be an illegal and unconstitutional court, and ... I refuse to plead at its bar.

Despite French and Manners, a censure was passed on 'unfounded and calumnious' charges. The House could go no further, having already got itself into a silly position.

The fact was that 'the greatest crime of which a Member of the House of Commons can, in the opinion of that wise and pure assembly, be guilty, is the crime of belonging to no party', declared the *Post*, which condemned 'this ridiculous piece of senatorial mummery'. A reader asserted that Ferrand was attacked by 'that little fretting wasp' Roebuck as 'the one man whom the Anti-Corn Law League feared'. Roebuck 'cut but a sorry figure' amid the merriment. To the *Standard*, the 'most extraordinary' affair closed with the Commons allowing Ferrand's 'demurrer to its jurisdiction'. *The Atlas* thought Ferrand 'highly meritorious' for stirring up the Commons' 'stagnant atmosphere', praised the 'honest, plain-speaking John Bull' who shocked the House 'by calling a lie a lie and a job a job' and noted his great popularity. And *The Britannia* considered that 'Ferrand began by being in the wrong; and he ended by being very nearly in the right'.

The country Press was also widely sympathetic to Ferrand. Halifax supported the workers' 'special representative' throughout the 'farce'; Newcastle attacked the 'ridiculous and farcical' affair; Manchester 'could not help thinking that there was yet something hidden . . .'; Liverpool praised the 'honest man – a lofty-minded and honest Englishman' and condemned the House. Much feeling was obviously represented by the *Tyne Mercury*:

> People who before suspected [Ferrand], as a professed Tory, now admire him as a fearless and honest man . . . As the House persecutes, the country embraces . . . on both points we believe Mr. Ferrand, and most potently disbelieve Graham, Hogg, Peel, Roebuck and the rest . . .

And *The Times* magisterially concluded that

> It is our entire belief that Mr. Ferrand owes the distinction with which he has been treated to the evident effect of his exertions in the factory cause. It is a practical object, worth while, to denounce him and put him under some stigma. The active parties against him are, almost to a man, they who are also active against a 10 hours bill. Others might, or others have said, what he has said, a hundred times over without animadversion. He has, in fact, only spoken the sense of the whole nation on the subject of election committees and official influence . . .

The final comments came from the cartoonists and humorists. One, by 'HB', entitled 'Bear-Baiting or Old English Pastimes Revived. Dedicated to Young England', featured Ferrand as a chained bear, Disraeli as his keeper and Roebuck, Hogg and Graham as attacking (and palpably losing) dogs. *The Age* published a long poem on 'The Wars of the Parliament', of which two lines set the standard:

> COL SIBTHORP: No they mustn't go out, for this reason – in future, If Ferrand kills Hogg, he'll be called a pork butcher.

While old allies remained loyally firm, *Punch* sourly pictured 'the lion-hearted Ferrand' as a kicked dog. Ferrand himself told Hogg that he thought his decision on Nottingham 'unjust and directly opposed to the evidence' and that he had acted under a bias – probably unconscious – in favour of Government. He had never charged him with corruption. He remained determined to deal with Graham later.

In response to readers' requests, the *Illustrated London News* revised its survey of Ferrand's career and its portrait of him (now giving what Johnson thought was 'a very good likeness'). Ferrand's 'popularity in the manufacturing districts', it stated,

> was sometime ago exceedingly great, but whether it has been impaired by the recent resolutions of the House of Commons . . . there has been as yet no opportunity of testing. One thing, however, he may be assured of, that the public will in future expect from him a greater degree of moderation, in tone and temper, and a greater respect for the feelings, as well as consideration for the failings of others.

As if in response to the first doubts, Irish friends rallied to Ferrand. Gregg's Dublin Protestant Operatives praised his defence of free speech and Cork Protestant Operatives thanked him for defending the Constitution. Ferrand had emerged from a potentially hazardous business almost unscathed.

IV

Other news was much less happy. The factory debates had continued in late April, with recitations of rival liberal and Tory viewpoints. At the Third Reading on 10 May Ashley was supported by Howick, Ralph Bernal, Buller, Muntz and Ferrand and opposed by Graham, Henry Liddell, Henry Knight, and Roebuck (in 'most vindictive and fiendish . . . oratory', according to operative delegates). Three days later the sides remained equally mixed: John Stuart-Wortley, Frederick Shaw, Forster McGeachy, Milnes and Pollington were joined by Macaulay, Russell and the Radical Benjamin Hawes, while Bright, Ward, John Manners-Sutton and Henry Labouchère were hostile. But Peel's threat to resign over the issue terrified many lukewarm Conservatives, still unable to visualise an alternative leadership: even staunch rural Protectionists could wobble from consistency. To Ferrand and Oastler the issue remained clear: farmers and factory workers alike deserved Protection and they distrusted Peel over both. To squires from sleepy bucolic areas, far removed from a Manchester, Leeds or Glasgow, the matter was sometimes less pressing; the paternalist benevolence on which many honestly and rightly prided themselves did not (despite Disraeli's and Smythe's attempts) always easily transfer to the grimmer industrial world.

Ashley was 'utterly, singularly, prodigiously defeated by a majority of 138!!' Even the Commons 'seemed aghast, perplexed, astonished.' But he quickly recognised that 'such was the power and such the exercise of Ministerial influence!!', for 'the majority was one to save the Government'. The 'great majority' (of 297 votes to 159), Ashley consoled himself, proved that there was no division against the principle, but one to save the Ministry. It [would] beget, too, a high reaction.

Ferrand could find some pleasure that at least most of his friends in the little Tory group as opposed to Peel's 'Great Conservative' coalition – had stood firm. And on May Day he, Manners and Tom Duncombe helped to kill a Master and Servant Bill which would have weakened trade unions.

V

After these traumatic events, Ferrand lived quietly at Harden, where Oastler joined him. Estate matters took time: with Currer (now a Keighley solicitor) Ferrand conveyed land to Oakworth school, which must

> at all times be in union with the incorporated National Society for promoting the education of the poor in the principles of the Established Church and conducted according to its principles and for the furtherance of its end and design.

But he also worked on a vindication of his actions over 'The Great Mott Question', which he published at the end of May, as a 36-page printed letter to Graham.

To many people, including Disraeli, the issue was a bore. But to Ferrand, having refused an adjudication by the Commons, it was essential to justify himself before the public. 'Sticking to his plain old English, [he] carefully abstained from extending to [Graham] the assurance that [he] was mistaken in supposing that he charged him with what was dishonest and dishonourable.' On evidence from Bolton Tories and Radicals, he claimed that Mott had made a false report on Bolton Union in 1841, which Graham had used against Bowring, the local Member. That report had been disproved in 1842, but Mott's attacks remained on record. Ferrand next examined the history of Keighley Union, founded by Assistant Commissioner Power in 1838 and organised from 1840 by Mott. He recalled Graham's surprising production of an unpublished Mott report in 1842, the Guardians' repudiation of many charges and the dismissal of Graham's 'poor tool . . . [and] degraded and ignominious instrument' when the Commissioners themselves admitted to possessing no substantiation. Ferrand bluntly repeated that Mott's Keighley report was untrue, that Graham secretly procured it despite Mott's Bolton record and that Graham knowingly used the dishonest Keighley report to crush him. Further, Graham had used his Parliamentary strength to have Ferrand's protests declared 'unfounded and calumnious'. The argument was 'between an honest, independent Member of Parliament on one side, and an unscrupulous, overbearing Secretary of State on the other'. Graham had 'made it the business of his office to oppress' the poor and trounce honest MPs; but Ferrand would continue his fight. Copies of this unrepentant and abrasive pamphlet – which certainly demonstrated the author's dislike of the Home Secretary – were sent to Graham, Peel and about 200 Members.

That the pamphlet was an instant success undoubtedly owed less to Ferrand's literary ability than to the widespread hostility to and suspicion of the former Whig

Minister. Graham was a hard-working Border baronet devoted to a form of liberal-conservatism, morosely convinced of gathering social dangers and given to arrogant and egoistical attacks on others while never daring to accept the premiership himself. He was certainly not a bad man, but his cold haughtiness and his *penchant* for 'putting down' earnest backbenchers made him few friends.

The Press was widely enthusiastic. 'We really cannot see how the most thorough partisan can read these facts', declared *The Times*, 'without coming to serious conclusions as to the value of Sir James Graham's affirmations'. For Graham 'was either utterly indifferent to truth, or so devoted to his special Commissioner as to be ludicrously blind to it'. Soon it welcomed other journals' similar comments. To the *Post*, Ferrand 'appeared to be perfectly successful'. Provincial papers cordially agreed. Ferrand 'completely proved' his case to the *Tyne Mercury*, 'made out an annihilating case' to the *Halifax Guardian* (which noted the 'strong sensation in the political world') and 'proved infinitely more than sufficient to justify the opinion he gave . . . at Leeds' according to the *Hull Packet*. 'He . . . convicts . . . Graham at almost every step', declared the *Manchester Courier*,

> if not of a *suppressio veri*, at least of a series of reticences which may be tolerated in a Minister of State, but would be denounced in the man of honour . . .

The Liverpool Standard would 'not, and few men would, like to be placed in the same position in which it left Sir James Graham'.

Another Poor Law official, Walsham, indignantly denied that he also had written a false report. Ferrand refused to argue: he had made his charge two years previously and would now deal with Graham, not subordinates. Walsham anxiously published his denials in the Press. But Ferrand left London after a last attack on the League.

The summer passed quietly, though Ferrand stirred up a local row in August by complaining to Leeds magistrates of drunkenness at Harden. Robert Milligan thereupon counselled villagers

> so to regulate your conduct that there may be no room for such remarks in future from one who appears to take so little interest in your welfare as Mr. Ferrand.

Ferrand was too busy on estate matters to be troubled: in addition to rural and moorland acres, there were urban properties in Keighley and Bradford (valued in 1844 at £6117 and £20,323 respectively), which raised special problems. And magisterial duties in an industrial area were undoubtedly heavy. Furthermore, in a Yorkshire community, there was the lure of both the moors and of cricket. Ferrand's Bingley cricket club was successful, if somewhat unorthodox. Local men recalled years later that having defeated a Keighley team, the Bingleians were once beaten off the field:

> Comparing notes on the fracas afterwards with one of his henchmen, the youthful Bingley captain remarked that, having been in the thick of it, he felt somewhat sore bodily. 'Tha should ha' done as I did', replied the more

experienced cricketer. 'And what's that?' 'I brayed mi way through 'em wi' mi bat.' This was the last match that the Ferrand organisation played in Keighley.

Milligan's sneer was soon disproved. Walker and Margaret Ferrand had long supported allotment schemes, setting aside fifteen Cottingley Bridge acres for 59 enthusiastic Bingley worker-gardeners, and Ferrand added gardens and a cricket ground. The annual dinner of the allotment association on 11 October was made a great local event, and 'Young England' was invited to join the festivities. Although Smythe and Walter could not attend, Ferrand's guests included Disraeli, Manners, the sporting 'squarson' Philip Savile, other Anglican clergymen and local surgeons and manufacturers, as well as the Bingley 'lads'. And, in line with 'Young England's' dreams, a cricket festival opened the celebrations. The resplendently-uniformed Bingley band hailed the teams – Manners' XI and Ferrand's 'locals' (who, not surprisingly, won two of the three matches). The scene had its extraordinary aspects, with Disraeli and a local shoemaker facing what was later reported to be Lord John's introduction of round-arm bowling to Airedale. 'Above-shoulder' bowling was illegal in MCC rules until 1862, but in 1902 Manners recalled that he had bowled over-hand from the left arm. The event was long remembered locally, in an area given to cricket folklore. Village cricket was less impressive than 'medieval' tournaments, but the message was the same.

The climax came at a dinner for 200, with Ferrand presiding, flanked by Disraeli and Manners and praised even by Milligan. The affair was conducted in true 'Young England' style. After the repast and amidst the toasts, Ferrand declared that this was 'the proudest . . . moment of his life',

> for if there be one position more than another in which an English country gentleman may stand proud and happy in his own parish, it is when he is surrounded by every grade of society within it . . . But . . . the pride of the moment is enhanced in a tenfold degree when I recollect that this meeting is assembled for the purpose of so much rejoicing, and when I also behold the operatives of our native parish placed for the evening on a level with ourselves . . . My friends, this is not the first time that such a glorious meeting has assembled in this parish. There has, God knows, too long been an intervening space between such cordial rejoicings. Shame on those who have neglected their duty in this respect . . . The working classes of this parish have not hesitated to tell me what was my duty. I listened to their counsel; I followed their advice; and it is the working classes who have placed me where I am.

And he predicted a 'traditionalist' future, in an uncharacteristically emotional 'purple passage'

> Behold, my friends, the dawn of the sunshine of ancient days on our native land! Behold this evening is new seed sown; some of you have already reaped the crops of former sowings. May God give the increase to all our fellow-countrymen! . . . May God grant that on the bed of death I may be enabled to offer Him a fervent but humble prayer that some redeeming point in my

character may be found in the fact that I have, so far as in me lay, endeavoured to do my duty towards you in that state of life into which it has pleased Him to call me.

These sentiments were echoed by Manners, to whom 'the peasant who had a stake in the hedge was more likely to be a better man, a better citizen and a better member of society than he who merely worked for another'. He believed that

> that allotment scheme . . . will go far to rectify what I cannot help looking upon as a serious and growing evil – I mean the extinction of every agricultural class between that of the rich tenant-farmer and that of the day-labourer . . . I do not say that it was ever the custom, or that it ever will become the custom, for many of the peasantry of England to rise from their condition and to become farmers; but . . . the system must be wrong which denies the possibility of such a picture being realised . . .

Disraeli spoke of an older, merrier England and of the little group's philosophy:

> We want . . . to impress upon society that there is such a thing as duty. We don't do that in any spirit of conceit or arrogance; we don't pretend that we are better than others, but we are anxious to do our duty and . . . call on others, whether rich or poor, to do theirs. If that principle of duty had not been lost sight of for the last fifty years, you would never have heard of the classes into which England is divided. We want to put an end to that political and social exclusiveness which we believe to be the bane of this country . . . We see but little hope for this country so long as that spirit of faction that has been so rampant of late years is fostered and encouraged . . . Of such a state of society the inevitable result is that public passions are excited for private ends, and popular improvement is lost sight of in particular aggrandisement.

On tours of the district 'Dizzy' carefully observed the countryside for use in his next and perhaps greatest novel, *Sybil, or The Two Nations* (1845). But 'Young England' itself, so brilliantly announced in *Coningsby, or The New Generation* (1844) and at Bingley and a Manchester *soirée*, was soon to disintegrate.

What the 'peasants', paying an average of 11s. *per-annum* for their holdings, thought of this high-flown oratory, as they munched through Ferrand's beef, mutton, pork, fowl, puddings, vegetables and personally-shot ten hares and sixteen rabbits and mellowed through his ales, wines and spirits, is impossible to estimate. Whether they saw the vision which 'Young England' itself only vaguely comprehended – but which, stripped of its verbiage, has some surprisingly 'modern' themes – is doubtful. They did know that Ferrand had defended the factory workers, the paupers and the land. Perhaps, as good Yorkshiremen, they followed the old injunction to

> See all, hear all, say nowt;
> Sup all, eat all, pay nowt.

VI

When his friends moved to visit Milnes at Fryston (where Disraeli first met Hardy's son Gathorne, his future colleague), Ferrand returned to rabbit-shooting. No doubt he has saddened by the *Intelligencer*'s claim that

> We have a right to anticipate great benefits from the introduction of the New Poor Law system into Leeds – an event which, it seems, is soon to take place.

Even Yorkshire Conservatism, shaken by the attitudes of some *quondam* allies, was becoming 'respectable'. But Ferrand would never desert old-style Tory principle to suit Tamworth pragmatism.

In December Ferrand underlined the point in an address to constituents in Knaresborough court house. He had maintained his election pledges. An unpublished report of the investigation into his attacks on the League 'exposed . . . a mass of iniquity, tyranny and plunder of the working classes that would disgrace a heathen nation'. His allegations on Cobden's Truck were proved. Against Government 'hatred and malice', he had 'pleaded the cause of the widows, the fatherless and the orphans'; against false accusations, he had secured a ban on Halifax's treadmill; yet 'at this very time, a plot had been laid for the purpose of expelling him . . .' Amid cheers and laughter, a supporter shouted 'Aye, but they would have summat to do, Sir'.

More dangerously, Ferrand asserted of the row in Parliament that

> Every statement I made stands uncontradicted, unrefuted; and I stand absolved . . . while Sir James Graham is convicted . . . of being a dishonest man and of having told . . . a wicked and deliberate falsehood.

He had supported re-introduction of the income tax and retention of the Corn Law; but the tariff changes 'could only have been brought forward by either a lunatic or a traitor'. Export of machinery was wrong; Government had enforced the Poor Law 'with greater tyranny, oppression and cold-blooded cruelty' than even the Whigs; above all, Peel had robbed the operatives of 'Ten Hours'. To Ferrand, Peel was Britain's 'most unconstitutional minister'. He condemned the unequal treatment of O'Connell and O'Connor, the unfairness to agriculturalists and the 'murder in cold blood' caused by the unsavoury, Radical-inspired 'Opium War' of 1839–42 with China.

However, Poor Law practices most greatly incensed Ferrand. As he revealed that Graham proposed to end the remaining 'Gilbert Unions', one listener affirmed 'he's a bad 'un'. The Commissioners had acted on the principle that 'killing the poor is no murder'; at Belper workhouse normal paupers mixed with starving maniacs, families were divided, talk was prohibited and children were disciplined like soldiers. 'England had become a nation of humbugs': a missionary at Exeter Hall telling of such cruelties 'among a nation of savages' would soon have 'a set of canting sleek-faced hypocrites' raising funds to help reform:

But here we have these things daily taking place in a nation professing to be governed according to the principles contained in the Bible. So long as a nation is ruled as this country is, she will receive no favour from Heaven . . .

As independent Member for Knaresborough, Ferrand warned constituents that

as Sir Robert Peel betrayed the Protestant Church in 1829, so he is going to betray the Protestant Church in Ireland in 1845. He keeps secret his intentions; but I say unto you, watch! for I can have no confidence in a man who obtained office by fraud, and who dares to trample under foot the best interests of the country.

By any standards, this was a remarkable 'end-of-term-report', and the Press noted it. *The Times* welcomed 'a striking effusion of sterling English home-sprung oratory . . . a good round circle of home truths' in 'audacious' not 'soft and glutinous' style: 'we have truth in a rough shape, but a little rough handling does no harm occasionally'. To the *Halifax Guardian* 'there would be many a responding bosom amongst the Conservatives of the West Riding', for Government 'had earned . . . much disfavour' over the Poor Law and Ten Hours. 'We sadly lack in the House of Commons a score of Ferrands to call things by their right names', declared the *Post*. The *Leeds Mercury* naturally thought differently, claiming that 'foul-mouthed' Ferrand was supported only by a handful of Tories and Chartists and would not be re-nominated. And Cobden told a London League meeting that Ferrand (elected 'on purpose[to] bait me') was 'in plain Knaresborough language, a slanderer and a————'. Before returning home, Ferrand distributed copies of his speech. He had now declared open war on the Government and was to find many Tory allies.

VII

Ferrand opened 1845 in determined fashion with a Rochdale speech on 9 January, when Walter and Fielden joined him in addressing some 2500 people against the Poor Law. Ferrand commended local Radical opponents urging them not to follow Yorkshire's 'degrading example': at Leeds

at the last general election the milk-and-water Conservatives shed crocodile tears while expatiating on the horrors of the New Poor Law, . . . that they might gull the public. Away with such falsehood. For God's sake let us have no more lying on the hustings.

He especially condemned the *Intelligencer* and its chief reporter, John Beckwith, who had just become clerk to the local Guardians.

William Bolland, a Leeds ironmaster and senior partner in the *Intelligencer*, protested in *The Times* that he had not known of Beckwith's appointment until hours before its announcement and that he disapproved of both it and the Act. In reply, Ferrand quoted a string of *Intelligencer* comments to prove its 'base apostasy'. At home he argued with fellow trustees of the sixteenth-century Wooller Charity, alleging misuse of funds and sending information to the Solicitor-General on the neglect of poor beneficiaries. Eventually, the trustees were ordered to make donations to local hospitals and to apprentice poor children.

In the Commons, on 20 February, Ferrand supported Tom Duncombe's campaign against Graham's selective opening of private mail. This was a long-standing argument. Graham had continued the Whig practice of authorising the opening of suspects' letters by the GPO's secret office: O'Connell, Chartists, Leaguers, Rebecca rioters, Giuseppe Mazzini and Duncombe had been selected. Duncombe had protested since 1844, backed by hypocritical Whigs eager to harass the Government and by *Punch* with its attacks on 'Paul Pry at the Post Office'. It was an unfair and largely dishonest campaign against Graham, who was constrained from giving details on security matters. Ferrand, it seems, was wrong in thinking that Leaguers had escaped investigation in 1842.

Ferrand maintained close contact with his Irish friends. In February Dublin operatives demanded an investigation into Peel's conduct, with a view to impeachment. These militant Protestants asked two religious Conservatives, Gladstone and Inglis, to take the lead. Both, naturally enough, refused. But Ferrand sent £2 to join the Association, and Gregg enthused over his support. Ferrand was now preparing to mount a frontal assault upon Irish policies and particularly the proposal to treble the public grant to the decrepit Roman Catholic seminary at Maynooth. In April he undertook to present the Dublin petition and

> rejoiced to say that a strong Protestant feeling was spreading through the country against Sir Robert Peel, who in his opinion was the greatest traitor who had existed since Judas Iscariot.

On Good Friday Ferrand was the guest of Bradford Oddfellows at a tea party to raise funds for widows and orphans. He was introduced by the tough Scoresby as 'a friend of yours and . . . of all working men', declared that he always regarded workers as 'the most valuable part of society' and praised Oddfellow colleagues for practically (rather than theoretically) aiding working families. 'The man blessed with wealth had an awful duty and great responsibility attached to the talent placed in his keeping; he had it to hold in fidelity towards his God, and for good service to his country . . .', and Ferrand prayed that his own attempts to help the operatives 'might cover a multitude of sins'.

In all these public activities family affections seemed to have receded into the background of Ferrand's life. Commander Crispin, ADC to the Queen and Captain of the Royal yacht, married his younger sister Caroline on 15 April in Bingley church, with a second Roman Catholic service in the drawing room at St Ives; but otherwise the family of Sarah Ferrand and Currer Busfeild had much diminished since 1832. Jane, Sarah, Mary, Anne and Benjamin were dead; Emily was widowed. Ferrand himself remained a solitary widower, rarely seeing his own two children, though family tradition suggests that he was not entirely bereft of female companionship. Lack of maternal care and long separation from their father probably contributed to the children's later problems. Ferrand's favourite Aunt Margaret tried to take the place of a mother for William and Sarah, but she was to die of cancer in 1846.

A papist brother-in-law in no way inhibited Ferrand from assailing Peel's 'Popish Bill' in the Commons on 18 April. The proposal to repair and further endow the ramshackle Maynooth seminary affronted Protestant Liberals and Evangelical Tories alike. To Ferrand, the subsidy cut across 'those principles which he had ever held most sacred and most dear – principles on which the Ministry had gained power.' Quoting forgotten addresses from 1841, he asked Ministers:

> Where is the great Conservative Party now? Your conduct has scattered it to the winds. You have no party – no constitutional party. The constitutional party which sits on this side of the House is, to a man, opposed to you . . . And where is public opinion? United against the rt. hon. baronet.

Peel had 'deserted the principles of his party', and Ferrand 'implored him no longer to drag his Conservative party through the kennel of apostasy'. When the Second Reading vote was taken early next morning 147 Tories opposed Peel and 159 supported him. Ferrand's predictions were proving true: over 3000 petitions were presented against Peel's proposals to incorporate and subsidise the institution (with the intention of improving the quality of quasi-literate peasant priests and restoring the older tradition of Continentally-educated intellectuals less prone to accept O'Connellite blandishments), and on the Third Reading Tories divided 149–148 against the Bill. If anyone could have altered the tragic course of subsequent British-Irish history, it was Peel. He tried hard, against bitter opposition from Erastian Radical and Anglican Tory alike. And he was badly let down by the bitter hostility of the O'Connellite 'Lion of Tuam' Archbishop MacHale (a rough student and teacher at Maynooth, the son of a publican, an obsessional Anglophobe, demagogue and controversialist) to priestly or other education. MacHale must bear a burden for what he wrought in Connaught and elsewhere.

At a time when the Church of England was under regular attack, it seemed monstrous to many Tories that public money should be devoted to 'training' a loutish, disaffected priesthood. Ferrand joined men like John Colquhoun and Inglis in angry opposition – though Gladstone (with much publicity) changed his mind. But the opposition was not entirely religious. Disraeli had already talked of Peel as 'catching the Whigs bathing, and walking away with their clothes', 'the political Petruchio, who had outbid them all', and declared that 'a Conservative Government was an organised hypocrisy'. 'The language of the Tory Party', recorded the astute Thomas Raikes on 19 April.

> is more bitter and violent against [Peel] than ever I heard in society of the older time from disappointed Whigs against Mr. Pitt. But I do not imagine this to be traced to a No-Popery cry. If Sir Robert Peel had left the Corn Laws untouched, he would have carried the Maynooth question by a triumphant majority without a schism . . .

Peel's crucial majority of 147 came from the Opposition.

'Peel's speech', recorded Greville, 'was considered as clearly indicative of a consciousness that his party was broken up and the termination of his tenure of office approaching'. Lord Winchilsea (who had duelled with Wellington in 1829 over 'Emancipation') led some Tories out of the Carlton to the new 'Protestant' National Club. Peel and Graham professed shock at the extent of squirearchical hostility and ingratitude. But, Graham told Croker in March,

> The country gentlemen cannot be more ready to give us the death-blow than we are prepared to receive it. If they will rush on to their own destruction, they must have their way. We have endeavoured to save them, and they regard us as enemies for so doing . . .

'The Bill will pass', he told Lord Heytesbury in April, 'but our party is destroyed'. And to Lord Hardinge he forecast that

> The Bill will pass and the Government will ultimately be overthrown in consequence. Our party is shivered and angry, and we have lost the slight hold which we ever possessed over the hearts and kind feelings of our followers.

As the Tories closed in to kill Conservatism, for once Graham's predictions tallied with Ferrand's.

CHAPTER FIVE

Defeats and Victories

In the late autumn of 1845 Peel was moving towards repeal of the Corn Laws. But the Cabinet was divided and on 6 December (as *The Times* revealed the plan, to be instantly denied) Peel resigned. Unable to form a Ministry, Russell eventually (as Disraeli put it) 'handed back with courtesy the poisoned chalice to Sir Robert.' On the 20th Peel returned and carried his leading colleagues (except Stanley) with him. Two months of argument, rumour, 'leaks', suspicions, dishonest denials and psychologically-damaging ill-kept secrecy were reaching a climax.

Two days before Christmas Ferrand made his annual report to constituents, 'at least two-thirds' of whom (including some noisy Leaguers) crowded into the Royal Oak at Knaresborough. He bitterly attacked Peel as 'a slippery eel' and 'had no hesitation in saying that he had been guilty of the grossest tergiversation and basest apostasy, and that he had broken every pledge he gave in his Tamworth Manifesto'. He thought Repeal impossible; but if Peel did yield to 'the wicked faction' and 'sacrificed the landed interest' he would be thrown from office. He asked typical questions on corn supplies, foreign exports and tariffs, mercantile engrossment, labourers' employment, farmers' survival, proprietors' compensation. And he answered Liberal threats:

> Mr. Cobden the other day said that he would back Stockport against Steyning. Good God!, gentlemen, if the League are so mad as to attempt to come to blows, the forces which they could muster would speedily be annihilated by the brawny arms of the agriculturists. I hope the League will fail in their attempt to produce bloodshed and civil war, and that all classes will continue to live in friendship, in harmony and in peace.

He would fight for Protection, social reform and Protestantism.

The Press soon commented on this fighting speech. It was 'a powerful view of the protection question' to the *Post*, 'and a no less powerful onslaught upon the Peel policy'. The *Wakefield Journal* praised Ferrand as 'honest in his intentions and straightforward in his conduct'. Ferrand told the *Post* that Protection must be comprehensive; indeed, he had refused to join the principal Protectionist body (the Duke of Richmond's aristocratic Central Agricultural Protection Society of 1844) 'because it was limited to the selfish object of protecting agriculture alone'. He also warned Manchester factory reformers against making any deals with Leaguers over 'Ten Hours'. But the *Mercury* sourly insisted that Knaresborough Tories had deserted him and that to collect an audience he had had to pay further election debts. Now Ferrand was to face new tests in Parliament and in Yorkshire.

I

On the death of Lord Wharncliffe on 19 December John Stuart-Wortley succeeded as 2nd Baron, thus causing a West Riding by-election. A week later Lord Morpeth issued an address as a Whig free-trader. The League had been gaining strength for some time by objecting to Tories at the registration and by selling parcels of land (with voting qualifications) to supporters: it was later claimed that 1483 Riding votes were thus created, though Cobden thought that the figure was 5000. Determined that the seat should not be lost without a fight, Ferrand resolved to organise a Protectionist campaign at this time of Tory dissension and bewilderment.

In January 1846 Ferrand sent a clarion call from Paris, where he had accompanied his ailing Aunt Margaret, to 'Brother Yorkshiremen' and 'the enemies of Popery, the supporters of the monarchy and the friends of native industry'. He announced the 'glorious news' that 'Conservatism in the West Riding was as dead as Whiggery':

> From this time forth let the 'thimblerigging' word 'Conservative' be struck out of the political vocabulary; it was coined to take in a nation, it has already destroyed a party. Let 'Protection' or 'Free Trade' henceforth be the rallying cries; let these two principles be again tested at the ensuing West Riding Election.

Ferrand promised to 'appear upon the hustings . . . to fight the battle of Labour against Capital' and to propose a 'Protestant', monarchist, Protectionist Ten Hours and anti-Poor Law candidate, supporting 'Protection for all, destruction to none'. The natural choice was Edwin Lascelles, brother of Lord Harewood (owner of 30,000 Yorkshire acres and almost hereditary leader of Yorkshire Toryism and of the Yorkshire Protective Committee for the Defence of British Industry from 1844). Ferrand would question Morpeth on dependence on imported corn, compensation, wage cuts and the Poor Law. 'One of the chief objects which the . . . League has in view', he still maintained, 'is to reduce wages to the Continental level and thus *to increase* the profits of capital, by *screwing down* the price of labour'. He urged workmen to attend the nomination, to give the League 'its death-blow in Yorkshire'.

Protectionists welcomed such a lead, calling for subscriptions to hire special trains for operatives. 'Henceforth', agreed the *Standard*,

> the rival standards must be inscribed with the mottoes of Protection and Abolition. Henceforth we must war not against Whigs, but against abolitionists; abolitionists of native produce and native skill, of English wages and English labour, of the Irish Church, including of course the Protestant religion, and, should it seem a probable speculation, of the union with Ireland, in a word, the abolition of everything – but the League . . .

It professed to find Ferrand 'confident in the wisdom and fidelity of Sir Robert Peel's Government' and only dissenting from repeal 'upon the broad and solid grounds of conscientious conviction'. The reality was different. And the *Mercury* lashed Ferrand's 'usual sulphuric style', 'little knot of Tory Chartists', 'the vapouring and tricks of the wild man of Harden Grange' and questions which 'evinced a degree of ignorance and wrong-headedness that made Mr. Ferrand more fit for any other place than a seat in Parliament'.

From the start, matters went wrong. Returning home, Ferrand found that Lascelles had been adopted at Ripon, where Harewood had some influence and where the redoubtable Miss Lawrence could virtually guarantee an unopposed return. After searching for a local candidate, on the 26th Ferrand proclaimed that George Lane Fox, son of his sporting friend and heir to 15,000 acres in Yorkshire and 24,000 in Ireland, would stand. Young George was well connected politically, and Ferrand optimistically suggested that 'it will probably only remain for [the electors] to declare by Show of Hands that he shall be our Representative'.

Ferrand, largely unaided, opened the campaign in Leeds Music Hall on the 28th. The meeting was constantly interrupted and sometimes violent. 'The riotous conduct which prevailed throughout the evening', declared *The Times*, 'was most disgraceful', and the *Mercury* confirmed that 'from beginning to end, the proceedings were one continual scene of indescribable disorder'. Ferrand roared above the noise against 'some men with good coats' who tried to prevent him from defending workers – who 'must take their stand or else become slaves for ever'. He turned on 'a most shabby set' of employers: 'the working men conducted themselves like gentlemen, and the master manufacturers like blackguards'. The opposition damaged £20 of fittings, but Ferrand urged his enemies to bring the foppish young Baines with them next time.

The climax came in Huddersfield Philosophical Hall on the 30th, when Ferrand was supported by 'a little knot of Chartists, members of the short-time-committee'. The cautious management having removed the chairs, the place was crowded, noisy and hot. There were angry exchanges, as Ferrand told the employer Frederick Schwann that he was a 'bully' who should return to his own country. After the meeting, reported *The Times*, Ferrand was kicked and beaten by some 'respectably-attired persons' and rescued by workmen. And the *Post* declared that

> The anger with which the wealth-worshippers regard the exposures that Mr. Ferrand has made in the North affords an amusing illustration of *Liberal* justice . . .

But it was enough to deter Lane-Fox, who announced on 2 February that ill-health prevented his candidature. Ferrand, whose 'unequalled audacity . . . tour of inflammation [and] . . . acts of instigation and delusion' incensed Baines, was alone – except for fellow Yeomanry officers with whom he dined in a tavern. He sadly declared that 'certain success' must be missed, as there was no time to obtain another candidate. And on the 4th Morpeth was returned unopposed, amid free trade enthusiasm, at Wakefield.

II

Parliament reassembled on 19 January, and the Queen's speech foreshadowed Peel's Free Trade plans. Party activity was mounting, noted Greville:

the Whig and Peelite (for now there are Peelites, as contra-distinguished from Tories) Whippers-in have been making lists, and they concur in giving Peel a large majority.

On the 27th Peel announced his scheme to abolish tariffs on many manufactured articles, cut duties on several foodstuffs and reduce the corn duty to a nominal 1s. per quarter by 1849. Agriculturalists who had doubted that their leader would go so far were now angrily disturbed, particularly by the lack of adequate compensation. 'The Protectionists were generally angry and discontented', commented Greville, 'none reconciled, and some who had cherished hopes of better things were indignant.'

To Lord Malmesbury the plan was 'mere mockery', and he became a firm Protectionist. Another previously lethargic politician, Lord George Bentinck – a Whig who reputedly became 'the most bigoted and violent of Tories', hitherto a rowdy racecourse gambler and eventual reformer of the turf – suddenly became active in the Protection Society and Commons alike, famously declaring that

> He kept horses in three counties, and they told him that he should save some £1500 a year by free trade. He didn't care for that: what he could not bear was being sold.

Already, during the debate on the Address on the 22nd, Sibthorp declared that he 'was neither surprised nor deceived by the course proposed' by Peel,

> for he had so often been deceived by him on important questions of religion as well as of agriculture, that he was determined to be deceived no more.

And Disraeli launched an attack on Peel which roused the Tory benches:

> We accepted him for a leader to accomplish the triumph of Protection, and now we are to attend the catastrophe of Protection.

It was this sense of betrayal, rather than any economic theory or even self-interest, which finally provoked the back-bench revolt against Peel.

A new party rapidly developed – 'a very strong and compact party', thought Russell, 'from 220 to 240 in the House of Commons, and no one knows how many in the Lords'. Long 'apolitical' county societies, in which farmers had urged squires to act since Robert Baker's Essex group of 1844, now burst into action, winning a crop of by-elections. Leaderless, unorganised but passionately angry, the Protectionists shocked Peel (who still controlled the Conservative centres of power) and made him finally realise that his party was doomed, albeit by supporters of a hopeless cause. Men who were outraged by the absence of any counterbalance for expected rural losses, men devoted to hustings pledges, men obeying patrons, men fearing ruin and men who believed in Ferrand's wide Protectionism now joined against those regarded by Bentinck as 'no better than Common Cheats'.

When Government hoped to go into committee on 9 February the Protectionists started a long debate ('the dullest on record' to Greville) on an amendment by Philip Miles and were 'very proud of the fight' they sustained, under George Bankes,

William Miles and Stafford O'Brien. Ferrand intervened on the 13th, to join in the baiting of Peelites. Lord Northland had announced his confidence in Peel. 'What confidence had you . . . when you were dragged from the coal-hole to vote for him' over Maynooth, Ferrand demanded, to Members' delight.

On the 24th Ferrand spoke at length. He claimed that League petitions were fraudulent: 'no working man who was employed by a . . . League manufacturer dare refuse to attach his signature'. He denied Ward's claim that he was paid £2000 to fight the Riding, claiming that if Lascelles 'had fought the battle as he ought to have done' he would have won. If the Peelites 'were honest men, [they] would stick to their pledges; if . . . [they] had changed their principles and opinions on this subject, let them resign their seats'. There passed under his scrutiny Beckett, Bickham Escott, William Cripps, Sir George Clerk, Sidney Herbert, Graham, Peel and Edward A'Court – pledged Protectionists converted to Free Trade. The people viewed 'with unmitigated disgust [Peel's] contemptible apostasy and tergiversation'. After reciting familiar selections of League announcements, Ferrand urged agriculturalists to save the labourers from rapacious capitalists. 'Such speakers', declared *The Times*, 'discharged a useful political function. Inconsistency should have its scourge.' Furthermore, Ferrand

> is consistent. He desires to see the labourer protected at the plough, the stockinger at his frame, the weaver at his loom. 'God made the country and man made the town' is his maxim . . . As far as they went, he agreed with the Conservative leaders. With them he demanded protection for the soil, though he went further, and asked it for the tiller thereof . . .

To some Churchmen, the speech was 'most useful and practical': 'its brilliancy, ability and, above all, its avenging truth, gave it a power which attended no other oration'; each attack left the offender 'naked to the public gaze, in all his apostate and repulsive deformity'. But Baines typically condemned Ferrand's 'outrageous calumnies':

> It was a bad sign for the cause of Protection when two of its principal champions . . . were Mr. Disraeli and Mr. Ferrand. Shallowness, conceit and intemperance would be poor substitutes to that party for the talent and statesmanship it had lost for ever.

Some MPs naturally attacked Ferrand, and Roebuck particularly lashed his opposition to rural migration. *The Times*, which enjoyed mocking both sides, disapproved of attacks on industry but thought Ferrand right to raise the sad problem of simple rural migrants, for

> The State has still to take the great towns in hand and devise more positive measures for their better security from the evils incident from accumulated numbers, poverty, improvidence and sin. We want a sound and vigorous system of municipal economy.

Ferrand vigorously defended himself: 'the public held Mr. Roebuck in such estimation that they would not give a quarter of a farthing for his opinions'; Bright's claim that Northern workers opposed Ten Hours was untrue; Bowring had misquoted him; and Morpeth was wrong on false League petitions. Disraeli supported him against Roebuck's sneers over the unjust and ridiculous 1844 resolution. He regretted Ferrand's hostility on industry and 'had often remonstrated with [him] on that subject; but in vain, for it was Mr. Ferrand's honest conviction that these attacks were necessary and just'. He challenged the House to investigate Peel's charge that Cobden had condoned murder – which Peel instantly withdrew. The Protectionists lost by 339 votes to 242.

Protectionists concentrated on delaying business until Easter. They were quickly becoming a powerful party, under Bentinck, William Miles, O'Brien and Bankes, with the still suspect Disraeli as counsellor and Newdegate and William Beresford as Whips; Stanley led in the Lords, with Eglinton and Malmesbury as Whips. Long concerned at League methods, Newdegate and Borthwick demanded an inquiry into 'fraudulent and vexatious objections' to Tory registrations. Ferrand asserted that this was regular League policy: his own vote had been opposed for four years until he threatened legal action. Charles Wood retorted that Ferrand had objected to many Liberals, including his uncle Busfeild, 'when he must have known the vote to have been as good as the vote of any man in the country'. There was merriment as Ferrand admitted signing objections:

> but upon this ground: for 3 years in succession a person had objected to his vote, and had received for his services a silver tea-pot – to which his relative was one of the principal subscribers. He had stated that if this person objected to him a fourth time, he would most certainly object to that of his relative . . . he thought he was perfectly justified.

This was not the only family division provoked by the Corn Laws in the Riding or elsewhere.

Only on 27 March was the Second Reading passed, by a majority of 88. Three days later an Irish Coercion Bill (passed by the Lords on the 13th) was accepted for debate in the Commons, as agrarian violence mounted. Protectionists toyed with the idea of an alliance with non-O'Connellite Irishmen: the militant 'Young Ireland' leader Smith O'Brien was at least sympathetic. The Bill passed a First Reading on 1 May by 274 votes to 125. Meanwhile, Repeal proceeded slowly, passing its Third Reading on 15 May by a majority of 100. The long debates virtually ended in the Lords on 28 May, when the Second Reading was carried by 211 votes to 164; the Corn and Customs Bills finally passed the Lords on 25 June.

Ferrand was absent through much of the debate. On 5 April cancer finally claimed his aunt Margaret, after long suffering, borne 'so meekly and with so divine a resignation'. Her place in Ferrand's affections may be judged from Manners' condolences of Easter Monday:

> Surely now that her spirit is at rest, and those agonies over, her sorrowing friends may take comfort in the belief that the great sacrifice consummated at this season was not made in vain for her. And to you, my dear friend, it should be a matter of thankfulness that her life was spared long enough to mould the

minds and discipline the hearts of your children, to watch over their progress until they arrived at years when they are old enough to treasure up and understand the benefit of her gentle teaching . . .

Manners' hopes for the Ferrand children were not to be justified.

When, on 15 June, the near-bankrupt Buckingham's motion to make permanent the sliding scale (planned to last until 1849) was lost by 130 votes to 103, the end was near. Ten days later the Lords passed the Corn and Customs Bills without dividing. That night the Commons debated coercion. The old view of what Graham called Protectionists' 'vindictive recklessness requires modification, despite their desire to punish Peel's "apostasy". Tories did have a sympathetic understanding of Ireland: as Bentinck told O'Brien, it lacked not food but cash with which to buy it. Furthermore, the new party could not determine how to act in the crucial debate: of 248 members, 69 (under Bentinck and Disraeli) opposed Peel and 105 supported him early on the 26th. Peel was defeated by 292 votes to 219 and promptly resigned.

III

Though overshadowed by the great corn-law contest, the factory issue still engaged the attention of reformers. During 1845 the Northern factory agitation had revived, urging Ashley to renew his Parliamentary efforts, and early in 1846 Balme and the new Lancashire secretary, Joseph Mullineaux, established new committees. Oastler could no longer help, having had to take a job in London. And Ashley moved for leave to introduce his Bill on 29 January only to leave Parliament two days later. Fielden now became Parliamentary leader, with Ferrand as his principal lieutenant: thus Tory-Radical co-operation was maintained, while Peelite-Liberal opposition, under Graham, Bright, Sir John Trelawney, Roebuck and Escott, remained bitter. But Ashley, Walker and many Anglican priests again roused the North during the spring, and the factory towns sent delegates to canvass MPs. When Fielden proposed the Second Reading on 29 April he was opposed by Graham and Hume – 'heartless and dishonest men!' to Ashley – with the usual prophecies of doom. On 13 May the allies were supported by Brotherton, William Cowper, Crawford, John Colquhoun, Inglis and Manners and opposed by Henry Labouchère, John Dennistoun, Trelawney, Roebuck and Edward Cardwell. On the 22nd Bankes, Bentinck, Beckett Denison, Russell and Macaulay favoured the Bill, against Bright, Cobden, Morpeth, Peel and Ward. Fielden was defeated by 203 votes to 193.

At last Ferrand's friends could be optimistic. 'Although not a victory, it is the next thing to one', thought Ashley. 'All hope of further successful resistance . . . was at an end', declared Mullineaux. 'The success of the measure was no longer a matter of doubt, but merely a question of time', asserted the Lancashire delegates. Supporters (including tellers) consisted of 117 Protectionists, 7 Peelites and 71 Whigs, Liberals and Radicals and opponents of 51, 73 and 81 respectively. The old pattern of primarily Tory support was thus maintained. Another encouraging sign was the support of some prominent Whigs by belated but important conversion – though most of them, like the ever-nervous Hindley, really favoured an 11-hours compromise. The future looked bright for the factory reformers.

The first great cause, Protection, was lost; the second, Ten Hours, was progressing; the third, the Poor Law, was undecided. In June Ferrand carried a vote of the Keighley Guardians against the Commissioners, whom he suspected of planning a local 'Bastille'. And he closely followed the proceedings of Lord Courtenay's Select Committee – set up only at the long insistence of Ralph Etwall – into the horrors of Andover workhouse, where underfed paupers engaged on crushing bones actually ate the rotting gristle and marrow. This scandal, long covered up by the Commissioners and then blamed on their juniors, was to be one of the steps by which the Commission of 1834 was to be destroyed. Despite recurring illness, Ferrand was determined to hammer home his nail in the coffin, particularly as Graham came out badly from the investigation.

Unfortunately, what he had in mind to 'reveal' was the continuing saga of the great Mott affair. Of course, the Commons' condemnation still rankled, founded as it was on incomplete evidence and subservience to a Minister. Naturally, Ferrand wished to clear his name. But another recital of Mott and Graham's iniquities must have filled friends with some unease, despite Ferrand's view that the Keighley and Andover cases were linked. From his sick-bed he wrote twice to *The Times*. The Andover investigation had proved that Graham had used untrue reports, and Ferrand would show in the next Session that Graham, Mott, Commissioner George Lewis and Walsham had joined in 'a foul and infamous conspiracy' to crush him. Lewis 'was guilty of the most deliberate falsehood for the purpose of deceiving the House of Commons, and of rescuing his "most confidential" friend, the arch-commissioner [Graham] from the infamy which awaits him'. Lewis had recently claimed that Mott was sent to Keighley simply because Ferrand had tried to obtain withdrawal of an order: 'nearly every word . . . was false', and if Lewis had been caught 'in such deliberate falsehood' at the Old Bailey he 'would be . . . indicted for perjury'. The evidence was that Mott reported on 13 April 1842, the order was dated on 30 April and Ferrand's notice followed two months later. Lewis was lying to save Graham from 'infamy'; he should 'receive condign punishment' for giving 'scandalously false evidence'. *The Times* agreed that Ferrand had a good case against the rascally debtor Mott, only one of whose reports had been used, simply against Ferrand: this 'was not administration of justice, but political intrigue'.

When Lewis corrected his own testimony to accommodate Ferrand's true chronology, *The Times*, 'without charging Mr. Lewis with deliberate falsehood . . . did not believe it':

> In the present dearth of the legitimate drama, we know not where better materials, or, we may add, better acting, are to be found . . . We believe that Mr. Mott was sent to Keighley, and his report put into Sir James's red box, not because the clerk of the Keighley Union had written a letter to the Commissioners [as Lewis claimed], but because the member for Knaresborough had very early announced his intention of waging war to the uttermost with the New Poor Law.

This was almost certainly the correct analysis, though proof was hindered by the Commissioners' loss of their instruction to Mott and curious habit of not filing 'private' letters. But Lewis, prompted by that lover of scandal Charles Greville, resolved to sue Ferrand for libel. When the case was heard in the Queen's Bench in November, the judges, headed by Lord Denman, absolved Lewis from blame and delivered a strong condemnation of Ferrand. On the facts this was inevitable, even though Press and public comment was that there was more to be said about the wider moral and political implications of the issue. But Ferrand was too prone to rely on Press and partisan sympathies.

IV

On 10 November Oastler, Fielden and Ferrand opened another Ten Hours crusade in Huddersfield Philosophical Hall, where 2000 people rallied under their vicar, Josiah Bateman. Oastler thereafter roused enthusiasm at Halifax, Bradford, Keighley, Dewsbury, Wakefield, Barnsley and Holmfirth, aided by Anglicans, doctors, Tories and Radicals (like Mark Crabtree, the Dewsbury Chartist and Yorkshire organiser), and met with great success. The Yorkshire campaign closed with a great rally in Leeds Music Hall on the 30th, under Hook, with the great friends as speakers. Ferrand reviewed the Factory Movement's history, recalling his conversion by Sadler and Oastler and the Bingley march to Low Moor in 1833 and ending with his recent 'ordeal'. In 1844, in the same room, he had charged Graham with procuring false reports, and 'he charged him again': the reports having now been produced, he 'meant to go further with them in the courts of law', for Denman's decision was 'a mockery, a delusion and a snare'.

The audience and the Press much enjoyed such fighting talk. 'A bolder, a more manly, a more unequivocal denial of any accusation, or a more direct countercharge against accusers, was never made and never brought . . .', declared *The Times*. But the speech actually provoked further trouble for Ferrand in the New Year. Meanwhile, Fielden was anxious that Liberal Scotland should be visited and it was agreed that Oastler, Ferrand and Rashleigh should tour the principal towns. When his colleagues were detained by business, Oastler alone spoke at Glasgow, Paisley and Dundee – with great success – before joining Ferrand for two Edinburgh meetings, in the Waterloo Rooms and the Music Hall, on the 24th and 28th. Having delivered a long attack on overworking and industrial accidents, Ferrand returned home for three weeks' sport before Parliament opened.

The Session of 1847 was to be important for Ferrand, but he spent early January coursing at Bingley, visiting constituents and friends – Milnes-Gaskell, Lane Fox and his Moss relatives at Otterspool – attending the Wakefield session and arranging to become a Deputy Lieutenant. He moved to London on the 18th, for Parliament's opening next day, instantly becoming active. On the 20th, during a debate on a motion by Pechell, he spoke against the Poor Law and gave notice that he would move for Returns on the Commissioners and Keighley Union, which the Home Secretary (Sir George Grey) agreed to provide.

Two days later Russell propounded his Poor Law scheme, by which control would pass from the Commissioners to a Board responsible to a Minister. This was a step in the right direction but did not go far enough for Ferrand – who instantly said so. He was determined that Government should never forget either the Andover tragedy or the Keighley scandal. He had written his letters 'for the purpose of courting legal proceedings' before a jury; he had just received a letter from Lewis's solicitor threatening a criminal information, which he regarded as 'an attempt to intimidate him'. Sustained by a great Protectionist dinner at the Carlton and regular meals with the Rashleighs, Ferrand threw himself into his favourite campaigns.

The Protectionists now constituted a party – as Disraeli and Bentinck demonstrated by taking Front Bench seats on the Opposition side – but did not agree on everything, as was shown in the debate on Ferrand's motion of the 28th. The proposal asked that a Committee should examine how Poor Law reports were obtained and what control Graham had, and Ferrand lengthily claimed that the Andover evidence proved Mott's dishonesty. Graham retorted equally verbosely, but Bowring attacked Mott's behaviour at Bolton, claiming that his complaints had caused his dismissal. Disraeli wearily re-examined 'the great Mott question', contending that 'although he thought him [Ferrand] often and egregiously mistaken, [he] was sincere and honest'. Ultimately on Disraeli's advice, Ferrand withdrew his motion.

When the great Ten Hours debate began on 10 February Bankes, Newdegate, Muntz, and above all Manners supported the bill against Hume, Philips, Bright, Bowring and the Chancellor, Wood; Grey and Russell were sympathetic but still favoured compromise. Seven days later Sir Andrew Leith Hay, Dennistoun, Roebuck, Trevelyan and Henry Marsland remained hostile, against Bernal, Crawford, Inglis, Strickland, Viscount Ebrington and T.S. Duncombe. Ferrand 'supported the prayer of the toiling millions' by quoting numerous descriptions of factory labour, condemning Liberals who 'argued about a 1/4 pound of cotton as if equal in importance with the lives of millions', denying Bright's lies about workers' opposition, recalling masters' broken pledges and bluntly threatening that 'the operatives (and he knew their feelings) were no longer to be trifled with'.

The Bill passed by 195 votes to 87 against an 11-hours amendment 'supported' (Ferrand bitterly noted) 'by all the despicable Peelites'. At this triumphant time the High-Tory *Standard* glowingly surveyed Ferrand's career:

> Five years ago Mr. Ferrand entered Parliament, and soon declared himself the determined enemy of the new Poor-law Commission and the factory system. All the *sober, moderate, prudent people*, who never do right for fear of being said to do wrong, affected to consider Mr. Ferrand as a mere violent agitator, one that could make a noise indeed, and delighted to make it, but one who could accomplish nothing. Mr. Ferrand, however, kept on his straight-forward course, though his path was made rugged by every dishonest and dishonourable artifice, by all the dirt and every other obstruction that could be thrown upon it. So violent were the efforts employed to repel or crush him, that on one occasion the House of Commons was prevailed upon to affirm an

untruth as a pretext for censuring the hon. gentleman. Still he kept on . . . and with what effect? Why, that the Poor-law Commission is under sentence of death, and the factory system reformed by the Ten Hours Bill. This is Mr. Ferrand's triumph – the triumph of courage and perseverance in a good cause; and Mr. Ferrand deserves it. It is true Lord Ashley's services are inestimable, but Mr. Ferrand has one claim more than Lord Ashley – [he] did not suffer himself to be cheated as Lord Ashley did – declaring himself favourable to the repeal of the corn laws, and losing his seat in Parliament, upon the promise of the millowners that, the corn laws once repealed, they would agree to a Ten Hours Bill. Between Mr. Ferrand and Lord Ashley there is, however, no feeling of rivalry, as was abundantly proved by the former's noble defence of his lordship on Wednesday, when attacked by Mr. Bright. We hope that Mr. Ferrand's glorious success will hold out an efficient encouragement to other men as honest and as brave as himself.

Thus cheered, Ferrand attended the Speaker's *levée* and on the 22nd went home for a few days' sport.

V

Ferrand regularly journeyed between Harden – where he superintended moorland planting – and London during the spring of 1847. There were walks with his daughter Sarah (now fifteen) in Kensington Gardens and pleasant dinners with the Rashleighs and Hoares, where there was the congenial Irish and Protectionist company of Gregg, O'Brien, Edward Grogan and Colonel Richard Howard Vyse of the Royal Horse Guards. There was the Factory Bill to support through its final stages in debates on 3 and 17 March, 21 April and 3 May – when it finally passed by 151 votes to 88, against Bright's last-ditch hostility. Above all, perhaps, as his political causes triumphed, Ferrand was seeing much of the beautiful Fanny Stuart, the daughter of Lord Blantyre, during regular visits to Rashleigh, whose wife Catherine (Fanny's sister) aided his cause. After days of planting and sowing oats on Harden moor, Ferrand would hurry to London to pursue his suit. The Rashleighs joined a house-party at Harden in April, with the Busfeilds, the Camerons and Dawson. On the 13th Ferrand. Sarah and the Rashleighs travelled together to London and on the 15th, armed with 7s.6d.-worth of flowers and an uncharacteristic 'Forget me not' entry in his diary, Ferrand dined at 16 Stratford Place yet again. Next day he 'dined and lunched at the Rashleighs. Explained.' The courtship had reached its climax. As Rashleigh went to Scotland to explain matters to the Stuarts, Ferrand bought a 6s. prayer book with which to accompany the sisters to church – twice. Through the following days Ferrand paid assiduous attendance at Stratford Place, and, when at last, on the 29th the Dowager Lady Blantyre gave her support, his expenditure on flowers rose to 15s. and even £1.

Despite all the occupations of courtship and the discussions of marriage settlements, however, Ferrand never neglected the House, where (as the *Standard* glowingly observed), the victorious termination of his two great labours, the passing of the Factory Bill, and the final demolition of the Somerset House despotism were reserved for the same evening [3 May] . . .

That since his entrance into Parliament Mr. Ferrand never gave a bad vote, or . . . failed to give a good one, we most firmly believe; but even they who may differ from us in this unreserved approbation of all his acts will at least allow that no man who ever sat in the House of Commons has exhibited more sincerity, zeal, energy, perseverance and courage in the cause of the humbler classes. 'The friend of the friendless', the champion of those who had no bribes either of wealth or honours with which to hire his service, he has fought the battle of the poor with great ability, and with a constancy and gallantry unsurpassed; in the most difficult of his two fields of combat he has fought it single-handed, and in both fields he has fought it with success . . .

Ferrand simply noted 'leading article in Standard upon me' – and ordered £5.4.2 worth of copies.

Everyone knew that an election was imminent, and on May Day Ferrand issued an address, explaining his Parliamentary career: he had 'no base apostacy to answer for, no broken pledges to explain away'. As promised, he had upheld 'Protestant institutions' and 'refused to support a religion which [as an MP he swore] contained a "damnable doctrine"'. As 'every interest except labour was amply represented . . . he . . . felt it his especial duty to fight the battle of the Poor': 'against fearful odds he had assisted a small but faithful band in Parliament' against the Poor Law – which

> not only violated the laws of God and man, but robbed the poor of their heritage, desolated their humble dwellings and placed them beyond the pale of the British Constitution.

He had 'aided' factory reform and introduced a 'general Inclosure Bill' which 'in all its essential parts' was subsequently adopted in an Act which

> was now bringing vast tracts of waste land into cultivation and was providing employment for large masses of the people.

Ferrand closed with the proud assertion that

> whilst in Parliament I have known no party but my Country, no interest but my Country's weal:- I have neither betrayed you, nor sold myself:- I therefore fearlessly ask you for a renewal of your confidence, and again to confer upon me the distinguished honour of being your Representative.

But dark manoeuvres were already afoot. In addition to the remaining Devonshire influence in the declining ducal borough, Ferrand faced the hostility of both the League and, incredibly, the Protectionist Harewood.

Though Ferrand found it difficult to credit and tried to obtain a denial, on 18 May Harewood effectively deserted him. He would not interfere at Knaresborough where he had little influence but he told Lascelles that 'although we may differ upon some points, I agree infinitely more with you than with Mr Ferrand'.

Bitterly disappointed, Ferrand withdrew his candidature:

> As this secret combination, which has been in existence since November last, will place many of my most earnest supporters in active opposition to Lord Harewood and his family if I contest the Borough against Mr. Lascelles, I have determined to save them from that painful position, but I should neither have performed my duty to you, nor to myself, if I had not exposed it, and, however deeply I regret being compelled thus to allude to the conduct of men, for whom I have hitherto had the greatest personal regard, still I will never allow private friendship to interfere with public duty.

For all the public gratitude of the Ten Hours campaigners in Yorkshire, Lancashire and Glasgow, and the sympathetic comments in the Press, it was perhaps the hardest blow of his political career up to that point.

In July, when the parliament elected in 1841 came to a close, Ferrand was left without a constituency to fight. A plan to stand at Carlisle fell through and the general election of 1847, which tenuously maintained the Whig ministers in office, saw the squire of Harden Grange engaged in more personal matters. His wedding with Fanny Stuart took place on 10 August in St. James's Church, London. It was a fashionable affair, largely because of the immense crowd of Stuart relatives and friends. His second marriage brought Ferrand into a higher stratum of society than anything he had previously experienced; but old political friends from the Young England days were not forgotten. Manners was best man and the Disraelis were present at the wedding breakfast. The honeymoon was spent at Alresford in Hampshire at a house belonging to Fanny's grandmother, the Dowager Lady Rodney, and was followed by a Stuart invasion of Harden. Later the couple went off to visit Fanny's family in Scotland and (for the bridegroom at least) a round of shooting and fishing. It was not on the whole a very satisfactory period in Ferrand's life. Fanny was intermittently ill; she did not get on well with her step-daughter; the weather was wet; and when she became pregnant early the following year there appeared disquieting symptoms. There were visits to Edinburgh to consult those eminent gynaecologists James Simpson and James Miller, and nearer the event the Ferrands took up residence there. On 1 October Ferrand recorded laconically, 'dearest Fanny confined at $8\frac{1}{2}$in evening at 5 Moray Place and delivered by Simpson under chloroform a splendid little boy – Hugo'.

In the intervening period Ferrand's largely social and sporting activities had been interrupted by the last important outbreak of Chartist violence in the spring of 1848. Though the famous April demonstration on London's Kennington Common passed off peacefully, the orderliness and good humour of the capital were not matched by events in the parts of the country where there were stauncher Radical traditions.

Ferrand and his type of Tory in the Northern manufacturing districts had often collaborated with local Chartists during the Factory and Poor Law agitations; and O'Connor first created his English base on causes founded by Oastler and Stephens. 'Tory Chartists' was a Whiggish term of obloquy from Glasgow to London and nowhere more regularly employed than in Bradford, Leeds, Manchester and Nottingham. A sympathy for the plight of the victims of the new industry and of the new economics had brought the old Right and old Left together.

Ferrand, however, was never prepared to condone illegal violence. On 24 May he warned the Home Office that drilling was going on among the Bingley militants and was in due course instructed to proceed against them. Ferrand acted promptly but with disastrous results. Two men were arrested and committed to York Castle; but they were rescued from the magistrates' office before the constables arrived to take them away and paraded in triumph round the town. The rescuers assaulted the magistrates' clerk and tried to ambush Ferrand on his way home. Though he escaped by making a detour, he was threatened with assassination and an attack on Harden Grange. Appeals for military protection proved useless. All the available forces in the locality were needed for Bradford where there were pitched battles on the streets. To keep the peace at Bingley Ferrand signed on dozens of special constables who patrolled the streets at night with apparently salutary effect; though this might also have been due to the torrential rain which providentially fell. He continued to besiege the Home Office, warning on Sunday 28 May that the government must not be deceived into thinking that the Chartists were a small body. 'They are an immense body in the manufacturing districts.' That same day he was informed, apparently by some humorist, that a great gathering was in progress on Harden Moor. Ferrand called for volunteers from Church and hastened to the spot only to find a peaceful congregation of Primitive Methodists: a fiasco which became part of Bingley folklore. Sterner measures followed. Within a few days he received a quota of military reservists, mostly aged Chelsea Pensioners (including one with a wooden leg) and on 31 May he proceeded to round up sixteen men and send them off to York under escort.

Though there was a slightly ludicrous side to these events, there was general agreement from the Home Office down to the local Press that Ferrand himself had acted with energy and skill, as well as personal courage. One eyewitness recalled many years later seeing him face the mob which invaded the magistrates' room at the Brown Cow at Bingley, giving them 'threat for threat, and browbeat them from passion into smouldering discontent – enjoying it all, no doubt, in his grim way – squared his jaw and roughened his voice, and astounded them all by that utter indifference to peril which was his strongest quality'. Though he was to endure taunts from political adversaries about his alleged brutality and hypocrisy in dealing with the Chartist rioters, at least he demonstrated that he was impartial in his severity against all law-breakers, whether political agitators or poachers on his estates.

CHAPTER SIX

Wool and Cotton

The year 1849 passed off more quietly in the now familiar round of sporting and social activities and visits to Scotland. But increasingly Ferrand was feeling the call of politics. His old mentor Oastler was still working to promote an alliance of working-classes and Protectionists as well as to uphold the provisions of the 1847 Factory Act against evading Liberal employers. By the end of 1849 Ferrand had decided to re-enter public life in support of what seemed a revival of protectionist feeling.

He began on 4 January, 1850, with a strong speech to a rally of the East Lothian Agricultural Protection Society in the George Inn at Haddington. Sir George Houston presided, supported by such local lairds as Sir John Hall of Dunglass and Sir James Walker-Drummond of Hawthornden and numerous farmers. Even in East Lothian, with the best farming in Britain, declared Ferrand, Free Trade brought ruin; and Ireland provided a classic warning:

> since the very year after Ireland had become a free trade country, 100,000 farmers had . . . left for America – a land of protection – taking with them £2,000,000 sterling [and] . . . hundreds of thousands [of labourers] settled down in England and Scotland, and in a few years the hordes of Irish labourers will eat out your vitals in Scotland through the poor law.

Ferrand talked of rioting Bradford workers' 'triumph [for] the principle of protection' against the North Midland Railway's free-trade wage cuts. And he enjoyably attacked Cobden, whose speeches contained 'very little but vulgar abuse'. In 1836 Cobden had forecast that Free Trade would not reduce farmers' prices and would end war, while a Ten Hours Act would ruin trade. The Factory Act actually was

> a law designed to protect the poor operatives from being worked to death one half of the day and starved to death the other half . . . Cobden himself had declared that they had had two of the most prosperous years of trade that the manufacturers ever enjoyed in this country.

Cobden's 'last prophecy was that the landed interest of England was to be destroyed – that the aristocracy and the farmers were to compound for their existence. [Ferrand] told him that that prophecy, like the others, would turn out to be false'.

Leaguers still dare not face their own workers. And Peelites were as bad: 'I look upon them as nobody', roared Ferrand. 'They are annihilated for ever . . . in the slough of degradation'. Peel 'had no authority. He had betrayed his party too often ever to be trusted again'. And Free Trade spelled ruin for agriculturalists, workers and Irish alike:

though we may have our Peels and Marshalls and Arkwrights making their millions, we shall have a nation impoverished and overwhelmed with misery, ruin and despair. I have no fear for England, if the landed interest will do their duty. If *you* allow yourselves to be trampled underfoot by a set of blustering knaves, you deserve every suffering which may befall you.

The speech, delivered with the old *panache*, was very well received, particularly by Blantyre's acquaintance, Sir David Baird of Newbyth. The Bairds became Ferrand's close friends.

After further sport, Ferrand repeated his Haddington success in the de Grey Rooms at York on the 23rd, following a rare night's dancing. Harewood presided over about 500 owners and farmers, both Whig and Tory, at a 'ticket-only' meeting (following League practice), supported by the Whig Duke of Cleveland (an old opponent of the League) and such squires as Edward Cayley, John Smyth, Octavius Duncombe, Joshua Crompton of Azerley Hall (brother of Ferrand's neighbour, Stansfield of Esholt), Ralph Creyke of Rawcliffe and Marton, owner of the expanding port of Goole, Harry Thompson of Kirby Hall, agriculturalist and railway director, James Legard of Welham, William Rutson of Newby Wiske and Nunnington and 'Single Speech' Pemberton Milnes of Fryston Hall, father of the Peelite MP for Pontefract.

Greeted by 'deafening and protracted cheering', Ferrand lived up to his reputation. He attacked the League for hiring 1500 armed Irish bullies to put down Manchester operatives: but 'let us only have a good flag, a fair field, and no favour in the town of Manchester, and I would not be afraid to meet the millowners even there'. Cobden might threaten violence, but 'the cotton-spinners of Lancashire were resting upon a volcano, and if it should explode they would be ruined'. Textile operatives were currently protesting at masters' breaches of the Factory Acts and threatening to 'take affairs into their own hands'. Such men would scarcely 'fight for their oppressors [or] be marshalled in Mr Cobden's rebel army – why, the first shot fired from such ranks would be through his own skull . . . if ever the Freetraders mustered their forces there would be a ragged crew . . .', routed by 'the bold yeomanry', with Cobden hanged and Bright saving himself by acting as 'Jack Ketch'. Ferrand's military picture simply followed Cobden's 'blustering' warlike threats: if O'Connor 'had made the speech at Leeds which Mr Cobden made, Sir George Grey would have sent the Attorney-General on his track'. He particularly condemned the 'most cruel, unjust and iniquitous' Opium War:

> We are now protecting Lancashire goods in the Chinese markets at the point of the bayonet . . . we are forming a sliding scale for the cotton spinners, which is composed of British bayonets, British cannon, British troops and British blood. [Free traders] have their permanent settlement in Hongkong with their commissioner there – Dr. Bowring, the late Poet Laureate of the League, who, if the British army were recalled, would have his ears nailed to his door within 24 hours by the Chinese . . .

And he bitterly condemned Wharncliffe (for whom he had 'worked like a slave' in 1841), Herbert and Denison for deserting the cause. He urged a union of Whigs and Tories for Protection, pledging to 'do his utmost to support the keenest Whig if he would stand by Protection'.

The speech thunderously applauded at York struck less responsive chords in London. *The Times*, now typically veering towards a liberal stance, was amused by Ferrand's call to arms: 'painful truths made pleasant fictions'. It contrasted Ferrand's imaginary battles with those of Walter Scott. The *Chronicle* was angrier, with talk of 'defeated cupidity truculent brutalities . . . strident and nerve-destroying . . . small spite and large rapacity . . . the gross suspicions of a vulgar imagination and the haphazard Billingsgate of a mendacious tongue . . . pictorial ingenuity . . . argumentative suicide' and so on:

> Your Ferrands are the blots and stains upon Conservatism . . . He is simply a person of a bad heart and worse temper . . . just the stuff out of which a good Jacobinical demagogue could be fashioned . . . His congenital malevolence and rancour have been roused by contact with the pioneers of Northern industry. Jealousy of his manufacturing neighbours, and hatred of their persons, have gradually become a passion with him.

It would meet 'the impudent libels of firebrands like Mr. Ferrand with demonstrations of steady and unqualified contempt'. But Ferrand still actually gained wide and long editorials. The *Observer* added its mite by reporting Ferrand's prosecution of several boys and men for poaching: they claimed that his game ruined their crops, a regular allegation during such 'rural wars'.

II

Protection remained an embracing social philosophy for Ferrand; to him, 'Protection for All' was more than an empty party cry. He had already demonstrated his concern for factory workers, miners, handicraftsmen and paupers. In 1850 – while still maintaining deep interest in Oastler's, Stephens' and the Fieldens' struggle to save the Ten Hours Act – he spoke primarily for the maligned Agricultural Interest. The rural community still represented all that was best in the old Britain which he loved. If a few hundred cotton masters could change national commercial policy, what could not a united agricultural movement achieve? If a League was the way to victory, then the Land must have its own League!

Ferrand envisaged something very different from the farmers' county societies or the aristocratic London organisation. The movement should include all the great host of country people—

> the landlords, clergy, freeholders, barristers, attorneys, physicians, surgeons, bankers, land surveyors, wine merchants, spirit merchants, innkeepers, beer sellers, builders, joiners, masons, mercers, linendrapers, tailors, butchers, bakers, grocers, druggists, veterinary surgeons, lime burners, saddlers, wheelwrights, cabinetmakers, carpenters, ironmongers, blacksmiths, nailmakers,

tinners, farm implement makers, corn-millers, tanners, shoemakers, horse breakers, horse dealers, seedsmen, gardeners, clock and watch makers, glaziers, plumbers, brickmakers, tilemakers, hatters, bonnetmakers, glovers, dressmakers, basketmakers, ropemakers, farm labourers, and every person depending upon agriculture . . .

When the rural hierarchy was thus listed, it appeared a mighty army.

Following talk of a three-year trial for Free Trade, Ferrand looked at its results since 1846. Wheat had fallen from 54s.8d. per quarter to 40s.3d. Barley and oats had also fallen; butter was selling at 'half the price for which it could be produced, meat at 2s. a stone less than what it could be fed for'; timber prices had fallen 50 per cent, bark by a third, willow by a half. This appeared to be a picture of a ruined agriculture:

> But amidst all this misery and suffering what are the farmers told? We are told that we are only in a state of transition. Transition! Where to? From our green fields to the back settlements of America; from our comfortable homesteads to the union workhouse; from full purses to empty purses; from a state of prosperity to ruin.

Ferrand and his friends, faced with declining rents, reduced profit margins, abandoned farms and dismissed labourers, could scarcely share Philip Pusey's dream of High Farming or imagine two decades of a 'golden age' in the future; nor, in 1850, could Pusey, who reverted to Protection of a sort.

The new agricultural League must campaign for the restoration of Protection to conserve rural society. But it must do more. It would take up Manchester's challenge and fight back against Liberal industrialists' sarcastic abuse. And thus Ferrand conceived the idea of substituting British wool and linen for cotton. The plan aroused many emotions – Protectionist, patriotic, self-interested, vengeful and simply 'social'. Ferrand now announced it to the farmers. On 23 March he addressed a big rally in the town hall at Pontefract, a typical old Yorkshire market town. The vital anti-Free Trade motion was seconded by Ferrand (received with 'loud and reiterated applause'), who delivered a typical onslaught on Leaguers and Peelites for ruining farmers. Parliament had rejected a return to Protection by 91 votes and a lightening of agricultural burdens by 21: united action was vital. Cobden had threatened to raise a revolution which would force landowners to 'compound for their existence'. Now, there were 200,000 landowners, over 50,000 owning under 30 acres: 'these were the men that were to compound – not the rich aristocracy':

> There are 700,000 farmers, who two years ago possessed a capital of £250,000,000. I should like to see the cotton lords of Lancashire [whom Ferrand numbered at 600] weighed up. I will stake my existence that three fourths of them could not pay 5s. in the £ . . .

Protection could be restored within two years if rural people united: 'they must all stand together or together fall . . .'

Ferrand's plan was a Farmers' Wool League. If all 'vowed that they would never again wear cotton if they could be provided with woollen or linen goods, in two years the cotton spinners of Lancashire would compound . . . cotton would be kept in America – let wool be kept in England'. Woollen masters would assist, while increased flax production would aid Ireland ('to help them to keep their labourers at home instead of over-running England'). Woollen profits could rise and a costly colonial empire maintained to consume the cotton masters' surplus production could be dismantled. The Landed Interest must fight the cotton magnates—

> men who turned their counting-houses into their church; their ledger was their Bible and their money was their god. They . . . span slave-grown cotton; they insisted upon sweetening their tea with slave-grown sugar; they daubed their calicoes to defraud the public, with slave-grown flour paste; they worked their women factory-slaves 15 hours a day in an atmosphere more destructive to human life than the climate of Sierra Leone; they were only prevented working little children to death by a stringent act of Parliament. They were themselves slaves of the Devil; and during the last 70 years the [British] cotton trade . . . had destroyed ten times more human beings than the cholera had destroyed in the whole of Europe . . .

As one who had 'spent thousands in their service and never received 6d. as a hired agitator' and who paid his own few labourers above normal rates, Ferrand warned workers that 'the shadow of desolation was fast approaching'; free traders would repeal the Ten Hours Act. He would 'as soon . . . wear a perpetual blister as a cotton shirt' and 'sooner pick a torpid serpent' than the local MP, Milnes: emigration was simply a substitution of white for black slaves. Finally, he castigated the landlords for past neglect:

> I would remind you that they have stood aloof at a period when you trusted – alas! too confidently – in the honour of English country gentlemen.

As Ferrand returned to Harden, to fish, sow potatoes, and attend magisterial and guardians' meetings, his strange new plan attracted wide attention. South Yorkshire Tories found that

> this honest, uncompromising and plain-speaking antagonist of the free-traders was more than usually felicitous in his smartness of invective and pungency of sarcasm . . .

But the free-trade London Press was less impressed. *The Times* resumed its humorous banter; it could not understand those who 'took a very serious view' of Ferrand – who was 'not a statesman, or a financier, or a statist, or any such high-and-dry commodity' – or even an M.P. – but 'a gentleman at large'. Ferrand was an amiable eccentric, ranking with Stanhope, Sibthorp, Brougham, Sheil, Osborne and Palmerston: 'let us cherish these pleasing diversities', proclaimed Walters' much-liberalised organ. The Peelite *Chronicle*, forgetting past pledges of silent contempt, was the most vicious opponent of Ferrand's 'folly and atrocity' and his 'brutalised conclaves': Ferrand was an 'unsavoury insect', full of 'grossness . . . coarseness and ruffianism . . . truculent revilings of everything which had the faintest savour of public virtue, moral courage, talent, sense, or patriotism'. The ever-sympathetic *Standard* considered such attention 'a high compliment to Mr. Ferrand's spirit and genius' and 'great excitement among the farmers of Yorkshire' led to requests for Ferrand to repeat his message at Doncaster, Beverley, Malton, Richmond, Snaith, Selby, Wetherby, Ripon, Knaresborough and Thirsk. Protectionist fervour appeared to be rising; even 'Scotland was thoroughly roused and up for protection from the ruinous effects of free trade' by April.

The Standard warned the new movement that it must 'secure a *great agricultural ascendancy*', for while 'many, indeed all other interests, except the monied interest, were concerned to restore protection, the misfortune was that almost all except the agricultural interest had particular objects . . .' Ferrand himself privately noted that 'Direct Protection to Corn I hold impossible, now'; however odd he might be considered, he was a realist. His creed remained all-embracing and was certainly never economically motivated. 'When James Caird, *The Times*' Liberal investigative journalist toured Yorkshire in November, even he reported that

> At Bingley is the estate of Mr. Ferrand, whose advocacy of the cause of protection cannot be charged to selfishness, in as much as his tenants, depending chiefly on grass, must be greatly benefited by the prosperity of their customers in the neighbouring mills, who buy all they have to sell, while the winter food for their dairy cattle is improved and cheapened by the choice afforded them in the different sorts of low priced grain now imported into the country.

However 'backhanded', coming from a convinced free trader, this was a tribute.

III

The wool and flax plan continued to dominate Ferrand's public activities. On 20 April he had a great reception in Doncaster, where as usual he attacked Peel, Cobden, and the cotton industry. He forecast an early victory, if farmers united:

> Don't let the cotton interest, stained with the blood of millions of lacerated slaves, be the predominant interest of England . . . The judgment of heaven will follow the oppressors of the slaves from America to Lancashire, if you dare to wear blood-stained cotton . . . I tell the Lancashire cotton lords – cotton, light as the air you breathe, has made you; wool, lasting as the Grampian hills, shall destroy you.

'Mr. Ferrand boldly aims at the extinction of cotton in this country', reported the local paper, and 'we think in a short time it might very well be dispensed with'. 'Let the anti-cotton war be vigorously prosecuted', *The Standard* observed of Ferrand's 'splendid meeting . . . and the victory will be won even too soon'. Newark men formed a branch of the National Association, and the London trades (at Oastler's prompting) vigorously condemned free trade. Nottingham Tories rejoiced that 'Protection's prospects . . . brightened daily':

> The manufacturers have now lowered their late exulting tone a little; and at Manchester they are completely chopfallen after the crushing speech delivered by Mr. Ferrand . . .

Liverpool Protectionists praised Ferrand's 'soul-stirring speeches [which] stood alone amongst the emasculated orations of modern politics', for

> He had the courage to speak out in plain, homely, intelligible English what is passing in the minds of most men of an earnest spirit, only that they have become so effeminate . . . [He was] almost the only out-speaking, truth-telling orator on their side of the question. They were glad beyond measure that a match had been found for those two single gentlemen rolled into one – Richard Cobden and John Bright. They understood that the latter worthy was quite crestfallen at having been thus superseded in his own peculiar style of mob oratory.

And Dublin loyalists praised the 'most powerful and thrilling speech', hoping that Ferrand would contest Dublin, as 'it was a loss to every cause with which the interests of the United Kingdom, and particularly of Ireland, were identified, not to have [him] once again in parliament'. By late April, reported *The Standard*,

> The Wool League is advancing with incredible rapidity in the northern counties, and an agitation for a Flax League has already commenced in the agricultural districts of the south. 'The spinning-wheel in every cottage' has, we hear it with pride, become a 'household phrase'.

On 4 May Ferrand spoke in Malton Corn Exchange, under one Parke, a Pickering miller and tenant farmer. 'Distress and misery were weighing down the heads of all classes too severely for any further trifling to be allowed': he estimated (by a series of statistics) a capital loss of £107 millions. The cotton lords were

> Yankees – in spirit, in principle, in all their actions . . . in their selfish disregard of the interests of England . . . in their disloyalty towards the institutions of their country – they were Yankee republicans . . .

Prince Albert's Great Exhibition was 'a grand example of national humbug' to support free trade: the Prince Consort was 'now licking the hand that was prepared to shed his blood'. Furthermore, 'the cotton trade employed only 1 in 26 of the population, and yet the country was to be ruined for the sake of the cotton lords'. Cotton production was

> horrible, damnable, and the judgment of God was upon them. It was to rescue England from this infamy, this shame and this disgrace that he called upon [them] to join [his] League.

The policy was engagingly simple: Britain, Ireland, the Cape and Australia would produce enough wool, flax and hemp to supplant cotton and 'form an interest so powerful and so wealthy as to make England no longer dependent upon foreigners, either for her clothing or her food'. As his own contribution, Ferrand was saving his own hundred lambs.

Ferrand was now 'deluged' by supporting letters. A Country Party rally on the 7th in the Crown and Anchor pledged aid and *The Standard* praised 'an able and courageous man': 'why not imitate Mr. Ferrand in every country?' On the 6th Ferrand addressed a big rally in Selby. Amid the usual attacks on free trade, he assailed Denison (though not the Beckett dynasty): Denison's

> cry of a man not being in office before is a bugbear, got up by the Tadpoles and Tapers of men in office. It is done to bamboozle and frighten the people. No, no; the clerks are the men who actually do the work; and though I am but a plain-spoken country gentleman myself, with the exception of foreign affairs which I have not studied very deeply, I would undertake to perform the duties of any government office . . . as well as any of her Majesty's ministers . . . because I should have to work for me men who have been in office, 20, 30, 40, 50 years; and under these circumstances I say the Protectionists could tomorrow form the strongest and ablest government since the days of Pitt.

He again condemned the Prince's show of 'machines to destroy labour', picturing the reactions of the poor needlewomen championed by Sidney Herbert, Lord Dudley Stuart's London tailors, Lord Ashley's ragged schoolboys, Cochrane's starving Leicester paupers and '100,000 wretched thieves who lived by plunder in the Metropolis': 'that's the picture for Prince Albert to look upon and study'. Ferrand roared that 'we won't submit to seeing England destroyed by 'quackery'.

On the 15th Ferrand spoke in the Scientific Hall at Goole. Undeterred by *The Times*' attack on his 'atrocious design' which would ruin cotton exports ('well, suppose we do', retorted Ferrand), he launched a succession of attacks – on Graham (currently advertising Netherby land for factories, with 'labour both abundant and cheap'), American slavery (causing 'sensations'), and the 'disgusting' imperialism of free trade – which had ruined India and caused Britain's 'most unprovoked, unjust and infamous war' against China. At the recent London Protectionist rally

> some used rather strong language – and I should have said they were faint-hearted cowards if they had not. What is the use of baited breath, whispering humbleness or simpering sighs, when the auctioneer is knocking at your doors?

Contrary to League slander, the farmers were most loyal citizens: they never threatened force or hissed the Queen in 1832, provoked arson, hindered troops in 1842 or talked of murdering Peel. But they must restore Protection, under Lord Stanley, and save Britain by destroying the power of Manchester:

> At present we are almost clothed in cotton; we mean to be clothed in flax and hemp and wool. What is so easy? Your grandfathers never wore cotton, and your grandchildren will forget it was ever used.

The reaction was overwhelming. A cheering crowd accompanied Ferrand to the railway station, and village folk applauded him along the line: 'it was indeed altogether a sort of ovation for the intrepid advocate of the Wool League'.

Whatever observers then or later thought of Ferrand's views, he had a charismatic quality in his native county, whether among operatives or rural people. He was rough, tough and abrasive, speaking the local vernacular with a local accent about local subjects on which he had local knowledge – from pauperism to swede growing, from child labour to estate management, from magisterial decisions to the sporting life, from political strife to village pastimes. He was patently honest, sincere, emotional and patriotic, a man of many moods, ranging from deep compassion (his charitable donations and his furtive sale of pictures to aid Oastler were well-hidden) to angry extrovert outbursts (for instance. against unforgivable 'traitorous' Peel or 'the foul – mouthed libeller Cobden') and angry, vengeful vendettas against those who treated him dishonestly (from poachers to Graham). And he was brave and blunt, giving and taking blows with equanimity. There were few like him – few visiting speakers, for example, troubled to know about Pontefract's obsession with willows or to consult the farmer John Almack before visiting Beverley, where Ferrand spoke on 1 June.

Beverley's chairman was Anthony Bannister, sheriff of Hull, but the most renowned member of the platform party was that doughty Wolds farmer Sir Tatton Sykes of Sledmere, greatest proprietor in the East Riding. The good 'old Tat' of Surtees was a renowned sportsman who saw 74 St. Legers, drove his own sheep to London, hunted and boxed – and was hidden from polite London society by his refined sons! Ferrand was joined by Edward Ball, a Cambridge Protectionist, and lengthily attacked Graham, Peel, Cobden, free trade, emigration schemes and the Plug Plot. Support was growing rapidly: he had replied to 78 letters in a day, and Downshire, president of the Royal Society for the Cultivation of Flax in Ireland, had accepted presidency of the Wool League. Later there were further speeches at a farmers' dinner in the Rose and Crown and a march.

Ferrand was indefatigable, although he had to miss the huge Liverpool meeting on the 6th. Invitations poured in, one asking Ferrand to tour Lincolnshire, to establish Association and League branches, another urging him to form a West Riding Voters' Emancipation Association against Cobden. On the 15th he spoke in East Retford Town Hall, supported by Sir Thomas White of Wallingwells, Arthur Duncombe, Henry Bevor and Henry Champion. He praised Disraeli, assailed Cobden's 'bludgeon men', Philips, Brotherton, W.J. Fox, George Wilson, Robert Tennant, John Brooks, John Bright and 'those canting, whining, hypocrites, the Quakers who made such an outcry against West Indian slavery' but were now 'spinning blood-stained cotton and coining gold out of their murdered fellow creatures': self-interest regularly dominated free traders. But 'well might [they] despair, for prophet Cobden was sinking more rapidly into contempt and ruin than Joanna Southcott's prophet robe'. By contrast,

> Our motto is 'Live and let live', from the monarch on the throne and the peer in the palace to the peasant in the cottage. We demand Protection for agriculture, because of the eighteen millions of people interested in it. We demand Protection for our ships, colonies and commerce that England may exist as a great nation and be mistress of the seas. We demand Protection to

national industry that we may not be converted into a nation of repudiating swindlers.

The remedy for depression lay not in the big rent reductions of the Duke of Portland – which were kindly but 'ruinous' – but in Protection.

This venture beyond the Yorkshire market towns was enormously successful, though doubtless tiring, as Ferrand could only spare a day. He was preparing speeches of up to two hours, publishing several of them, answering a vast correspondence from almost every county and running his estate. On the 17th he went to London, to arrange the formation of a central committee with Downshire, and two days later addressed some 600 Wiltshire farmers (largely sheep breeders) at Salisbury, delivering what the *Morning Herald* considered 'perhaps the most important pronouncement that has yet been made in behalf of protection'. There was the usual range of supporters – a Mr. Mills of Elston, the Rev. Frederick Baring, the local Protectionist leader George Brown and a national leader George Young – of Limehouse shipyards. And Ferrand told them what they wanted to hear: they must tell Peel and Herbert (a local M.P.) that voting for them was voting 'themselves into the union workhouse'. He joked that Bright, having to close his cotton mills, might join the new League, boasted that of over 10,000 Yorkshire auditors only one (a Doncaster pawnbroker) was hostile, praised Bingley's woollen workers, lambasted the immoral, diseased, thieving 'refuse of the scamps of the neighbourhood' in the local cotton mill and 'pledged his word and honour' that the free traders had tried to promote revolution in 1842, while Graham – who had the evidence – simply punished working-class dupes. Manchester would soon become the English equivalent of Paris, as a national revolutionary centre – unless they 'checked these demagogues and democrats'. The new League would aid English labour, help to destroy American slavery and revitalise Britain. Ferrand called for help

> in the name of the wretched slave, in the name of humanity, in the name of the God of the slave, in the name of Him who created the slave in his own image, to assist in enabling Great Britain, with one universal shout of joy and triumph, to exclaim, 'These hands, so far as slavery is concerned, are clean!'

'Pelted by children', Ferrand tersely noted. 'Slept all night at White Hart.'

On the 29th, after Palmerston had triumphed in the *Civis Romanus Sum* debate on his bullying of Greece over the rascally Portuguese-Gibraltarian Jew Don Pacifico (by 310 to 264 mainly Tory votes), Peel was thrown from his horse, dying four days later. As many towns mourned – as their monuments testify – British politics was greatly affected: 'Peelites' spent a decade finding a new political home. With no reason to regret the event, Ferrand and Downshire went to Reading public hall on 6 July, to address some 300 farmers. Downshire rather patronisingly 'took up cudgels for the yeomanry of England', declared 'war *a l'outrance* [by] the farmers against the Manchester cotton manufacturers', advocated a boycott of cotton, expressed 'disgust and contempt' at *The Times*' mendacious 'infamy' and rather spoiled the effect by a deal of self – praise. Ferrand then launched himself into familiar waters, calling for a self-sufficient Mercantilism:

Let England depend upon herself. Let her no longer go begging on bended knees to foreigners for their blood-stained cotton or corn. Let her grow her own corn, produce her own clothing, and provide her labourers with employment, and she is free and independent of the world, whilst her enemies will be as powerless to destroy her as the sea which lashes her iron-bound coast.

The Times maintained a jocular attitude: 'the great anti-cotton league was assuming a formidable aspect', with Ferrand 'like another Father Mathew administering the pledge to thousands' and Downshire surpassing him in denunciations. On the 19th Ferrand went to a great dinner at Exeter given by Devon Protectionists to Young; some 800 men dined, under Yarde-Buller, Earl Talbot, Earl Stanhope and other local notabilities. Once more Ferrand delivered a rousing address, trying to stir those squires who still considered agitation ungentlemanly and condemning 'blood-stained cotton'. He returned to London by the first mail train. The *Chronicle* predictably found the proceedings of 'the vagabond camp' full of 'drivel and shrieking execration ... truisms, fictions and assertions immediately suggestive of a suicidal inference ... self-stultifying argument ... Micawberian ...' and blamed Ferrand's 'very soft head, though a somewhat hot one'; he was 'exquisitely silly ... malevolent', using 'mock lunacy and imbecility ... unmitigated Billingsgate ... cant, rant and ruffianism ...' The Peelite organ was no demurely respectable sheet.

Back in London Ferrand dined with the Halifax Tory worsted manufacturer Henry Edwards, attended 'the Scotch church' with Fanny and Lady Harriet Suttie and had his portrait painted. On the 25th he travelled overnight to a Suffolk banquet at Stowmarket, attended by 950 squires and farmers, Ferrand giving his usual attack on Free Trade and urging support for the Association. 'He had been at work upon this movement some four or five months', he asserted, 'and he had ... [raised] the price of wool more than 3d. per pound!' By now the Press and Ferrand were preparing for his next foray, to a mass meeting of Lincolnshire men at Boston on the 31st. Local farmers solicited the visit and they made it memorable. They wrote of Ferrand's 'almost unparalleled position ... unquestioned sincerity and integrity'; he was 'a man of family, education and great wealth – above the suspicion of bribery or selfishness'. They arranged special trains and invited many local celebrities. The county paper even published a supplement, which (not altogether correctly) described the hero – 'brought up to the bar ...', of 'ancient and honourable family', a great reformer who turned down three safe seats in 1847, retiring from public life 'until the end of three years [the period demanded by Free traders to test their experiment]'. The founder of the Wool League – which had thousands of members, including Lords Downshire, Talbot and Stradbroke and Christopher – was aged 48 (he was actually 41), 5 feet 10 inches tall, with a 'firm yet strong build and a voice of great power and fine tone': he had 'a ready wit ... the courage of a lion ... [and] unbounded charity'. He was also 'a great and original thinker', whose plan was succeeding.

The huge rally of perhaps 8000 people in the Old Mart Yard at Boston was headed by 200 dignitaries perched on farm waggons. The chairman was James

Stanhope of Revesby Abbey, backed by an array of squires, clergy and farmers. For the first time, there was Liberal heckling as Ferrand delivered his usual assaults. Ferrand's disturbed friend Frederick Cooke asked mayor Staniland to turn the police on the mob. But Ferrand knew how to deal with 50 hired bullies, asked the support of the audience (which beat the disturbers from the yard) and enjoyably told off the local free trader John Norton, who laughed during his anti-slavery peroration: he 'envied not' his 'brutal feeling'—

> Such men were more fit for a land of slavery than a land of freemen. They are just the men to hire a mob to shout down the expression of free opinion.

Lincolnshire amateurs could not put down the experienced orator; but a policeman was seriously injured in a subsequent fracas.

IV

August was spent pleasantly enough. Manners and Smythe arrived for the shooting, reviving 'Young England' memories and touring the neighbourhood. One celebrity the two must meet was that 'Currer Bell' whose novels *Jane Eyre* (1847) and *Shirley* (1849) had been sensational successes. Accordingly, a note was sent to Haworth parsonage. 'I forgot to tell you', Charlotte Brontë wrote to her friend Ellen Nussey,

> that about a week before I went to Westmorland, there came an invitation to Harden Grange; which, of course, I declined. Two or three days after, a large party made their appearance here, consisting of Mrs F[errand], and sundry other ladies and two gentlemen; one tall and stately, black haired and whiskered, who turned out to be Lord John Manners – the other not so distinguished-looking, shy, and a little queer, who was Mr. Smythe, the son of Lord Strangford. I found Mrs. F. a true lady in manners and appearance, very gentle and unassuming. Lord John Manners brought in his hand a brace of grouse for Papa, which was a well-timed present: a day or two before Papa had been wishing for some.

Manners reported the visit to Granby:

> We pilgrimaged yesterday to Jane Eyre's village. It is a manufacturing village on the side of a steep bleak moorland. Her father is the rector. The streets are narrow and paved; the parsonage [is] unapproachable in a carriage. She is very shy and retiring, but after a short delay came into the room: pale, thin, pretty manners, very intelligent countenance. A drawing of her by Richmond hung on the wall, rather like her but far more like 'Becky Sharp' in *Vanity Fair*. She had been a month this year in London, but was glad to get back to her Yorkshire solitude. Her father is a tipsy old Tory parson, named Brontë.

Meanwhile Oastler added his advice. 'The love which I bear towards you induces me on all occasions to view your proceedings with a feeling of friendship', he wrote. 'I never can, and I never will, forget your past exertions in my favour. When I was in prison, but not forsaken, you exerted yourself on my behalf with a vigour and perseverance that knew no limits.' He praised Ferrand's Poor Law campaign, his exertions for 'the defenceless and unprotected' and his courageous defence of 'the true interests of the people and the Crown'. And he thought the Association timely and useful:

> Very great care will, however, be required in the detail, and in forming the rules . . . You will pardon me, I am sure, if I hint that hitherto you have not been sufficiently careful to secure the co-operation of the working-classes. I am the more surprised at the omission, as the interests of the working men are directly involved in your movement, and without their support your efforts will prove useless. Always remember that as the well-being of the working men is your great object, to secure their concurrence and active support should be your aim.

He was convinced that workers' support could be gained for such a laudable project.

On 11 September Ferrand left home to address the Association's last big open meeting, at Ross in Herefordshire. Next morning a procession of Free traders demonstrated outside Ferrand's room in Barrett's Royal Hotel. The little rally, of some 400 people, in a meadow, under Henry Chellingworth of Grendon Court, soon became riotous, as 'about 15 or 20 men of the lowest class, some of whom were evidently the worse for liquor', twice stormed the hustings waggon and stoned Ferrand; he 'only escaped broken limbs or loss of life by running at full speed from his brutal persecutors'. Having avoided being thrown into a cesspool, Ferrand completed his speech at a chastened dinner for 50 men in his hotel, urging farmers to take sticks and labourers for protection at meetings and to support the Tory Thomas Booker at a forthcoming by-election.

Despite this setback – which greatly cheered the *Chronicle* – the Association grew. A speech by Lord Clarendon on flax made the *Post* think him 'a disciple of Mr. Ferrand'. It supported Christopher's pleas for increased flax production and the appeal for a chartered limited liability company to encourage Irish flax. *The Standard* rejoiced that almost forty peers and MPs had joined the committee. And even the *Northern Star* devoted a long editorial to 'a British Mine of Real Wealth' as Ferrand's Association 'involved a sound idea'.

V

Early in 1851, as the first snow fell, Ferrand went to Pocklington in East Yorkshire, to address 500 people in the Oddfellows Hall, with Arthur Duncombe. He attacked the Tory gentry for deserting the farmers – a Whig had called the York Protectionist meeting! He talked of Bingley strikes against wage cuts, revealed that his own labourers used to have 15s. weekly but now got 12s., while 16 Irishmen had 9s. and he had rejected 200 others in a month, who would work for less. And he urged support for wool and flax. *The Times* was verbosely sarcastic on 'the Persian fire eater', well suited to 'a lion skin and a club', whose 'imagination was not so much inventive as plastic' – sure proof to *The Standard* of Ferrand's 'unanswerable' case; Liverpool Tories condemned 'laboured and coarse abuse' by 'this Jew paper, the most unprincipled print in Europe, preserved by capital and written for profit, and not for the high aims of an honest reputation . . .'

The Ferrands moved to London on 1 March, and Ferrand soon hurried on to Norfolk. On the 4th he spoke at the county's second Protectionist rally in a huge barnyard at Aylsham, crowded with 2000 farmers and labourers under Lord Orford. Ferrand talked of a Protectionist revival against the free trade system of Graham ('the farmers' greatest enemy and the labourers' bitterest foe'), the apostate Peel and the 'Jacobin . . . League' and quoted *The Times*' approving comment on his own speeches of 1842—

> *Neque enim lex justior ulla est*
> *Quam necis artifices arte perire sua.*
> [For there is not a juster law
> Than for authors of destruction to perish by their own device]

Free trade had completed Ireland's ruin (he personally now employed 40 Irishmen at half of English wages) and was exporting Irish problems. He instanced Liberal masters' wage cuts in Bingley and Keighley. Free trade thus harmed both agricultural and industrial workers. He read out *The Times*' report on his property and admitted that

> if this Free-trade were continued, my income might be quadrupled, but . . . I do not wish to flourish at the expense of my fellow countrymen . . . It is not by agriculture that my income is to be increased; it is not by what be grown on the surface of the soil, but what is growing under it; by the coal, the iron and the stone beneath the surface and by supplying the town of Bingley with water . . . The estate with which I am connected has had a low rental for a long period; and yet, owing to the low prices of agricultural produce consequent upon the repeal of the Corn Laws, its rental has been reduced 5 p c., and the next largest proprietor, who is a retired manufacturer and a Free – trader, has been compelled to reduce his rents 10pc. Now, that has been the effect of Free-trade on agriculture in the manufacturing districts.

He repeated his challenge to public debate, after 'one of the best, if not the very best, Protection speeches [*The Standard*] had ever heard'.

Later that spring more exciting news reached Harden. Frederick Calvert, the Liberal MP for Aylesbury, was about to be unseated on petition. Since 1847 the borough had returned one Protectionist and one Free Trader, but optimists believed that Toryism might take over entirely and Ferrand was the accepted champion. The farmers, lacemakers, straw-platters and duckling-breeders of the town and district were independent men, recently relieved of residual loyalty to the bankrupt Duke of Buckingham, with his humiliatingly-wrecked empire at Stowe. Ferrand thought it right to call on the fallen magnate in his London railway hotel, where his Grace morosely recorded past Greenville glories. Apart from a chat with Forbes Mackenzie, a former Tory whip, Ferrand made no further preparations.

On 3 April Ferrand heard of Calvert's probable rejection and hastened to Aylesbury by night train. Next day he issued a placard from the George:

> I quit a happy rural life again to enter the turmoil of Politics – but duty calls me and I cheerfully obey... Let Labour be Protected and Capital will receive its due reward, whether invested in the Soil, in Manufactures or in Commerce... Our Protestant faith, engrafted on our Native Land by the blood of Martyrs, purified by the Gospel and handed down to us by our Forefathers as our best inheritance, shall ever find a Defender in me...

The Standard was loyally delighted: no one had better claims to defeat the unpopular Whig Richard Bethell; and local Tories welcomed Ferrand to 'the very citadel of the Agricultural Interest':

> No triumph would be greater to the Whig party, no defeat more disastrous and discreditable to the Conservative and Agricultural Interest than the return on this occasion of a Whig Member for Aylesbury.

Whigs would obviously try every tactic, even in their preference for Bethell over John Houghton (who had split the Liberal vote in December) – which was understandable.

Ferrand's message to 200 supporters at the George was unequivocally Protectionist: 'our ancestors found this country a desert waste, but by their industry and capital they have made it a fertile plantation', he declared. 'Shall we allow the Manchester cotton lords to make it a barren waste again?' He canvassed assiduously, only taking Sunday off for a London consultation; but the fight was difficult. Most great local proprietors – Baron Mayer de Rothschild of Mentmore (and his relations) and his fellow-banker, Lord Carrington of Wycombe Abbey (but not all of his Smith relations) – were Liberals, far surpassing the Tory influence of Lady Frankland Russell of Chequers Court and small farmers, particularly as de Rothschild and Calvert actively worked for Bethell. Nor was the Tory Press very helpful. The *Post* reported a 'very active political contest', the support of the popular Calvert and John Abel Smith for Bethell and its own ambivalent beliefs: 'we may frankly and freely say to Mr. Ferrand that he is not altogether the man, in regard of temper, discretion and moderation, whom we should look upon as our model legislator', while recommending him as a 'constitutional' and honest man. On nomination day both Ferrand and Bethell received rough receptions. Ferrand lost the show of hands (by 'a large majority', said *The Times*) and his proposers, Messrs. Lovett (a brewer) and Hale (a magistrate) demanded a poll. After a 'dull and insipid' campaign (to *The Times*) the poll was held on the 11th. After an hour, at 9 a.m. Bethell led by 65 votes to 27, at noon by 344 to 329 and at 3 p.m. he won, by 544 to 518, the majority (by 227 to 121) coming from the town.

Manners was, typically, the first to commiserate, from 'pretty' Tunbridge Wells, where he was staying with his 'Ladye Love and her mother'. 'If you need consolation for a defeat which was so nearly a victory and which disgraces only the constituency that permitted it', he wrote,

> You may find it in the universal expression of regret that was heard among our friends when the news was received. Strangers to you said in my presence 'I am so sorry Ferrand has lost' – and to those who know and appreciate you, like

myself, you may fancy how great the disappointment has been. I will trust, however, that it is only a temporary defeat and the spirit, pluck and gallantry with which you fought the battle cannot fail to encrease your popularity and enhance your reputation not only in the borough but in the country at large.

Ferrand issued a courteous placard to friend and foe, promising to return, while supporters less felicitously blamed rich 'German Jews, a wealthy Lord Lieutenant and ten attornies, Whig threats and treating' and 'the intrusive family of German Jew Barons' deceit'. Tories had fought their best fight for years, but must work harder now that the ducal influence had gone. The contest 'excited immense interest all over England'.

Local enemies gloated: but sympathy came elsewhere. 'My dear Ferrand', wrote Disraeli,

> I wd. not annoy you, at the time, with condolence, but I don't like to leave the country without telling you that you have left golden opinions here, and have established a good interest, if you ever care to avail yourself of it again.
>
> It wd. have given me sincere pleasure to have found you fighting in our parliamentary as well as our political ranks, but, I hope, that time may yet arrive.

Bethell and his agent were ceremonially expelled from the London Conservative Club and a group of county Tories invited Ferrand to an Aylesbury dinner in his honour. The dinner in the George on 21 May was enthusiastically supported by 300 Tories (at 3s.6d. each), and Ferrand gave a lone speech against free trade, quoting the Manchester Chartist worker James Leach – 'one of the ablest and most honest men whom I ever met in my life' – on operatives' declining wages and employment. He hoped to return as joint MP for Aylesbury with his chairman (Lowndes), the sitting millionaire Protectionist, Quintin Dick, being about to retire. He went on to a second dinner at the Golden Lion, earning further praise. Local Tories claimed 'a moral victory' and *The Standard* asserted that

> There was not a man in England whom all classes and degrees of revolutionists, whether Parliamentary Reformers, Financial Reformers, Free-traders, grinders of the poor or Socialists so anxiously desire to exclude from Parliament as Mr. Ferrand.

For once paid his expenses by his hosts, and cheered by news of a petition against Bethell's election, Ferrand went home in good humour. His political future seemed settled. But in fact it was to be very different from Ferrand's previous experience.

CHAPTER SEVEN

St Ives and Devonport

As it turned out, all further parliamentary ambitions had for the moment to be laid aside. From the summer of 1851 to the late spring of 1852 the Ferrands were abroad. The reason lay in Fanny's health. All through her marriage she had been an intermittent invalid and her family was growing increasingly concerned. After a meeting with her mother in June it was settled that her husband should take her for a prolonged period of rest and recuperation on the Continent. Together with Ferrand's daughter Sarah (now nearly eighteen) they left home in July, following a leisurely and meandering course to Bad Ems, down the Rhine, into Italy, back into France, on to Spain, and finally crossing France once more on their way to England. After a ten months' absence the party returned to Harden in May 1852 to be greeted by church bells.

They had gone into winter retreat at Malaga on the south coast of Spain, over a thousand miles away, when the exciting news reached them that the Whig ministry under Lord John Russell was first tottering and then fell. 'Lord Derby of course will be sent for', added Manners, their correspondent, who had already reported in official quarters Ferrand's wish to be provided with a Conservative seat. 'How I wish you were at home and in Parliament. A dissolution will probably take place in a couple of months' time.' Derby did form a ministry of sorts – something he had found impossible when Russell had offered his resignation the previous year – but the outlook was not auspicious. He owed his position in office simply to the divisions among Whigs, Liberals, Radicals and Peelites, whose combined forces outnumbered his own in the Commons; and there was little certainty that a general election would improve matters. Still, office was a breath of oxygen to the Conservative Party and its supporters. Ferrand certainly was not indifferent to the change. In March Disraeli wrote that

> I think you are quite justified, and every man in public life is, in looking to office as the legitimate acknowledgment of his political position, and I would not have hesitated, had you been in Parliament, to have submitted to Lord Derby your name in the list from which, as far as the H. of Comm. was concerned, it was expedient that he should select the members of his administration – but I think that you must, on reflection, feel the insuperable barrier which your absence from parliament offered to yr. promotion to parliamentary office. This I deplore, but time may remedy the annoyance.

On 3 May Ferrand crossed from Calais to hear the latest news in London, meeting Manners and Disraeli that evening. After a few days at Harden and Osgodby he returned to London to be 'advised [at the Carlton] to stay and not to go to Paris'. There was a possible by-election approaching at St. Albans, where the Liberal Jacob Bell was disqualified; but in the event the borough was disfranchised for bribery and corruption. Attempts to retain the seat failed on the 10th and Ferrand returned to Paris next day.

With his party in office there might at least be a consolatory chance of securing something for his son William over whose future he had been pondering. 'I have been thinking over what you say about your son', wrote Manners in July:

> Your services to the Party have been such that I think you have every claim upon the Government: and if you continue to think that an Attacheship would be beneficial to your son I should be most happy to press upon Malmesbury the propriety of giving him one. But I think you should consider well before coming to that decision.
>
> If the Army be an idle and dangerous life to a young man in easy circumstances, I should conceive a Diplomatic residence in Paris, Vienna or Florence must be much more so.
>
> To a young fellow with no means, who feels he must work his way up to independence by zealous attention to his duties, Diplomacy may not be a more dangerous profession than any other: but to one circumstanced as your son is, what field of mental exertion would it open? He would see and feel himself to be in possession of means greatly above the reach of his companions, and would be so tempted at once into luxury and idleness.
>
> Excuse the freedom of this; but what I have seen and heard of English Attaches to Embassies abroad makes me say it . . .

Manners' comment was curiously prophetic, but Ferrand was determined to persevere. 'I spoke last week to Lord Malmesbury about William', Manners wrote in November,

> and was pleased to find that he had already put his name down in the list of attacheships. You would have been gratified to hear the frank way in which he agreed with my estimate of your claims on the party. You will however understand without my telling you that the number of applicants for such places is very great, and the claims of many very pressing . . .

For the rest of the year Ferrand could only be a spectator of the political scene. It was not an edifying spectacle for a Conservative loyalist. Lord Derby had honourable scruples about abandoning Protection before a general election had demonstrated the true opinion of the electorate. On the other hand, Disraeli, as chancellor of the exchequer and leader of the Commons, was more concerned with retaining power and, as his free-trade and income-tax budget showed, he was ready to accept diluted Peelism if the country wanted it. As a result, when the inevitable general election was held, the Conservative Party was in a state of intellectual and moral confusion which was not improved by the desperate and in some constituencies disreputable use of government influence to win much-needed seats. Though the party gained some ground (for the first time since 1846) it was not enough, and in December 1852 a

Whig-Peelite coalition came into office under Lord Aberdeen. To any impartial observer the new ministry seemed to possess both talent and numbers; and it attracted a fair amount of cross-bench support. The prospects for the opposition were once more dimmed; and Ferrand's hopes with them.

II

The long continental sojourn does not appear to have been a particularly happy time for Ferrand, who tended to react to foreigners and foreign sights with a certain John Bull suspicion. The weather had been poor, accommodation at hotels indifferent, and the enforced and prolonged travelling intimacy had not improved the prickly relationship between Fanny and her step-daughter, known in the family as Lilla. It seems clear that Lilla, a plain and moody girl, felt neglected and unloved; equally clear that her family saw little that was lovable in her general behaviour. Early the following year there was a blazing row with both her parents in which both Ferrand and Fanny used unforgiveable and unforgettable words. It was followed by Lilla's departure from the family home to take up residence with her uncle, Johnson Busfeild, to whose son she was (temporarily) engaged. Johnson, who tried to pacify both sides, suffered the usual fate of peacemakers. Relations with his brother at Harden Grange cooled markedly, and though he provided the sullen Lilla with a home at Ryshworth, she evinced little gratitude. It was a relief when in 1855 she married Edward Hailstone of Horton Hall.

The previous year had seen a more important family landmark with the death of Ferrand's mother in May 1854. Ferrand now had complete control of a valuable estate. His mother left him, 'in token of her affection', her painted glass windows, the Ferrand family portraits and her husband's presentation silver and antique china for Fanny. Her daughters received clothes, jewels, plate and books and there were small sums of money for children and friends. By settlement on the estate, some larger amounts were to be paid. The Crispin twins received £4000, Walker and his children £6000, Currer's young son Currer £6000, Johnson's son William £6000, and the same amount to each of her three married daughters. With £40,000 charged on the property, Ferrand would obviously have to exercise some managerial care. But he immediately re-engaged the St. Ives staff and workers. And already he had major plans for the estate.

At the age of 45, Ferrand was now a man of considerable property; the estimated sale value of his mother's estate was almost £150,000. Agricultural rents produced over £5000 *per annum*, to which were added mineral rents, produce sales and profits from railway, canal and other investments; annual fixed payments took about £850. The award for the enclosure of Harden Moor in 1855 had added about a square mile, and Ferrand soon organised digging, manuring, draining and planting schemes. Such wealth demanded (to Ferrand's mind) the maintenance of considerable state, after Sarah's long absence. Ferrand kept a butler, a footman, two domestic gardeners, two gamekeepers, numerous female servants, two carriages, a pony cart and dog cart, a hunter, twelve greyhounds and eleven dogs. Maids, pantry-boys, grooms, lodgekeepers and home farm employees added to a sizeable community.

He himself moved to St Ives and on New Year's Day 1855 presided for the first time at the estate rent-dinner. To mark his new position he now dropped his middle name of Busfeild. The transition from the shabby-genteel family of Currer Busfeild to the landlord magnificence of the Ferrands was complete. One sign that a new era had commenced was the decision to pull down the old house of St Ives and build a great new mansion more in keeping with the family's status. The scheme seems to have been greatly favoured by Fanny and her mother who took a leading part in planning the new house. His brother Johnson on the other hand regarded it as 'an act of lamentable folly'. In the event Harden Grange formed the basis of the new St Ives, while old St Ives was largely destroyed and became Grange Farm. While the new mansion was certainly more modern and commodious, many regretted the loss of the old house which had been widely admired. Friends of Ferrand at a distance were able to applaud more easily. 'You will make Harden Grange a splendid place', Manners wrote in October 1856:

> It has great capabilities, and you know how to develop them . . . It is very kind of you to regret that we do not now meet often, but for your sake I am not sorry that it is so: '*non sum qualis eram*' – but I am and always shall be
>
> Yours very truly

Though meetings were rarer, however, Ferrand still kept in touch with his old political friends through correspondence and, in Disraeli's case, at any rate, by regular despatches of game:

> Your grouse reached me in the West, but the stupid servant did not tell me they were yours. I ought to have guessed it, since, for several years, your birds have been the first to fly here. They were capital, and worthy of their donor, wh. is saying much.
>
> Your idea of the festival is most alluring, and we should like above all things to pay a visit to Mrs. Ferrand, whom we remember always with so much pleasure and have never seen enough – but alas! duty is imperative. It is more than ten months since we were at home, except a day at Whitsuntide, and our wanderings, wh. were very brief, are over.
>
> Politics are quite dead, and the chickenhearted are all despairing – but I am an orthodox believer in the resurrection of the fractions [*sic*] and am too old a stager ever to give up the game.

Disraeli was writing in August 1853; but by then Ferrand was preparing to launch another personal political initiative.

III

That he did so was a mark of his characteristic energy and restlessness. Even in the quietest of times he usually had some cause to pursue, some enemy to hound. His forays into local politics and administration were an inextricable part of his life. All these years he continued to feud with the Bingley Charitable Trustees and kept a vigilant eye on their property and financial dealings. Another object of his suspicious scrutiny were the local Poor Law Guardians against some of whom he made serious charges of financial malpractices in 1855. By 1854 he had also become increasingly concerned at the activities of Bradford Corporation waterworks, which appeared to be robbing him, as lord of the manor, of water in the Hewenden valley and on moorland gathering grounds. Such action would drain Harden beck, harm local mills (two of which Ferrand owned) and destroy fish. In March he discussed the matter with Milnes Gaskell and lawyers in London, Leeds and Bradford, before appearing before a Commons Committee on the Waterworks Bill. But on 4 April 'the Committee came to an iniquitous decision' in favour of the Corporation. Ferrand would not allow the matter to rest. By a coincidence, the *Post* published comments on the dangers of large reservoirs in late April, and Ferrand seized the opportunity to write a series of letters against the Bradford undertaking.

Ferrand had a reasonable case; he saw waterworks becoming a mania like the railways in the 1840s, in the hands of shady promoters. 'I have had good cause to watch the proceedings of these audacious and unscrupulous speculators', he wrote, 'for I am now defending my property from their fourth attack in 14 years, and for the third time before committees of the House of Commons, at a ruinous expense.' He would expose plans

> to oppress the poor, to secretly plunder private property for their own self-interest, to bamboozle the Parliamentary committee by the grossest falsehoods and violate even the paltry compensation clauses of their own Acts of Parliament.

The issue was one of those important, though neglected, by-roads of Victorian history. Obviously the great towns urgently needed better and purer water supplies, as Chadwick's investigations had proved. But with control in the hands of business speculators, the means of obtaining water were often open to objection. No warning was given to owners of a Bill's promotion, and no thought was given to the requirements of local communities and industries. An owner's first knowledge might be the drying of his streams and the death of his fish. Ferrand recalled the 'unprincipled and outrageous attacks' on his property by Bradford undertakers since 1839. Another stream had been taken under Act in 1841 and another, without notice, in 1852. He had tried a settlement by obtaining a promise not to repeat the theft, but in 1853 found that his guaranteed supply was being diverted. Now he strongly protested against the 'German Jews' who had taken nearly 600,000 gallons of pure spring water, selling it at 10 per cent profit and paying no compensation. Ferrand's trout stream was now dried up and mill refuse was emptied on the bare bed, making life at St Ives very unpleasant for his mother and creating a danger to health. The *Post* supported his onslaught on 'the water robbers'.

Yet important as these matters were to Ferrand personally, they were no substitute for the larger stage on which he had appeared in earlier years. Not long after Disraeli's letter in the summer of 1853 he had embarked on something even nearer to his heart.

On 6 September Ferrand went to Manchester for the first committee meeting of a

Labour League. The idea was basically Oastler's. His metropolitan campaigns had led such London Protectionist workers as Robert Essery to form 'the Labour League for the Protection and Regulation of the Interests of Native Producers', advocating local 'boards of trade' to arbitrate on industrial disputes, further limitation of working hours, abolition of Truck and repeal of the Poor Law. Now Ferrand was to lead a 'Labour League of Lancashire, Yorkshire and Cheshire' with the same aims, announced at Manchester on 4 August. Ferrand's vice-chairmen were John Horsfall of Royton, Luke Swallow of Ashton, George Robinson of Clitheroe and John Myers, John McDouall, Richard Yorke, William Grocott and James Ruse of Manchester; the secretaries, James English and John Hull, and the treasurer, James Heaton, a Clitheroe councillor, completed the committee. Just important as these mainly Tory manufacturers and reformers were the trustees, Robert Alexander and two Anglican priests, G. H. Moore and Charles Whitaker, Ferrand's congenial new friend. Most important, as the League's propagandists, were Ferrand himself, the young Whig squire of Huntroyde (recently elected at a Clitheroe by-election), Le Gendre Nicholas Starkie, and Samuel Kydd, a prominent Chartist leader – a poor Arbroath weaver who became Oastler's secretary, the first historian of factory reform, the winner of Ferrand's prize for the best essay on the effects of free trade and eventually a self-taught barrister.

Reactions to this largely neglected episode in labour history were predictable. William Burroughs, leader of the ever-declining Spitalfields silk weavers, called for proletarian unity over 'the Labour Question', under 'such men as the Cobbetts, the Bulls, the Fieldens, the Ferrands, the Oastlers . . .' Jeremiah Briggs of Derby, with his National Labour Alliance (demanding 'the division of wealth') agreed. Oastler's 'hope' was 'strengthened'. Auty thought the League 'just what is wanted': its 'principles and objects'

> mean real and substantial benefits for the working classes of this country, in opposition to Cobden and Co's flimsy, hollow and delusive free-trade League. But will the working men believe in it? The old cuckoo cry of 'Tory trick', or some other, will, no doubt, be raised by the enemies of the 'workies', and, I fear, will, as usual, succeed.

The socialist Chartist dictator Ernest Jones, the barrister son of a Hanoverian courtier, followed Auty's predictions. To him the League was 'a Tory factory lords' Protection dodge', a 'trick' on 'an impracticable question': 'the fault lay not in Trade's being *free*, but in Labour's being *enslaved*'.

Kydd opened the campaign at Clitheroe on 3 October, when 600 workers heard him speak on 'strikes – their causes and remedies'. Next day Ferrand and Starkie joined him at Padiham. Kydd went on to Burnley, Bury, Todmorden, Preston (where Horsfall, a victimised Royton weaver who became a bookseller and printer, gave support), Colne, Haslingden, Bacup, Blackburn, Bingley, Bradford, Halifax, Oldham and Stockport (where Ferrand joined him on the 21st, aided by the 'Ten Hours' veteran Thomas Smith). The campaign was part of a wider Protectionist involvement in working-class causes, exemplified by Sir John Tyrell's donation of £500 to Preston operatives (led by the factory reformer Mortimer Grimshaw) during their great winter lockout and strike. It was a development which worried Jones: the aristocrats, he thought, 'hoped . . . to bribe the people into a love of aristocratic institutions . . . [and] to melt the hearts and win the enthusiastic love of the factory population'.

Ferrand missed much of the campaign in order to meet the Keighley Guardians on cholera prevention and highways and to attend Keighley petty sessions and the quarter sessions at Knaresborough, Leeds and Doncaster. But he and his League colleagues unanimously condemned 'unrestricted competition' and 'some . . . said that their desire was to re-impose a duty on all foreign agricultural produce'. Nevertheless, the much-diminished Chartists remained sadly aloof: one Pate 'thought [at Padiham] the only protection wanted was Universal Suffrage – and he knew the men on the platform would not go for that, neither would the manufacturers'. He was right: even Starkie and his father (a former MP for Pontefract, with whom Ferrand stayed at Huntroyde) would go no further than £5 suffrage. Instead, the League generally repeated old Tory social doctrines. 'As to the Poor Law', asked Whitaker (Ferrand's host at Simonstone Hall),

> What said the Word of GOD with regard to the treatment of the poor? – It said, 'Thou shalt not harden thy heart nor shut thy hand from thy poor brother, but shalt open thy hand wide unto him'. Now, he would ask whether the present Law was either conceived or administered in that spirit? He thought it was not . . . Bring down prices because of competition, and you bring down profits. Low prices, low profits and low wages are inseparable.

Kydd concentrated on 'the Labour League [as] the Cure for Strikes', whether at a big meeting in Burnley Literary Institution or a small one in Bury Assembly Rooms. He charged 1d. admission, estimated total audiences 'at not fewer than 12,000' and met with no 'direct and effective opposition'.

At Ferrand's last meeting, in the Stockport Lyceum where he was introduced to a small audience by Smith as 'one of the cleverest and most fearless friends of the labouring classes that ever set foot upon the threshold of the House of Commons', he spoke in old style, supporting the restoration of wage cuts:

> The same party who opposed the Ten Hours Bill now opposed the 10 *p.c.*, because, they said, they could not afford to give it. What had unrestricted competition done for the people of this country. If it could not afford the 10 *p.c.* Free Trade had been a dead failure.

He attacked Manchester's statue to Peel, who 'did more to trample underfoot the rights of labour than any other man who ever filled public office': the monument should bear the legend 'Peel, Popery and Poverty'. He advocated unity, mutual protection and peaceful agitation:

> The Labour League was not for the protection of any particular class, but for the benefit of all, inasmuch as it craved to be protected from the evils of unrestricted competition here as well as abroad – to protect mill property as

well as landed estates – and furthermore to place labour under legislative protection.

In his final speech Kydd explained that the League existed 'to provide practical remedies for practical grievances'. Glutted markets and low prices caused low wages, which were harmful socially and politically. Kydd opposed Free Traders' 'buy cheap, sell dear' philosophy: 'the very nature of Labour required protection, whereas Capital could protect itself'. Labour – the workers' capital – needed protection from over-use, and local boards of trade should settle disputes impartially. The League wanted arbitration, limitation of hours, abolition of Truck, Poor Law reform, an end to centralisation, reform of 'the middleman system', trade colleges, union ownership of estates to provide jobs and comprehensive protection. When an operative claimed that Tory as well as Liberal masters had employed Southern rural workers, Kydd agreed that Ferrand went too far on that point but was right in principle.

The Labour League certainly had some success in cementing the alliance between Tories and workers. Ferrand was, 'as you know', Kydd told Oastler, 'a very powerful, popular orator'. But Auty's prophecy soon came true. 'Political power could alone give protection', asserted Jones, 'and real protection could alone consist in Social Rights':

> Let Mr. Busfeild Ferrand and his new allies know that the people are not to be caught by any state protective trick, although it comes clothed under the guise of sympathy for the industrious classes, and 'protection for Labour against Capital'. Although it is backed up by parsons, joined by a sprinkling of the ranks of toil. The protection of Labour is to set it free – so that it will want no artificial protection at all.

The League gradually disappeared. Liberal Britain had little sympathy for such Protectionist bodies particularly when the mid-Victorian boom began. Jones himself dropped futile Chartism and became a Liberal.

IV

In April 1854, a month before the death of Ferrand's mother, Manners' greatly-loved wife had died and the two men had exchanged letters of mutual condolence. In August Disraeli's annual acknowledgement of grouse ('I have an especial relish for yr. Harden grouse, wh. always remind me of the old moor and the happy visit we paid in 1844!') referred to this among other matters:

> I wrote to John Manners with the hope that he wd. come to me, as I am living in perfect solitude, and prepare himself by conversation for a return to that public life in wh. he will find the surest solace, because the most powerful distraction but alas! he does not appear in any degree to rally, but sends me quite a broken-hearted reply. He has not been even to his nearest relations, and is now, I believe, by this time at Pau, with Mrs. Marlay [his wife's mother].

Politics was dead:

> There is no news. All is suspense, and will be, I apprehend, for a month. If the great expedition fail, Austria will play us a trick, for wh. she has long prepared.

This last was a reference to the war in the East. In March the government had finally declared war on Russia, and by the time Disraeli wrote it was known that a joint Anglo-French attack on the Crimean peninsula was being prepared.

The outbreak of hostilities had brought some personal interest to the Ferrand household since in February Fanny's younger brother departed with his regiment to take part in the campaign. But life at Harden and St Ives followed its customary routine unaffected by the events at the further end of the Mediterranean or even by the early disasters which brought about the end of Aberdeen's government, the installation of Palmerston as prime minister, and the ultimate resignation of the Peelites as a body from the new administration. The autumn of 1854 which saw the bloody battles of Alma and Inkerman was spent by Ferrand in superintending his harvest, buying sheep, and moving into the house at St Ives. Early next year as Aberdeen's ministry reeled and finally collapsed, he was coursing, shooting, marking timber, sowing turnips, serving a writ on the Bradford waterworks, laying out allotments at Cottingley and supporting local relief funds.

In the summer of 1855 the family moved south; Hugo and his nurse went down to Cornwall while Ferrand took Fanny to Bournemouth and Weymouth, bathing daily – at which Fanny 'exhibited bravery equal to Balaclava charge'. 'I breakfasted off grouse today', wrote one of her admirers, Disraeli, in August. 'Excellent! I delight in them above all birds.' He solicited Ferrand's views. 'I think I have contrived, at last, to turn the flanks of those imposters "the great Liberal Party" ', he wrote. He always liked Fanny. 'We often regret our ill fortune', he insisted 'in having had so few opportunities of cultivating the friendship of one whom we always, and from the first, thought so charming.' His appreciative phraseology was now developing. 'I am sure we shall be very glad to see Harden Grange again', he declared,

> and, still more, Mrs. Ferrand, whose hand, in imagination, I venture to press to my lips – but, at present, we have little prospect of relaxation except a stroll in our own woods. The Recess will be very busy, and the business must soon recommence.

But the flanks of the Liberal Party refused to be turned so easily and for a few more years Ferrand had to be content with a life bounded by estate business, sport, local politics, travel, and endless social visits. In 1857 he even embarked on a new country activity by starting his own pack of hounds, aided by friends like Sir Charles Slingsby and Hugo Meynell-Ingram, son of the wealthy squire of Temple Newsam. That enthusiastic Tory sportsman, the Duke of Beaufort, sent him three of his own hounds, complete with detailed pedigree; and the Whig Duke of Devonshire gave him permission to hunt over his somewhat dilapidated Bolton Abbey estate. More hounds were promised by Manners (from the pack belonging to his brother the Duke of Rutland) and by the Duke of Cleveland. Ferrand's pack met for the first time at Harden in January 1859. His enthusiasm for fox-hunting grew with experience and he began to turn out with such famous packs as the Bramham Moor Hunt and the Duke of Rutland's Belvoir Hunt. Like many squires who started a pack of their own, however, he probably found it both expensive and time-consuming, and after another year he gave up hunting on his own account.

Meanwhile there was other game to be pursued. In 1858 one of the not infrequent displays by the House of Commons in these years of factious politics and temporary popular excitement resulted in the defeat of the government over Palmerston's Orsini conspiracy bill. Ferrand was up in Scotland when Derby formed his second minority administration with Disraeli as Chancellor of the Exchequer and Manners as First Commissioner of Works. Though there could be no place for Ferrand, the sight of his friends in office stirred once more his political instincts. In March he met Derby and Disraeli several times and watched from close quarters the death-throes of yet another Conservative government. Defeated by 330 to 291 on the 31st, Derby dissolved parliament and for a second time went to the country in a bid to secure that elusive prize, a majority in the Commons for his party. Ferrand stayed on in London to pursue that equally elusive prize, a seat in the House for himself; and after various negotiations was offered the candidature for Devonport.

Since its creation (with the adjacent parishes of Stoke and Stonehouse) in 1832, Devonport had been generally regarded as a 'government' borough. 'A candidate's connexions at the Admiralty, Treasury, & c, have much weight in a town where employment in government establishments constitutes the main support of the residents', observed Charles Dod in 1852. 'The ministry of the day is, therefore, usually powerful at Devonport!' In consequence it returned two Whigs, often without opposition, until, in 1852, Sir George Berkeley won one seat against three Liberals. Since Berkeley's death in 1857, the naval town had reverted to Liberalism, under the prominent lawyer Sir Thomas Perry and the well-known owner-editor of *The Economist*, James Wilson. It was no easy contest that Ferrand agreed to fight, with his nervous fellow-Tory, Archibald Peel, the inexperienced 30-year-old son of General Jonathan Peel, the new Conservative Secretary of State for War.

Ferrand sent an early manifesto to Devonport. 'As a public man, my motto has been "the Bible, the Throne and the Cottage"', he wrote: he was

> ever anxious to diffuse our pure Protestant faith at home and abroad; to uphold the authority of our Constitutional Monarchy: to improve the condition and increase the comforts of our sons of toil.
>
> To the shipping interest England is greatly indebted for her security and her vast colonial empire, and it shall always find in me an earnest defender.
>
> No doubt, Lord Derby's government will, as soon as they have leisure, introduce a Reform Bill which all moderate men may support . . .

He would relieve dissenters from Church rates, 'redress every grievance of which the public could justly complain', cut taxes and especially reduce income tax, 'which the present government were pledged to abolish'.

As Perry and Wilson had opened their campaign, Ferrand and Peel started work quickly, addressing 1800 people (and 500 outside) at the town hall on 19 April. The rally seemed 'a splendid reception' to Ferrand, who told of his campaigns on industry, Truck, allotments and the Poor Law. There were numerous disturbances during Peel's halting speech, but Ferrand's 'stentorian lungs' carried the message of an £8 franchise (with £5 for educated urban workmen) and against the Ballot (for 'he would rather endure a slight national injury than a great national degradation'). Next day there was an enthusiastic gathering at Stonehouse and local Tories grew more hopeful:

> Mr. Ferrand, with a noble voice and a genius which difficulty only encourages, is a real orator. More, he is a thoroughly sincere and earnest man. There is perhaps no man in England who has done for the poor so much as Mr. Ferrand.

'From the time when he rescued that poor little child from death in the bitter snowdrift, he had devoted himself to the cause of the working classes.' He and Peel were almost unanimously adopted as 'champions of loyal Conservatism'.

Liberals soon retaliated against the 'two mysterious personages'. Peel's only claim was as son of the War Secretary and nephew of Sir Robert and of George Dawson (thrice rejected at Devonport, in 1835, 1840 and 1841). But their real vituperation was reserved for 'one of the most violent advocates of the Corn Laws', with his 'virulent and abusive tirade . . . self-laudation . . . pathetic tales . . . clap-trap . . . most unChristian sentiments . . . political turpitude and inconsistency'. Simultaneously, an anonymous rhymer mockingly penned thirteen verses on *The Babe in the Snow, or Ferrand in a Mist and Peel in a Mire* which made it clear that the dramatic story of the factory child rescued from the snowdrift which he had related to the Duke of Newcastle in 1852 was now known to a wide audience:

> He can fawn and can flatter, and tell what fine things
> For the poor men to do he is able;
> Tho' he often has stood, and did all that he could
> To keep the Cheap Loaf from their table.
> He has sat with the 'Commons' in years that have past,
> And his value was understood fully;
> He was shunned by them all, as a 'Firebrand' should
> And by all he was voted a 'Bully'.
> And tho' he can rise, and with tears in his eyes,
> Blubber out such a pitiful story;
> Of 'the Babe in the Snow' that he saved long ago,
> Yet we can't nor we won't have a Tory.

And there was some shock when Ferrand supported large armed forces because

> My conviction is that Louis Napoleon intends to raise a war of annihilation throughout Europe . . . for [he] is determined, as he believes he is someday destined . . . to revenge Waterloo.

The dockworkers were inevitably a major target. On the 21st too many of them attended the Tory meeting, so Ferrand spoke outside the Albert Hotel (which Peel could not do) and boisterously shouted to a good-natured rally of 'at least 6000 people', with much egoistic showmanship about his lonely work for reform. He had supported Protection to maintain wages (which Whigs had reduced locally), but added that

> he that would now try for the re-enactment of the Corn Laws would be fitter for an asylum than to stand . . . as a candidate . . .

The workers mainly supported him, and he went off to dine with the captain of H.M.S. *Impregnable*.

'If strong lungs and violent language can carry the day, Mr. Ferrand has certainly a very excellent chance', declared the 'radical' *Devonport Telegraph*, as polling started on the 30th; Peel would be merely a 'cypher'. Ferrand himself appears to have expected to win, with Wilson, and Liberals reserved their real bitterness for him – the 'Tory Chartist with his silly wool league, his torch-light meetings on Lancashire moors and his roaring, frothy oratory', his 'inveterate prejudices, bitter personalities, violent declamation, unscrupulous personal attacks, intemperate and uninstructed zeal and exploded sophistries' was 'beneath contempt' – though not beneath such heated observations. At the poll the Liberals soon established a lead. At 9 o'clock they had 168 votes each to the Tories' 99, at 9.30, 261 to 183. The emergence of some split voters had little effect. By 1 o'clock Wilson had 988 votes, Perry 974, Ferrand 851 and Peel 836. At the 4 p.m. close Wilson and Perry triumphed by 1216 and 1198 to Ferrand's 1075 and Peel's 1039. Bitterly disappointed and blaming 'the gross misconduct of Mr. Beer, the principal agent', Ferrand went home for the Riding election.

V

Back in London the gossip was of Disraelian Reform and Government's danger, whenever the assorted liberals could get together to present a common front. Derby had won about 30 seats but was still in a minority if Whigs, Peelites, Liberals and Radicals could all unite. Meanwhile Ferrand stayed on in the capital. He attended 'the grand dinner at Merchant Tailors Hall given by the Conservative Party to Derby and Dizzy'. He also spent eight days at the Admiralty with Sir John Pakington, who, as First Lord, was Devonport's patron and from whom Ferrand secured a cadetship and four clerkships for supplicant electors.

Ferrand was reluctant to leave London because of Perry's rumoured resignation, which seemed to be verbally confirmed when Wilson asked him not to stand in April, dangling the acceptable (because inexpensive) bait of a future unopposed election. Disraeli sagely urged him to get a written pledge, but Wilson turned up with Sir William Clay to say that he only wanted to know Ferrand's intentions. Ferrand was carefully non-committal to the inquisitive enemy. On 3 August he heard at Plymouth that the second Devonport seat was also to be vacated: the Whigs obviously hoped to hold both seats by two quick campaigns. On the 5th *The Times* confirmed that both Perry and Wilson were retiring, to take Indian jobs. Ferrand telegraphed Devonport Tories promising to return, though he was informed in London that the party had decided not to oppose the popular Admiral Sir Michael Seymour.

Arriving at midnight, intending to contest Wilson's seat, Ferrand had 'a splendid reception' in the town hall on Saturday the 6th. On Monday he was 'nominated against [his] consent' and had to withdraw his assurance to Seymour, because of the enthusiasm of one Dr. Raw. He had a single day in which to canvass and to explain at Stonehouse his policies against the warlike Napoleon, Whig deception and dockyard unfairness and for relief of dissenters. At the show of hands the candidates were equally balanced, and at the poll on the 9th Ferrand drew ahead, by 329 votes to 167 at 9 o'clock, 808 to 680 at noon and 993 to 941 at 3 p.m. But in the last hour 155 new (and, to Tories, suspect) Liberals appeared, giving Seymour 1096 votes and a majority of 49.

Local Liberals maintained that Ferrand had deceived Seymour – and uneasily noted that dockers and sailors supported him. His late arrival was proof of his real intentions. He had established a sound 'interest' and base, and the Tories promised to pay his expenses if he would stand again at the second contest. In London, Disraeli advised waiting until the writ was issued. Hopes of shooting were dashed. Ferrand went home on the 11th; the writ was issued that night; next morning was torrentially wet and on the 13th he was in Devonport for his third election campaign, to find that yet another Indian enthusiast, Sir Arthur Buller, was already actively attacking him. Ferrand first addressed workers leaving the dockyards on the 15th and a 'splendid' evening meeting in the town hall (which was actually very noisy). He condemned recent Members' 'desertions', 'cowardly' anonymous pamphleteers, dockyard management and Palmerston, who was

> accused of having conspired with Napoleon to trample down liberty in Italy ... Napoleon's sole idea in keeping up the vast armaments which caused so much apprehension, was to invade our native land at the first fitting opportunity.

He was triumphantly re-adopted.

At the Guildhall nomination next day Buller launched personal attacks, which Ferrand answered lengthily, defending himself from the 1844 censure, ascribing Gladstone's new dockyard superannuation scheme to his candidature and threatening a petition against Seymour. A body of sailors gave delighted support, and Ferrand narrowly won the show of hands (though *The Times* blamed this on the mayor's casting vote), then holding another 'very good meeting'. No doubt the asperities of the battle were increased by Ferrand's recollections of Buller's Radical brother, Charles.

Voting on the 17th was excitingly close. At 9 o'clock Buller had a lead of four (177 to 173), at 9:30 Ferrand one of sixteen (373 to 357); at 10 both sides had 450 votes. From 10:30 (by 563 to 547) Ferrand took the lead for an hour, but from 11:30 the poll was neck and neck (Buller 713, Ferrand 712). At noon Buller led by 784–783, at 12:30 by 849–847, at 1 by 961–960, at 2 by 1010–1008. But thereafter Buller's lead grew (1097–1044 at 2:30, 1108–1054 at 3, 1161–1097 at 3:30 and at the close 1189–1114). Defeat by 75 was a blow; but Ferrand had palpably enjoyed a noisy little campaign, revived local Toryism, gained the largest Tory vote ever in the history of the constituency, and promised to return.

Echoes of the three contests reverberated in triumphant Liberal publications. The ever-hostile *Globe* with heavy topical allusions to the characters in Dickens' *Bleak House*, observed that

> Personalities are still [Ferrand's] stock-in-trade and he has, of course, showered them right and left upon all his opponents. Mr Ferrand has signally gibbetted himself at Devonport. He is a man who has evidently mistaken his mission instead of striving to be a Member of Parliament, he should have made himself the champion of the Red Republicans, or the male advocate of the rights of Borio-boola-gha. In short, he should have striven to be the Mr JELLYBY of public life, and then, although he might have found rivals, he would have found no equals.

Ferrand's numerous compliments to local women were mocked. Liberals recalled that Dawson had flirted with them all, while Perry had claimed that his only enemies were ugly Tory women from the crowded slums. 'Mr. Ferrand, we must say, does not improve on acquaintance', claimed the Liberal *Telegraph*:

> At first there was something in the fluent, roystering orator which caught the popular ear and tickled the popular palate. But we expect, after all, in a would-be Member of Parliament, something more than more ability to split the ears of the groundlings. Mr. Ferrand rants and roars like the Citizen in *King John* . . .
>
> He is headstrong, intemperate, not at all scrupulous in his language, and in his acts pretending to a chivalry which was badly exemplified indeed in his behaviour towards Admiral Seymour. The most harmless thing about him is his conceit. He is brimful of assurance . . .

'One contest more and Victory awaits you', Ferrand had told the Tories in his address of the 10th. His promise was only postponed, as he returned North with his Press cuttings.

At 50 Ferrand was robust, energetic and determined. His staunch Toryism withstood any mockery from liberals or trimmers. He was an assiduous 'low' Anglican attender of churches from Cornwall to Edinburgh. He was a crack shot and intrepid rider, a kindly squire but stern defender of his rights, a fair-minded magistrate and sympathetic Guardian of the Poor. No Scottish or London 'High Society' blandishment ever seduced him from his blunt Yorkshire attitudes. He carried out his duties without fear or favour. He hated corruption, in any form, and was prepared to fight against the perpetrator, Whig noble, Radical tradesman or even Anglican priest. He never deserted workers' causes; he remained an ebullient, certain and never despondent exemplar of an old-style Toryism which could appeal to all classes.

His second marriage had certainly led to changes of lifestyle: sport on wild, misty moors was now supplemented by attendance at sophisticated metropolitan drawing rooms: bleak old manor houses gave way to sleek Victorian mansions: dour old retainers from the stable and moor yielded to a hierarchy of servants. In 1859 Ferrand paid tax on a butler, a footman, a running footman, a groom, two keepers, two gardeners, two carriages, a pony carriage, a cab, 36 hounds, two setters, two springers, a terrier, a retriever, a pointer, three saddle horses and his armorial bearings. He was an avid traveller by railway and had seen far more of Britain and Ireland (and the Continent) than generations of his ancestors put together. But his first love remained Yorkshire.

VI

The year 1860 opened with a rent dinner in the White Horse, followed by daily hunting. Ferrand subscribed to a Todmorden statue of his Radical ally of 'Ten Hours' days John Fielden and on 14 January went to stay with another old friend, John Manners at Belvoir Castle. On 11 April he took Fanny and Hugo to London and on the 14th travelled to Devonport for a long-planned event, with a Haddington friend, Admiral Wallace Houstoun, now of Sissinghurst, as his travelling companion. A 'great crowd' met him and the Tories gave him dinner. Cheered by the dockers, he expressed his pride at the event, ending:

> I have just one favour to ask of you, which is that every man who has a wife or sweetheart will give my kindest regards to them.

On the 15th Ferrand was at church and dined with his loyal chairman, John Thierens. And next day there was a great rally in St. George's Hall, attended by 2600 people. Here Ferrand received a 'beautiful' silver vase, with a pedestal bearing the figures of Justice, Truth, Charity and Labour. 'Completely overcome', Ferrand nevertheless delivered a lengthy explanation of his work on Truck, Ten Hours, the Poor Law (for which he had been 'blessed' by the dying Walter), allotments and 'tyranny' in the dockyard. He went on to denounce the 'cotton lords' and the Cobden Treaty in familiar terms, before 'thanking [Devonport] with all his heart' for a gift which his family would always cherish. The Tory Press welcomed 'his admirable exposure of the millocratic conspiracy', for

> if Manchester wins, the working men of England will lose their liberty – for cotton spinners are tyrants. If Manchester wins, England will lose her place among the nations – for cotton spinners are cowards . . . and joyfully reported another banquet attended by over 700, when Ferrand promised to return.

Inevitably, local Liberals did not share these sentiments. Admitting that it had 'rarely met with such a case of love on first sight' and that 'boldness he possesses in an eminent degree and there is in him no symptom of that faint heart which never won fair lady', one paper assailed Ferrand's factory campaign and his methods: 'if [facts] are on one side and he on the other, so much the worse for them'. He had been a friend of 'the mad Chartist', and 'Mr. O'Connor's revolutionaryism was not one whit worse than Mr. Ferrand's . . . he still endeavours to set class against class and employed against employers . . .' The *Telegraph* alleged that the Tories were drunk and that Ferrand ('the political McNaghten' with his 'disgusting . . . calumny [and] bare-faced exaggeration') had to fight to get out of the meeting: he damaged any cause and 'could hardly make a single statement without distorting it'. The *Independent* wrote of drunken 'uproar', as Ferrand 'blazed away like an unwholesome squib' with 'ferocious energy . . . noise and insult . . . and untruth'. Northern newspapers joined in the quarrel: the *Leeds Intelligencer* reported what was obviously a remarkable event, while the *Manchester Guardian* defended its supporters against 'furious and puerile attacks'.

Some Liberals questioned Ferrand's statements, and one Bingham Snell sent Ferrand's 'absurd rigmarole' to Bright, who 'supposed the speaker either drunk or mad' and expressed surprise that anyone should check on 'the correctness of anything said' by Ferrand. In fact, as the *Mail* pointed out, Snell had used an incorrect *News* report of Ferrand's comments on Bright's 'perish Savoy' speech. As usual, Ferrand left amid controversy. But he left also – after seeing Heenan draw with Sayers in a 'Great Champion fight' – with his vase and a testimonial parchment signed by representatives of 2539 contributors, praising his work:

> You have stood in the breach, and fought our battle inch by inch. You have not disdained the title of the Working Men's Friend, and we are proud to hail you by that Title.

CHAPTER EIGHT

Back at Westminster

No recollection of his recent animadversions on Napoleon III and Bonapartist military aims inhibited Ferrand from escorting Fanny on another long visit to France in April 1860. Taking Hugo, now twelve, with them, they rented a house in Paris and, though Ferrand himself went back to England several times, it was June 1861 before Fanny returned to the new house at St Ives. She clearly enjoyed life abroad and Ferrand himself perhaps was learning to appreciate European ways, since they went on more continental holidays in 1862 (Holland and Belgium) and in 1863 (Germany).

Yet for all her visits to such health resorts as Bad Kissingen, Fanny continued to suffer from regular bouts of illness and her small son seemed to have inherited some profound weakness. He was almost constantly ill. Ferrand too in these years was afflicted by various ailments, including gout, bronchitis, rheumatism and skin trouble. Nevertheless, his basic robustness and energy remained and he hunted regularly with the Belvoir hounds each winter. Much of the early part of 1862, for example, was spent with the Manners set at Belvoir and Grantham. 'Young England' was now growing, if not old, at least middle-aged and Ferrand by this date 'weighed 15 Stones in hunting dress'. A year earlier, in August 1861, he had lost an important link with the past when his early mentor, the 72-year-old Oastler died at Harrogate on a rare Yorkshire visit. Ferrand was pall-bearer at the funeral in Kirkstall with such Ten Hours veterans as William Walker, Sam Fielden, Joshua Pollard and Samuel Kydd.

His own family circle was thinning out. By July 1865, when he and his brother Johnson attended the funeral of their fifty-year-old sister Elizabeth (Mrs. Rawson), of the original family of Currer Busfeild and Sarah Ferrand – five sons and eight daughters – only two sons and two daughters were still alive. Worse was to follow. On 1 September he received a telegram announcing that his elder son William had died in Jersey at the age of 33. Grief at the loss of his son and heir did not soften his heart towards the other child of his first marriage. When Lilla sent a letter of commiseration, Ferrand returned it with a request to receive no further communications from her. He subsequently made a new will excluding Lilla from any share in his money or property. But at least he was now reconciled to Johnson, whom Lilla had been instrumental in alienating from him twelve years earlier.

There was still more than enough in estate affairs, local administration and sport to fill his life; and the year 1860 in fact had seen an additional outlet for his energies. The deep national distrust of France, which Ferrand fully shared, and the sudden fears roused by Napoleon III's diplomatic and military exploits since the Crimean

War, brought about a national Volunteer Movement in 1859–60 designed to provide a corps of patriotic military units in every county to support the regular army, the yeomanry, and the militia. By 1861 they numbered over 160,000. Ferrand's temperament and social position made it almost inevitable that he would take part, and in the course of 1860 he became Captain and Commanding Officer of the Airedale Volunteer Rifle Corps. In October, in their light-grey uniforms with red cuffs and collars, black belts and grey shakos with red pompoms, the Rifle Volunteers first drilled at Keighley with their old Enfield muzzle-loaders.

Ferrand threw himself with characteristic enthusiasm into his new military role. He engaged at his own expense a certain Sergeant Chipp to teach him drill, held parades for his men and marched them to church on Sundays, exercised them twice a week, gave them dinners and presented prizes for efficiency. As time passed discipline and attendance at parades were not always what he expected. 'I record my deep regret and indignation', he was obliged to write on 12 August 1861, 'at the miserable muster of Saturday last.' Of 108 men, only 39 had turned up. A week before a Corporal Brown (subsequently reduced to the ranks) had played truant to take part in a cricket match; and Ferrand threatened future defaulters with public dismissal. Things improved and on 25 September he took his contingent to a great review at York. Unfortunately for their smart new uniforms and accoutrements, and for Captain Ferrand already suffering from influenza, the heavens opened and a fearful thunderstorm drenched everybody. Three days later the chastened company were inspected at Keighley without much comment. Though Ferrand's early martial ardour may have waned slightly, he still carried on with his Volunteer duties the following year. In the autumn he organised a two-day rifle competition on Harden Moor and presented the prizes. There was better luck with the weather in October when a sham battle took place in St Ives park with the Eccleshill, Guiseley, Keighley and Bingley Rifles forming the defending force against an attack by five Bradford Companies. There was music and fireworks; the day was lovely and warm; special trains brought enthusiastic crowds; and more than £60 was taken at the gates to swell the Corps funds.

The rank and file of the volunteers were working-class men for the most part and local working-class politics still had pride of place in Ferrand's heart. He took a lead in raising money for the erection of a statue of Oastler in Bradford; and when Conservative Working Men's Associations began to appear in greater numbers in the 1860s, he gave them every support. Leeds was a pioneer in the movement and in January 1865 Ferrand accepted an invitation to speak at the Leeds Association dinner. Flanked by other local gentry, he proposed the toast to Lord Derby and the Conservative Party amid 'deafening cheers'; even he thought it 'a good speech'. He made his usual attacks, praised the aristocracy and condemned 'sham reform' and Wellington's 'great mistake' of 1830. Intelligent workmen (but not patrons of dog fights) should now have the vote restored. And, he declared,

> search the whole of the Black Book, and . . . you will not find concentrated one-twentieth part as much jobbery and corruption as is to be found in the Charity Board alone.

Almost exactly a year later he was back again addressing some 200 members of the Leeds Association in the Music Hall. 'He looked upon the protection of [workers'] interests as the paramount duty of Englishmen' for 40 years, he declared, recalling Sadler, Oastler, the Becketts and Robert Hall:

> He did not intend to taunt his opponents, but he challenged them to call over their muster roll and produce a list of men like those he had mentioned, who had struggled through life to advance the rights of the working classes. He denied that there ever was a great measure upon which the working classes had set their heart with which Mr. Bright had identified himself. Who was the bitterest opponent of the Ten Hours Bill? Who was one of the first manufacturers in Lancashire who was fined for violating it? Who was the man who was constantly opposed to the Tory party in the House of Commons when they were endeavouring to repeal the harsh clauses of the Poor Law Bill? Why, John Bright and the Manchester school.

He contrasted the conduct of Manners, Stanley, Pakington, Northcote, Hardy, Walpole and Cairns with that of 'the rank republican, the violent demagogue, the abuser of his sovereign and the enemy to the institutions of our native country'. But for all that he went on to condemn a £6 rental franchise, 'which would make working men the dominant party in the state, [for] the working men as a mass were unfit for the franchise . . .'

The speech delighted Tories. 'We do not always follow Mr. Ferrand in his opinions', commented *The Standard*,

> but we certainly commend his speech at Leeds to the study of working men, who are continually informed that they exist to be patronised by Whigs and championed by Radicals.

The Press also praised Ferrand:

> The hon. gentleman's services with reference to the Ten Hours Bill alone more than outweigh anything that Radical agitators have accomplished . . . There is not a man in England better qualified by his acts during a long public career to grapple with the false accusation that the Conservatives are opposed to the interests of the working classes than Mr. Ferrand, and his exposure of the fallacy was complete . . .

II

All the while letters from old friends kept Ferrand in touch with politics as seen from Westminster. In the summer of 1861, for instance, there was concern over the Plymouth by-election made necessary by the succession of the sitting Conservative member to the Mount Edgcumbe earldom. 'I trust that all will go well at Plymouth', wrote Manners. Disraeli mentioned it in his annual grouse letter which also touched on electioneering at home and hostilities abroad:

It gave me great pleasure to be remembered by you. The grouse were worthy of yr. famous moor. What think you of affairs? It is worth living in an age of such rapid and strange events. I hope we shall not lose Plymouth – but it looks queer.

We have had a splendid harvest here in quality, quantity and time. I wish you had sent us good accounts of your charming wife.

Plymouth did fall – to the wealthy Radical landowner Walter Morrison who beat the new Conservative candidate by nearly 200 votes. On the other side of the Atlantic the American Civil War had broken out and at Bull Run in July the Federal troops had been defeated.

Whatever his views on the war in America, Ferrand could not be concerned by what had happened at Plymouth for he was still carefully nursing the other west-country dockyard constituency at Devonport. He dined the mayor of Devonport when he visited London in 1860 and in the autumn of the following year was gratified by the news that the annual registration of voters showed that the Conservative majority had risen to 96. Then, early in 1863, the long-awaited news of Admiral Seymour's acceptance of the Chiltern Hundreds finally arrived. On 3 February Ferrand and the Whig Vice-Admiral Sir Frederick Grey, senior Naval Lord of the Admiralty and third son of Earl Grey, arrived in Devonport almost simultaneously and started campaigning even before Seymour's official retirement on the 5th.

Ferrand energetically canvassed yet again from the 4th and spoke at Devonport and Stonehouse. His address condemned underhand Whig manoeuvres and his speeches bitterly attacked Somerset. By the time the writ arrived on the 6th, the battle was well under way. Archie Peel loyally returned to speak and canvass; and Manners wrote from Rutland's sickroom 'anxiously expecting glorious news from Devonport'. At the nomination on the 11th Ferrand won the show. As he toured the polling stations at 8 next morning, queues of electors were forming, and he took an instant lead: 44 to 26 at 8.30, 138 to 109 at 8.45, 231 to 184 at 9 (when Liberal counters gave 276–212). By 11 Ferrand led by 705 to 618, at noon by 817 to 734, at 2 by 1079 to 1028 and at the 4 o'clock close by 1234 to 1204. Ferrand had won by a record vote, and Tories welcomed a double victory: for the Bradfordian Francis Powell of Horton Old Hall had just won Cambridge. 'Hurrah!' wrote Manners that night, after an anxious day with Rutland:

> The news has come, and most heartily do we all rejoice at your glorious triumph – I write in the name of all.

Disconsolate Liberals could only rake up old slanders; but nothing could spoil the victory, as Ferrand was drawn to his hotel by (he thought) 20,000 people and typically thanked supporters – especially

> the lovely ladies of this borough, for they have rallied round me in a manner which makes me love the whole of them.

For a few days Ferrand remained in Devonport with his lieutenants, Thierens and Beer, before visiting Rashleigh and moving to London on the 16th. His fortnight's expenses, including train fares, totalled £46.6.10d. Excitedly determined to resume his Commons career as quickly as possible, Ferrand asked Manners and General Peel to act as his sponsors. 'It will not be a slight cause that shall keep me away from your side in the House of Commons at 3.45 on Tuesday next', replied Lord John,

> and I shall esteem it one of my happiest parliamentary moments when I walk up the floor with you to the table.
>
> I had the pleasure of reading your letter out to the Duke this morning; and it appeared to interest and cheer him . . .
>
> The account of your election in the Western News is very graphic and confirms the idea I had previously formed that you fought the battle with consummate tact and dauntless pluck.

In London Ferrand took Pakington, Elphinstone, Sir John Hay, Cochrane and Edmunds to dinner, re-entered the House to great cheers (and instantly gave notice of a question on the dockyards) and attended Disraeli's Parliamentary dinner.

Back in the House after sixteen years' absence, Ferrand made his first speech on the 24th, during the debate on Hay's motion on Navy pay and promotion. 'He never was more astonished in his life than when he saw the cowed spirit of the dockyard men, occasioned by the tyranny of the Board of Admiralty': neither workers nor Naval officers dared to complain openly. He welcomed Palmerston's promised inquiry, but wanted a broad investigation:

> He could view the Naval service in no other light than as a lottery with a great many blanks and very few prizes, and he had heard the Naval officers at Devonport protesting against the manner in which the great prizes were monopolised by a few influential families . . . [while the dockers,] a highly distinguished body of workmen, had had their spirit roused by intimidation and oppression, not on the part of the Conservatives but of the Whig party.

A day out with Trollope's hounds at Belvoir and a weekend at home prepared him for Parliamentary rigours. By early March he was again an active and contentious Member.

Ferrand's range of interests had expanded to include his constituents' naval involvements. When he raised an unpopular Admiralty order of 1861 and received a discourteous reply from the Secretary, Lord Clarence Paget, he followed with five further questions and spoke during Cobden's Naval debate. But old issues still concerned him. On 6 March he strongly opposed the Dundee flax magnate W.E. Baxter's Scottish Education of Factory Children Bill, which 'he viewed with great alarm, for it was introducing the thin end of the wedge for the purpose of upsetting the Factory Act'. He urged Baxter – an old enemy of factory legislation – to postpone the Second Reading and was successful.

Next he secured a promise of a debate on the cotton famine from Palmerston and regularly called for alleviation by Government of the widening distress – against counter-proposals by Edmund Potter, a Free Trade leader, who wanted a time-wasting Commission. The subject had all the makings of a traditional Ferrand-style 'blow-up' against Free Trade and the masters. But he also complained of 'the open and flagrant interference of the Duke of Somerset and his minions in election matters within the influence and control of the Admiralty'. He was, asserted a new ally, 'one of the most uncompromising foes Liberal corruptionists had ever met with before the public or within the walls of Parliament'.

On 27 April he had a 'great success' with a 2½ hour speech on the distress in Lancashire caused by the American Civil War and the resulting 'cotton famine'. The speech was a full-scale attack on the employers, past and present, who had 'destroyed nine generations of factory operatives'. Ferrand reminded Liberals that 'it was you who opposed the Factory Bill with all your force and . . . we who carried it and who rescued the people from consequences that were appalling'. Furthermore,

> You are indebted to the noble conduct and to the magnanimous bearing of the factory operatives themselves for the peace of Lancashire. Recollect, you have no claim on them, because you have broken faith with them and violated your pledges . . .

But the workers

> are the same men they were in 1841, 1842 and 1848. When the rebellion of the belly takes place no living man can control it; and you know that this is on the verge of taking place now.

Workers wanted work, not pauper relief. And Ferrand condemned Lancashire's 'cruel injustice' to Indian outworkers and China. Instead of soliciting long-rejected Government aid and ruining other industries, Lancashire should return to old regulatory principles. An 8-hours Act (with 4 hours for children) would both share work and prevent periodic gluts.

To Ferrand, workers had lost their political powers in 1832 and had been deceived by Cobdenites over Free Trade prosperity. They 'had no steady work; they were either worked to death or kept in idleness; and the labour was most seriously increased, and was continually increasing, by the improvements in machinery': not only did one man often tend four looms but machine speeds had been doubled since 1825. Many now opted for Bright's talk of free trade in labour: 'they asked to be allowed to go away, [but] were too poor to go themselves', and required help. Even Thomas Bazley saw the need for emigration, and even Ferrand favoured help for families to go to the colonies. But his plan was broader. Children and (especially married) women should now, he thought, be barred from the factories. His resolution (seconded by Baillie) was

> That, in the opinion of this House, it is the duty of the Government to take into consideration, without delay, what measures may be necessary to relieve the distress which prevails in the cotton manufacturing districts, so that the people may no longer continue unemployed.

That night he dined with Walker and Kydd, two veteran and experienced allies.

Presumably on the principle that all publicity was helpful, Ferrand noted 'excellent article in Times on my speech' and 'another very good article on my speech in

Times'. In fact, *The Times* was ponderously sarcastic. The speech was 'in the style we all remember so well' and 'the time was singularly opportune for the reappearance of Mr. Ferrand . . . We may safely agree with every word . . . till we come to the assumption which appears to lurk under it, that all other classes and industries are not in the same evil case as the manufacturers of cotton'. To Cobden's *Star* Ferrand was

> more than an eccentricity. He is an anachronism . . . though [he] has learned nothing and forgotten nothing, he has kept his watchful eye upon his old enemies. He has treasured up in an unforgiving memory every incident that seemed to him at all capable of being used against them, and that includes well-nigh every occurrence in the British empire . . . He champions the workmen only for the sake of assailing the employers.

The *Manchester Examiner* typically called Ferrand a 'grievance-monger', repeating 'old calumnies': 'as he was twenty years ago, so he is now'. Its London correspondent wrote that

> to hear him last night carried one back at once to that period, which already seems so far off, when he thundered against 'cotton lords' and stood up for protection . . . He looks every inch the burly agitator: tall, broad-shouldered, with one of those massive faces, low, heavy, square forehead and powerful jaws, which denote unmistakable force and power of some sort or other. The scowling, lowering expression of his countenance is, however, unpleasant, and you are quite prepared for the coarseness of [his] vituperation . . . He has a hard but powerful voice, of a piercing quality . . . his speech was one long angry shout . . .

Another old opponent, the *Leeds Mercury*, sarcastically assailed Ferrand's 'unintelligibleness in the midst of a great blotch and blaze of high colouring', while welcoming Villiers' plan to use Poor Law labour on public works: 'perhaps such an assurance was not dearly bought even at such a price'.

Even *The Standard* regretted Ferrand's revival of 'old political or personal feuds' and 'bitter and not unnatural feelings of antipathy against the manufacturers of Lancashire'. He 'spoiled the effect . . . of a very powerful argument' by his 'vehement spirit of antagonism' to old 'sins'; but

> It is impossible not to respect his earnestness, his eloquence and his sincerity and . . . not to regret that his honesty and his talents should be so misapplied . . . But men of Mr. Ferrand's stamp – men who will speak the truth without fear or favour – are peculiarly liable to exaggeration and error on the side unpopular to their audience, for they have little respect for public opinion, and opposition rather provokes them to excessive vehemence than controls them within the bounds of reason . . .

Other Tories were more unreservedly enthusiastic. The *Intelligencer* could not entirely agree, but praised the 'well-timed' speech, its 'beneficial effect' and Ferrand's 'moral courage'. The *St. James's Chronicle* welcomed a good speech and also thought that Ferrand's 'moral courage deserved credit'. And the *Herald* believed that Ferrand's proposal

> answered its chief purpose admirably. It compelled the government to make up its mind to take some course or other. So long as no pressure was put upon them, or put upon them only to be withdrawn, they were content to do nothing and let matters drift. But with a serious motion in prospect, threatened by a man not to be cajoled or lectured into withdrawal, they were compelled to act . . .

Ferrand had demolished the ineffective Potter's amendment for a delaying Commission and had gained Villiers' promise on public works. He was proud of his speech and, aided by Kydd, published it as a 32-page pamphlet. In this form it attracted the attention of a heavily-bearded German Jewish refugee, Hegelian and revolutionary theorist, who himself largely lived on cotton profits while he worked on his *magnum opus* in the British Museum. In *Das Kapital* (of which the first volume appeared in 1867) Karl Marx thrice quoted the speech, thus giving Ferrand a strange place in history.

After this episode Ferrand had a quieter period, but when Villiers' Lancashire Relief bill was debated on 18 June Ferrand (contrary to Villiers' sneers) 'not only approved [of it] as far as it went but regretted that it did not go far enough'. Villiers had called Ferrand obsolete, but it was his own free trade policy which was 'obsolete', because 'he was asking the House to protect the cotton industry'. Forecasting a worsening situation, Ferrand considered a loan of £1,500,000 too little. Amid widespread distress and misery Palmerston 'came down to the House . . . and asked it to vote half a million of money to buy those old rotten buildings of Kensington'. Furthermore, the Bill proposed to give work on ponds, ditches and sewers to men accustomed to heated factories: 'such men' (as Ferrand knew from experience) 'were utterly unfit for the occupations contemplated by the Bill'. Government must provide dry jobs and assist emigration.

The speech was highly successful. One Western commentator ('no particular admirer of Ferrand') found it 'fine', particularly 'that great outburst' on the Kensington affair:

> The effect . . . was terrific. I, who have sat out debates of every imaginable character, never remember anything more electrical in its effect . . . The cheering was long and demonstrative . . .

Ferrand returned to the subject with what he regarded as a 'strong speech in favour of Emigration' on the 26th and again on the 29th. He feared the effect of winter; the Bill would employ only 27,000 men (with their families, 82,000) of a total of 400,000 people – and no single women. He would not inflame opinions and indeed had refused recent invitations to Lancashire. However, demoralised men grew restive; he would serve against rioters as in 1842 and 1848, but

> he earnestly hoped the House would remember how nobly the poor operatives had behaved, how patiently they had borne their sufferings, and would act

> mercifully and kindly towards them. Let them have the means of emigrating to a certain extent, so that some of them might go where they could live in comfort, instead of remaining in their present state of semi-starvation at home.

No constituent could complain that Ferrand was inactive. But he contrived also to participate in a round of social engagements. Scarcely a night passed without a dinner in Hill Street, Belgrave Square, Grafton Street, Curzon Street, Cavendish Square and the like.

The House remained central to Ferrand's life, however, and his range of interests steadily grew. On 3 July he 'spoke at night on Indian Cotton [and] showed Cobden up'. The Liberal agricultural writer James Caird had proposed to substitute Indian for American cotton, and Ferrand could not resist lecturing the free traders: they

> had urged upon that House to become a great protection society for the growth of cotton for Lancashire . . . Now, he would advise [them] to trust to supply and demand for the future. Let them not come down there whining for protection. At all events, if they abandoned their principles, let them like honest men say that they had failed and that protection to native industry must be applied once more in the case of the cotton trade as well as the agricultural interest.

Ferrand never forgot that as recently as 1860 some masters had recruited operatives from the agricultural counties and had even asked Villiers for workhouse children. Later he supported John Laird's briefly successful Chain and Cables Bill to test Naval equipment and made an attack on Edward Reed's appointment as chief constructor of the Navy – 'a gross and scandalous job, an insult to every man employed in Her Majesty's dockyards': despite Hay's and Elphinstone's support, Ferrand lost to Paget by 14 votes to 23 at 2 a.m. Undeterred, he raised questions on Admiralty misbehaviour and pensions for dockyard workers and dined with Backwood and Laird, the great Tory shipbuilder. It had been a busy and contentious few months and he had demonstrated that his long absence from the Commons had not diminished his appetite for controversy.

When he returned home in the autumn, after a holiday abroad with Fanny, he revived a Knaresborough habit by reporting to his constituents and enjoyed a few days addressing large meetings at Devonport and Stonehouse. He reviewed all his votes and condemned Government's 'indecent conduct', Palmerston's dishonesty ('no greater political impostor [existed] within these realms'), the failure of Reform and a disastrous foreign policy ('England was either engaged in or drifting into seven wars – in America, Afghanistan, China, Japan, New Zealand, Russia and Prussia'). There was great enthusiasm and a unanimous vote of confidence. But *The Times* waxed sarcastic over a speech

> three columns long, undertaking a dozen different quarrels and charging twenty distinguished functionaries with falsehood and wrong dealing.

Manners, however, was delighted with 'the capital and stirring speech':

> I believe the public has recognised the justice of your delineation of Palmerston's and Russell's careers. It was really refreshing to read your sturdy Saxon sentences weighty with truth and good sense.

Tories were again progressing in the country and Manners

> quite agreed with you that if some of our friends would not talk rubbish about Palmerston the electoral successes would find their counterpart in Parliament; as it is, the country declares it has no confidence in the Government which the House of Commons supports.

Ferrand's energetic years ended quietly, with shooting, hunting and examining Bradford waterworks' accounts.

III

1864 opened quietly enough at St. Ives, with the rent dinner, tree marking and pruning, magisterial duties, shooting, days out with the harriers, family church attendance, discussions of water charges and intermittent concern over Hugo's health. But the unnatural calm presaged a coming storm. As soon as Parliament met on 4 February Ferrand gave notice of a motion for a Select Committee on the Charity Commission and for a return on its activities. On the 11th, he recorded, 'Government [was] obliged to yield Returns. Made speech showing up Board. Party supported me well'. He later boasted to constituents that

> When those returns were laid upon the table of the House they exposed a most disgraceful robbery of public money. Those returns are in existence now; there is not denying what I say. My statements have never been denied or refuted.

Ferrand asked for a return of members and officials appointed under the Charitable Estates and Trusts Acts of 1853 and 1855, with dates, salaries, expenses and professions. He agreed with widespread complaints of neglect, alleged that the second Act was passed under false pretences and denounced the appointment as an Inspector of one Boase as a reward for deserting Sir John Trelawny at the notorious Liskeard election of March 1854 (which scandalised the West) in favour of the Premier's secretary, Ralph Grey. The Board had been used to reward Whigs at huge cost to the public, without any accountability to Parliament; and the secretary's salary had recently been secretly increased. In reply, Robert Lowe claimed that the increase was authorised by Act, discounted Ferrand's charges and agreed to the return, except on professions. Powell and Richard Malins supported Ferrand and, shorn of the reference to professions, the motion was agreed.

Even Ferrand could scarcely have dreamed of the rich seams he was to mine in his obsessional pursuit of Whig nepotism and corruption. Before the controversy really commenced, however, he went home to examine Denholme reservoir and give evidence to arbitrators at Bradford. He prepared for the Commons fray by writing to *The Times*, quoting Lowe against the Commission. Lowe referred to the Charity Commission Act of 1860 and denied that he had attacked the Commissioners for fraud. When Ferrand rose, the Speaker called him to order. Manners and Disraeli, doubtless dreading another interminable 'great Mott' row, 'pressed [him] to withdraw', but he moved an adjournment *pro-forma* to explain that Lowe had told another Member that Ferrand was right to oppose frauds in his district and that the Commissioners would act on them; that, thought Ferrand, 'floored him'.

Next, Ferrand turned to Naval and dockyard affairs, preparing a 'speech on naval commission showing Duke of Somerset and B. Walker's conduct'. On the 22nd, observing that the Dockyard Commission consisted of four Whigs and one Tory and that 'therefore he had not much confidence in its reports', he condemned Admiralty 'tyranny' over dockyard workers and the appointment of the incompetent Reed. In 1863 Charles Wood had instanced Ferrand's election as proof of Admiralty fairness at Devonport; the truth was that the superintendant, Admiral Thomas Symonds, allowed a free vote, whereas in 1859 Walker had kept jobs vacant as an incentive. While the War Office threatened a military supporter of Ferrand, the Admiralty promoted a Whig Naval officer who led his own side. Ferrand launched a detailed attack on Somerset's selective promotions and intimidation.

The Tories were reluctant to be involved in the Boase scandal, which seemed unprovable, but were curious about the more substantial charges, which brought Ferrand prominently before the public again. A humorous paper sarcastically epitomised hostile views:

> To judge from Dod, he was not educated at all . . . [He] is a rabidly democratic Conservative. He is a Protectionist and generally of the sort of politics one would expect – of the fossil man of Neanderthal . . . He is one of those blatant friends of the working-man who are always talking of the dignity of labour, and recommending the poor fellow to stick to it . . . As an orator he would be unsurpassed if fluency implied wisdom, or a loud voice deep convictions . . . His opinions are labouring on a stage coach to try and keep up with an express train . . . he is sure before long to plunge headlong into some frightful scrape which will render his retirement necessary.

Undeterred, Ferrand led Devonport delegates to the Admiralty. He saw Laird's Bill sent to a Select Committee on 2 March, attended the Speaker's levée and next day launched his assault.

Ferrand bluntly asserted that the principal persecutors of the 'noble-hearted' Stafford over his partisan patronage in 1852 were, under Somerset and Walker, much worse offenders. There had been large-scale Admiralty interference against Ferrand in 1859, including a poster and the appearance of Captain (now Admiral) Robert Robinson, in uniform at the nomination (on which he produced written evidence). He

> wished with all his heart that poor Augustus Stafford had been spared to sit on those benches. He was a persecuted and, politically speaking, a murdered man. His bitterest enemies were the Duke of Somerset and Sir Baldwin Walker, men who had violated the law ten times more than he had.

What Bernal Osborne characterised as a mere 'electioneering brawl' caused a storm. The Tory Hay felt obliged to defend his Service, and Paget haughtily defended Walker from 'unfounded and slanderous attacks': 'he would rather take Sir Baldwin Walker's word than [Ferrand's] oath', whereupon Sir William Fraser moved that his words 'be taken down' and Pakington urged him to withdraw. Paget clumsily apologised, still attacking Ferrand, and Buller joined in. Manners praised Ferrand's 'pluck and courage' and hoped that he would continue to expose such matters; but Osborne attacked him as one who 'never withdrew an imputation or made an apology when he was proved to be wrong'. Ferrand had won the day and sent 250 copies of *The Times* report to Devonport.

The exchanges provoked wide comment. The *Mercury* acknowledged Ferrand's 'great talents for a bore' and his 'insane animosity' and 'pachydermatous nature' in the 'very pretty disturbance'. More importantly, the *Herald* noted that Ferrand's charges 'had not been disproved', despite Paget's 'outrageous insolence', and believed that 'public opinion . . . would decide in favour of the pursuer'. Ferrand was

> certainly the most formidable censor which the Board of Admiralty – composed . . . of the Duke of Somerset and Lord Clarence Paget, its Alpha and Omega – had ever encountered. He told home truths, and brought into court such downright, unmistakable facts about the Whigs that . . . even Mr. Bernal Osborne, the soul of mirth and good humour . . . got angry – so angry that it looked as if even he were afraid of revelations respecting his own tenure of office . . .

The *Standard* also attacked 'hot-headed Paget [and] flippant Osborne':

> Mr. Ferrand is not to be put down by clamour. The Conservatives are not to be frightened by bluster, nor are the people of England to be blindfolded by the mists raised up by anger and cunning. There was corruption; there was partiality; there was gross political partisanship; there was disgraceful Whig jobbery. Mr. Ferrand was a sufferer . . . When Sir Baldwin Walker disappeared from the kingdom without meeting the charges against him, he became himself his gravest accuser; and all the noise of his *claqueurs* but renders his absence the more conspicuous.

As if to vindicate this praise, on the 18th Ferrand opened a new campaign by attacking the 'bad state of Bradford Waterworks', following a catastrophe at Sheffield's Bradfield reservoir: Doe Park and Silsden reservoirs were now dangerous. Grey sent a Home Office inspector, who agreed about the former works. *Punch* featured Ferrand as one 'whose amiable business it was to bring up wretched old grievances, which were not much when they occurred and were now utterly stale . . .' and satirised 'Don Ferrando of fair Devonport' as a latter-day Don Quixote tilting at windmills. But concern over reservoir safety, after the Sheffield collapse had drowned 238 people and ruined £400,000 of property, was hardly a Quixotic illusion. A coroner's jury echoed Ferrand's demand for regular inspection. He continued to question Grey over waterworks safety. His own local situation he regarded as dangerous. Doe Park, with 110 million gallons, had leaked on completion and only Ferrand's warning had prompted repairs, on seven occasions. Another, with 11,000,000 cubic feet of water, had almost overflowed: it could drown 300 people in Ferrand's valley and inundate Shipley and Leeds. He wanted official inspection of all reservoirs.

Ferrand had now made three issues his own – malpractices in the dockyards, corruption in the Charity Commission and waterworks safety. He was about to add a fourth.

IV

By mid-century the development of high-pressure industrial boilers was causing a succession of explosions, killing and maiming workers and others and destroying property. Shoddy workmanship, careless supervision, lack of maintenance and – as pioneer insurance companies discovered – sheer neglect of basic precautions and unrepaired breakages all contributed to the gory record. Ferrand now prepared a Bill for compensation to families of people killed by boiler explosions caused by owners' neglect or default; he brought it in on 3 May. With Government sanction, the measure was later enlarged into Accidents Amendment Bill, altering Lord Campbell's Act of 1846 which allowed compensation but effectively prevented workers' participation, because of ignorance, absence of administrators and legal costs. 'Here was a law for the rich and another for the poor', Ferrand told his supporters in November:

> I have seen the injustice of this in my own neighbourhood, where four or five hundred people have suffered death through accidents like this and, on an average, in nine cases out of ten, those accidents have occurred through the recklessness of the owners of the boilers, or those employed by them. I think that it is high time to put a stop to it.

He had introduced a general measure, quickly passed, and

> if I had done nothing else since I went into Parliament, I have by that written my name in the legislation of this country, and I expect hereafter to receive the blessings of many a working man's family for being placed in comfort and saved from the miseries of penury on the loss of a husband or father.

The Accidents Bill, which passed its Third Reading on 23 June, was accepted by a Lords Committee (with some amendment) on 14 July and received the Royal Assent on the 29th.

The previous month, on 16 June, despite the misgivings of some of his friends, Ferrand moved for a Select Committee on the Charity Board and its forty (Whig) employees. He examined the Board's history (on which he had received hundreds of letters) from 1818, hotly condemning its work and appointments. Much of all this was a defence of ancient local trusts against central interference; the Commissioners' 14-year investigation of public and grammar schools' endowments still rankled, and Ferrand recalled rows at both Bingley and Giggleswick. But his masterpiece was an analysis of the officials. There was, for instance, the fascinating biography of John Simons, unsuccessful coal and potato dealer of Hampstead Road, who fled from his creditors in 1853, became a hired labourer in Australia, returned in 1856 as a Board inspector at £800 *per annum*, again defrauded his creditors in 1857 and was presented at Court by Palmerston in 1859! 'This odious and corrupt appointment' was followed by others, equally disgraceful to the Board.

The speech provoked sarcastic laughter, a revival of old controversies and righteous indignation. Walter Morrison opposed Ferrand because of his personal attacks. Powell, as a Bingley trustee, disagreed over Martin but favoured investigation. Henry Bruce defended the Commissioners from individual charges, but Osborne (while recalling the Cheadle case) favoured inquiry, as did Adderley. Lowe defended the Board and grimly observed that Ferrand

> had special reasons connected with his past career in that House for being particularly cautious in the exercise of the right of freedom of speech . . .

Ferrand's interventions being ruled out of order, Abel Smith ventured to quote the 1844 resolution, asserting, amid tumult, that Ferrand 'had forfeited his right to expect any consideration to be given to charges which he might bring forward'. Malins attacked Ferrand, and Galway attacked the expensive Board. At the count Ferrand and Hennessy could only raise 40 votes against 116 (including Gladstone, Bright and Palmerston) for the Government's postponing motion.

The Press was inevitably divided. The *Standard* hoped that Ferrand's 'voluminous style' would not detract from public enjoyment of 'the most delicious anecdote of Whig patronage which the oldest inhabitant of official premises can remember'; Simons' history was 'unique' in 'the wonderful medley of corruption painted, like the representation of a masque, by the indomitable, vivid and indefatigable [Ferrand]. The whole story is shameful . . .' The *Herald* regretted that Ferrand

> had not the art of sharpening his axe to the fineness of a razor, and consequently when he had made the House ring with his trenchant blows he was told that he was too rough in tone and temper, and that consequently he would not get what he sought.

It supported an inquiry:

> For such light as we have on the subject we are indebted to [Ferrand] who has been well abused for his pains, but who has specially in the interests of the Charity trustees – the latter a numerous body, as will appear when we consider that the charities of the kingdom are something like 50,000 in number.

But another disappointment was to follow. On 11 July Ferrand attended the last 'Sewage' meeting. For three months he had fought against river pollution, missing only a single Committee meeting; he was to be bitterly frustrated three days later: the report was 'an abortion'. That night he 'brought Reservoirs before the House', as he tersely recorded. Actually, he lengthily attacked reservoir policy. He held that in regard to the supply of water there ought to be no speculation whatever. It ought to be furnished at the cheapest possible price as a necessity of life; and ample protection ought to be afforded to the inhabitants in the neighbourhood of every reservoir for their life and property. The sole aim of the companies, however, seemed to be to obtain high dividends; and in order to effect that object the reservoirs were too often badly constructed in the first instance, and afterwards grossly neglected.

The consequence was the disasters. Bradford's five reservoirs had been proved unsafe; the promoters had bought the Duke of Devonshire's support for £10,000 while ignoring local people's protests:

> in many instances in his own neighbourhood farmers and others had been deprived of their spring water; and on three occasions his own property had been deprived of it by stealth, and once he was obliged to apply to the Court of Chancery for redress.

He asked for Government inspection before reservoirs were used. But Grey airily declined responsibility, told Ferrand to take legal action and insultingly told him that 'he sometimes spoke under great excitement and was not really aware of what he said'. Northern Liberals – such as George Hadfield of Sheffield (who had fought Bradford in 1835) and Bradford's William Forster-vigorously defended their fellow nonconformist capitalist supporters, though the latter (while opposing inspection) would accept an inquiry.

While Ferrand could scarcely expect to budge a *laisser-faire* Ministry, he certainly achieved his purpose in raising public interest. And the M.P.s who defended the waterworks companies were not backed by those barometers of local opinion, the provincial journals. Ferrand's speech seemed highly appropriate in Sheffield after the 'terrible catastrophe' of March; and even the *Bradford Observer* was sympathetic for once. 'Mr. Ferrand's speech', it very fairly commented,

> has been described by a contemporary looking upon the subject from a neutral stand-point as 'temperate and practical' . . . For our part we think Mr. Ferrand has done well in forcing upon the Government the subject of reservoirs. Dissenting from, and thinking several of his statements overdrawn or erroneous, we yet coincide with his general view of the dangers of these great waterworks which exist in the North of England, and in the vicinity of populous districts in other parts of the country; and think Sir George Grey has treated the matter in a spirit of levity quite unsuitable to its importance.

It favoured inspection. And when later in the summer T. Barham Foster of Manchester impartially reported on the Bradford waterworks, he found considerable wastage and recommended further safety precautions.

The end of the session set Ferrand free for the usual late summer and autumn round of grouse, partridge and pheasant shooting, country house visits, and magisterial duties. But he did not neglect his constituents. In late October he went to London to meet his new colleague John Fleming, a Devon squire, merchant and shipowner, with whom he travelled to Devonport on 2 November.

The visit was a triumph. Even Ferrand's usually laconic diary entries were excited: on the 3rd he

> Addressed constituents. Immense meeting. 1/2 an hour before I could get in. Again addressed them outside. Immense enthusiasm. Fleming first rate. Unanimous vote of approval. Lovely day.

And on the 4th he was at Stonehouse:

> Lunched at Thierens. Addressed constituents at St. George's Hall – great meeting. Fleming excellent. Thierens' best speech. Unanimous vote of approval. Fleming adopted at both meetings unanimously.

Ferrand was indeed rapturously received, from his arrival, when he spoke to a crowd from the Royal Hotel balcony. He thanked local women with his usual gallantry: 'from my heart I wish that all the single were married, and all the married happy'. In the Town Hall he praised the dockworkers who had risked their jobs to support him and bitterly attacked the Government:

> Palmerston had been in every Ministry except three since 1804. As the Tory Secretary for War, he thanked the Yeomanry for what the Radicals called the massacre of the reformers on the field of [Peterloo]. In 1859 he promised Mr. John Bright and the Manchester Radicals a Reform Bill which, if carried, would have had the effect of converting the country into a British Republic.

Furthermore,

> Since Lord Palmerston went into office we have had a series of little, disgraceful, cold-blooded wars – wars which the people are ashamed of – wars which no man in the House of Commons has ever attempted to support without a blush upon his face; and indeed there has been no war in which we have engaged that has not brought a stain upon this country. What causes have led us into war? It is not because of flags insulted or privileges invaded, but it has been to force the trade of this country.

Palmerston had reneged on Reform and Denmark alike.

Ferrand could point to a remarkable personal record. His Boiler Explosions Bill had grown into the Accident Amendment Act, guaranteeing the rights of poor families to claim compensation. He had consistently supported rises in naval and dockyard pay and had brought in the Factory Extension Act. The Charity returns which he had obtained 'exposed a most disgraceful robbery of the public money', and a Government

> so lost to principle, to honour, to justice, to truth and to political honesty was unfit to govern even a nation of savages . . .

Finally he had exposed the reservoir danger; if they burst, 'upon Sir George Grey's head would rest the consequences . . .' Amidst 'prolonged and deafening applause' he pledged his future service, and with Fleming was adopted as prospective candidate.

As he approached his 56th year Ferrand still retained the strange mixture of reputation which he had earned two decades earlier. To manufacturing, dissenting Radicals he epitomised all that they loathed in Toryism and still appeared as the quixotic champion of an older, departing, rural England. There was, certainly, an element of truth in this view. He enjoyed the role of the paternalist, the caring squire and generous host, the honest justice and the all-round sportsman. But there was, of course, much more to Ferrand. His paternalism and Protectionism – so easily denounced as 'socialism' – spilled over into the industrial world, on which he was embarrassingly well-informed. He still disliked the Mancunian ethic, with its uncaring domestic attitudes and its penchant for often brutal colonial policies; he was, in a sense, a pioneer of the 'liberal origins of imperialism' school. And he cared intensely throughout his life about social conditions in the dismal urban conurbations, as well as the time-honoured rites and delights of the countryside. He could still spoil a good case by repetition of old arguments; but his involvement was sincere enough. His new reputation as the exposer of those devious corruptions for which the Whigs were notorious was sometimes similarly marred. His dislike of turncoats (largely Peelites) was boundless: of the current Cabinet 'only three . . . had not bolted'. Whatever cause he espoused gained a resolute champion in the 'Bingley Bull'.

CHAPTER NINE

Triumphs and Tragedies

When Ferrand went up to London for the parliamentary session of 1865 his first calls were on the Institution of Civil Engineers and Bateman, the sureyor who had examined the Bradford reservoirs. Ferrand had looked at them himself during the Christmas vacation and found that the promised repairs had still not been carried out. He urged the Home Secretary to give instructions for the dangerous Doe Park reservoir to be drained off and told him in January that

> The Corporation has been secretly conveying water to Bradford for more than a year, in violation of their Act of Parliament, and when found out, to prevent legal proceedings, they proposed to pay over the money they had received for it to the persons they had robbed . . .

He explained the payments fully in the *Observer* and offered to publish the 'damning facts' of the Corporation's thefts and blatant lies. By 22 January the reservoir was leaking and on the 27th Bateman found 'the leakages seriously increased'. Ferrand joined nine other worried local proprietors in offering to demonstrate the dangers in the Hewenden valley. As he attended the Volunteers' dinner on the 30th, Ferrand must have thought that he had won. But further work lay ahead in the House of Commons.

The February debates produced little excitement, but on 6 March Ferrand delivered his promised speech on 'Dockyard wages . . . contrasted with private gangs'; it was 'very favourably received', thought really a recitation of familiar complaints. By this time he was interested in another topic. Sir Richard Bethell, Ferrand's opponent at Aylesbury in 1851 and subsequently twice Attorney-General, had become Lord Chancellor (as Lord Westbury) in 1861. Gladstone's remark that Whigs acted with a more close and marked preference for the claims of consanguinity and affinity than was to be found among other politicians' was amply demonstrated by Westbury. By March his habit of appointing relatives to official posts was becoming a scandal. Ferrand's interest and detective instinct were now aroused.

Though Lord Westbury was not the only mid-Victorian minister to indulge in political jobbery, his distinction was that he did so not for party interests or personal friendships but on behalf of his own sons. A certain Leonard Edmunds, who was Clerk of Patents and Reading Clerk to the House of Lords, had embezzled large sums of money. He was allowed to resign his offices and the Chancellor, with full knowledge of the facts, recommended to a Select Committee (of which Westbury was member) that he should receive a pension of £800 *per annum*. The Committee, not knowing that Edmunds was an embezzler, accepted the recommendation. Westbury then appointed his own younger son Slingsby as Reading Clerk and his son-in-law Captain Carler as Clerk of Patents. It was at this stage that Ferrand unearthed further damaging details, which he discussed with the Party's lawyer-agent, Markham Spofforth. Eventually he put his evidence before Manners. It was to cause a sensation.

Lord John carefully examined the papers at the Party offices in Victoria Street and discussed them with Pakington and the lawyer-MP, William Bovill. If a Commons committee were to look at the case, he wrote,

> I do not think you would be safe in relying upon the female witnesses and the letters to prove the case against the great criminal. The committee would be under no judicial guidance, could not examine upon oath, would be strongly prejudiced in favour of the criminal, would disbelieve the women and reject the evidence of the letters. Such at any rate is my conviction – I cannot therefore advise you to encounter the risk of making such a charge on such evidence.

However, he thought that a Committee could be requested 'safely and successfully'. Furthermore, Westbury's recent setting up of a new Lords' Committee would facilitate the motion and had 'prepared the public mind for the discovery of fresh scandals'. But if others advised otherwise, Lord John modestly wrote,

> pray don't let anything I have written have weight with you – for I never was more embarrassed in forming a judgment and am quite prepared to be convinced that I am wrong.

Certainly, he would help in the House and greatly admired the tracing of the case: 'the pains, skill and patience exhibited were astonishing'. Ferrand bided his time.

When the new Lords Select Committee reported on Westbury's shady contacts and in particular on the scandal of Edmunds' resignation and his previous misappropriation of public money, the press immediately sensed a gathering *cause célèbre*. The revelations, asserted the *Evening Standard*, constituted the 'strongest condemnation that could possibly be passed upon the Lord Chancellor's conduct'. The Committee (by one vote) had censured the Chancellor for his silence over Edmund's record and the pension was revoked, though not the new appointments. Westbury offered his resignation to the Prime Minister but Palmerston refused to receive it. There, perhaps, the matter might have ended had it not been for the fresh scandal of the Leeds Registry. A certain Mr. Wilde, the Registrar of the Leeds Bankruptcy Court, unable to explain his financial accounts satisfactorily, had been permitted to retire with a pension on grounds of illness, though the only grounds he could adduce were that he had consulted his doctor about his eyesight. His successor, Mr Welch, was alleged to be also physically infirm and to be holding his office only until the Chancellor's elder son Richard, an outlawed bankrupt, had obtained a judicial annulment of his bankruptcy. Richard Bethel, a man of notoriously bad character, had received money from Welch in consideration of the influence he claimed he possessed with his father, and had boasted that he would himself have the reversion of the Leeds post, though in the event he was never actually appointed to it.

On 11 May Ferrand gave notice of a question to the Attorney-General, Sir Roundell Palmer, on the resignation of Henry Sedgwick Wilde, the Registrar of the Leeds Bankruptcy Court. This seemingly innocuous question was followed on the 15th by a request for papers and on the 16th by a demand for a committee on the matter. Regular attenders at the Commons and newspaper reporters now knew that further trouble was brewing for the Lord Chancellor.

Ferrand's questions were whether Wilde had been ordered to resign and refused, was subsequently offered £600 *p.a.* pension if he retired through ill health and accepted, was granted this sum by Westbury, was succeeded by one Welch (who was already ill) who was told to keep the post until the reversal of outlawry on Westbury's eldest son Richard, and whether Richard Bethell had been appointed, as he claimed, on 24 February. William Murray further asked whether Wilde had petitioned Westbury on his retirement. Palmer blandly replied that Wilde had merely been asked to explain the Commissioner's complaints, gave unsatisfactory replies and was allowed to resign because of bad eyesight; Welch had been strongly recommended to Westbury, who never met him and did not know of his illness; there was no plot to help Bethell (whose outlawry ended on 15 December 1864, while Welch was appointed on 30 July); and, although Bethell had resigned his London post, he had not been appointed at Leeds and the Lord Chancellor knew of no such claim. To Whig cheers, Palmer scored the first victory.

Whig relief at the old habit of 'putting down Ferrand' was premature. Next day (the 16th) Palmer triumphantly added that he had evidence from Wilde and Bethell backing his statement. Ferrand then gave notice of a motion for a committee to inquire into the resignation of Wilde, appointment of Welch and intended appointment of Bethell. On the 17th he maintained pressure by asking Palmer by whose authority his statement had been prepared and for production of the original and the letters from Welch and Bethell.

The discomfited Palmer 'thought that probably on no former occasion had the House heard so extraordinary a question'; he had given his replies in good faith, but the documents were private, though he would show them to Ferrand privately. Lord Robert Cecil instantly asked whether it was proper for Ministers to quote letters which they would not make public. The Speaker decided that Palmer's 'distinction [was] a just one'. Round two was marginally Ferrand's.

Ferrand worked on his case, consulting Disraeli and Cecil on the 21st, while simultaneously serving on the Waterworks Committee. On the 23rd his motion for a Select Committee was due. Palmerston tried to forestall trouble by stating that as Westbury 'courted inquiry', Government would not oppose the motion. Ferrand formally moved his proposal, adding that he did not accept accusations of 'defalcation' against Wilde; Palmer amended his charge to one of borrowing and bad book-keeping; Ferrand further defended Wilde; Disraeli, Roebuck and Grey, in rare unison, called for a fair, non-partisan committee; William Heygate, noting that further charges were to follow, wanted a committee without lawyers, while Cecil wanted a general inquiry, with lawyers; Malins hoped for a clearance of Westbury and Horsman simply hoped for a full inquiry. Round three was clearly Ferrand's.

From 8 June Ferrand regularly attended the committee on Wilde. But on the 15th came news that the Liberal M.P. for Devonport, Sir A. Buller, had resigned and Ferrand hurried off to his constituency to aid Fleming in the resultant by-election. The new Liberal candidate, as had been known for some time, was Thomas Brassey, son of the millionaire railway contractor. On the 17th the two Tories addressed 'a great meeting outside Town Hall', on the 19th had an 'enthusiastic reception' from 6000 people at the dockyards, on the 20th (though Ferrand, suffering from gout, was 'very poorly') spoke at Stonehouse and on the 21st won the show of hands; Fleming's canvass gave him 1385 votes. But on the 22nd Brassey won by 1264 to 1208. Convinced that there had been the 'grossest bribery', Ferrand set his own canvassers to work. Back in London he read the committee's report on the 'grievous scandal'.

Ferrand might have contentedly basked in reflected glory from the Select Committee's denunciation of recent official appointments. *The Times*, professedly horrified by the revelations, noted fairly that much of the evidence was 'extremely unsatisfactory and contradictory'. And so it was. But the Committee untangled some points from an appalling undergrowth. Mid-Victorian politicians were unaccustomed to probing matters which so closely and delicately affected the Lord High Chancellor.

Basically, the Committee condemned Westbury's policy of allowing Wilde to resign and then granting a pension. It rather weakly tackled the morass of evidence on Welch. He was a close friend of Westbury's heir, Richard Bethell, involved in his furtive financial transactions and (according to the Rev. George Harding of St. Ann's, Wandsworth) had agreed to pay £1500 to Bethell for getting him a job from his father. The awful priest (who was to receive £333.6.8) claimed that Bethell threatened to shoot him if he gave evidence. Bethell and Welch claimed that the £1060 which the latter actually 'found' was a loan, but disagreed over the rate of interest. Welch, apparently, quite often lent cash to influential people, in the hope of a job. Harding, said Bethell, was a liar and a blackmailer. The Committee could only (in their 45th paragraph)

> consider it their duty to observe that the indisputable facts are such as to render it essential to the public interest that the case should as soon as possible be made the subject of legal investigation.

On the question of whether Welch was to move to London, leaving the Leeds post to Bethell, the Committee prevaricated, but worked out a rough chronology of events. In May 1864 Westbury heard that his heir was deeply in debt but hoping to arrange matters with creditors and for reconciliation with his father, whom he asked for a clerkship in the Commons (which was refused) and another post as a London registrar (also refused); but on 22 February Westbury had apparently offered him the Leeds registrarship, if he paid off his debts. The Chief Registrar had prepared documents for this appointment. But Westbury claimed not to know of these events, and on the 26th stopped the appointment. The Committee politely exonerated the

Chancellor, except for his 'haste and want of caution in granting a pension to Mr. Wilde', but urged further inquiry. The final rounds had surely gone to Ferrand.

The dreadful business, which deeply offended some Tories (and not only on partisan grounds) was dismissed by later writers as some little local difficulty; the quasi-official view that 'in using his position to favour his relatives he had been following a long, if an evil, tradition' was jejune. Westbury had been brazenly and arrogantly dishonest and Ferrand unmasked him. Much more was to emerge from the sleazy side of Victorian politics.

Devonport's reaction was immediate. As the Lord Chancellor planned to resign, a large poster praised Ferrand. It quoted Hennessy's speech of the 25th:

> every word uttered by the hon. Member for Devonport was true, whilst every allegation made by the Attorney General was untrue.

The 'True Liberal' author also quoted an unnamed London journal:

> [Government] wished to stifle inquiry and but for Mr. Ferrand's determination and pluck they would have succeeded . . . One constituency must take an especial interest in this matter. It is to Mr. Ferrand that we owe the exposure and punishment of a great public delinquent. He alone, with a rare and resolute moral courage, ventured, in spite of Ministerial denunciations and lukewarm support, to press an unpleasant charge to trial and conviction; and his constituents of Deveonport will do well to take prompt measures to repress the disreputable intrigues by which his enemies are trying to exclude from the next Parliament an opponent whom they would easily forgive for his vehemence and impetuosity, but whom they cannot pardon for the honest hatred he manifests for a job, the keen scent with which he detects and tracks it to its origin, and the pertinacity with which he pursues its authors to exposure and punishment. While we have Whigs in office and Whig cousins eager for employment, we cannot afford to lose Mr. Ferrand from the House of Commons.

This provided a pleasant welcome to Ferrand when he returned to Devonport on the 26th. Concerned by Fleming's failure, he started an extensive canvass and issued an address in preparation for the general election due that summer.

II

Friends were delighted at Ferrand's triumph. 'I have very little doubt that your view is correct, and that these practices have been going on to a very large extent', wrote Lord Cranborne:

> More investigation is urgently required and I hope you shall be able to [persuade] the government to give it – or if not to compel them to do so. I most earnestly hope you will be successful at Devonport – not only on personal grounds because of the great loss the House will sustain in a [losing] event but because also, at this present juncture, it will certainly act as an encouragement to the Chancellor and encourage him in his corruption

The final stroke was delivered by Ward Hunt, the Conservative member for Northamptonshire who had been chairman of the Committee of Enquiry. On 3 July, in the dying days of the parliament elected in 1859, he proposed a direct motion of censure on the Lord Chancellor on the grounds that 'a great facility existed for obtaining public appointments by corrupt means' and, with the evidence before the Lords on the case of Edmunds, showed 'a laxity of practice and want of caution' on the part of the Lord Chancellor in pensioning off suspect officials and 'making highly reprehensible' appointments. A government amendment merely requiring that in future legal pensions should only be granted by the Treasury on the recommendation of the Lord Chancellor, was defeated by 177 votes to 163 and Hunt's motion was then adopted. The minority included Ashley, Baines, Gladstone, Grey and Palmerston; the majority Adderley, Cranborne, Manners and Disraeli. Next day the Prime Minister announced Westbury's resignation and on the 5th Westbury made his personal statement in the House of Lords. Parliament was now dissolved and Ferrand returned to Devonport.

At the nomination at the Guildhall on the 11th a 'disgraceful' drunken Tory mob shouted down the Liberals, and Ferrand declared that Fleming had been unfairly defeated. When the second Liberal candidate, Thomas Phinn, asserted that the Tories had distributed free grog for 18 months and defended Westbury, Ferrand revealed that he would make further charges shortly. Brassey and Phinn surprisingly won the 'show', though Ferrand thought it was '2 to 1 in our favour'.

Next day, according to the Liberal Press, the behaviour of the Tories was even worse, as they waited at polling booths from 5 am to waylay voters and deter Liberals; Ferrand drove round before 6 o'clock and organised a coffee distribution. By 9 am 360 electors had voted and the Tory lead was 252; at 10, when 891 more voters had turned out, Liberals gave the lead as 173, while Tories claimed 202. The gap narrowed as more prosperous voters appeared. At 12.30 the Tory lead was 96, at 2.30 36, at 3.30 17, and at 3.45 only 8 – according to Liberals. There was the largest poll in the division's history, and a huge crowd gathered for the result. 'The only change', wrote a Liberal journalist,

> that has taken place since the late contest in the position of the two parties is the abandonment by the Liberals of public-house committee rooms, and it is stated that the Conservatives have received the support of nearly all the victuallers and beer-house keepers.

Publicans' Tory leanings were demonstrated by a still drunken Tory mob, noisily fighting both Liberals and police, while singing

> Slap, bang, here we are again! Jolly dogs are we.

The workers' enthusiasm was rewarded by the declaration: Fleming had 1307 votes, Ferrand 1290, Brassey 1279 and Phinn 1243. For the first time Devonport had two Conservative MPs.

It was, as Ferrand observed, a 'great victory', partly planned with Disraeli; and he warmly thanked the electors, expressed his pride and promised his continued hard work. As always, John Manners was the first with praise:

One line of hearty congratulations on your well earned triumph. That double event is the climax of the General Election of 1865: and all honour and glory to you for it!

As the Devonport Tory chairman, the unfortunately-named John Beer, told electors, 'that man who was the means of unseating the Lord Chancellor was no ordinary, common man'. Ferrand had certainly worked hard for his victory, even addressing an agricultural dinner and making 'one of my best speeches' at Stonehouse. Gout still marred much of Ferrand's pleasure and he missed a Grand Ball (attended by the Prince and Princess of Wales) for visiting French officers. However, he met the Prince during a night's stay with Colonel Augustus Coryton at Pentillie Castle. In London he met 'Dizzy' and Pakington at the Carlton and was 'greatly congratulated on Victory'.

III

The autumn of 1865 which saw the death of Ferrand's son William was to be marked by a more momentous event. Palmerston died on 18 October and his old rival Russell succeeded. The great bar to Reform had been removed and Government could be expected to indulge in more active domestic policies. As Ferrand entertained his guests at St. Ives in November, he watched the new man in charge of Palmerston's old Government. The now Liberal *Times* expressed misgivings:

> The Government without Lord Palmerston, and with the addition of Lord Clarendon, is assuming once more the air of an arrangement by which place and power are distributed among a few great families. Mr. Gladstone is the striking exception, but Mr. Gladstone is declared too young for the first place, and almost every other member of the Cabinet can trace his position to some other influence beyond his personal merits and abilities . . .

But while Ferrand enjoyed such comments, he faced difficulties over his own position.

Ferrand had collected evidence of Liberal corruption at the by-election but had not used it. Liberals were less forgiving and, despite an affidavit by Ferrand denying any bribery, they put forward a petition against the successful Tory candidates. Having recently vacated the taverns themselves, they welcomed an embarrassing bill by a publican named Collins for refreshments allegedly supplied to thirsty Tory partisans. Ferrand hastened to London to repeat his assertion that he had authorised no such expenditure. 'I read yesterday . . . a report of your Devonport examination' [by arbitrators], wrote Manners cheerily. 'You seem to have come triumphantly out of it: and I hope the verdict will be such as to deter the Radicals from petitioning.' The business involved Ferrand in two London visits and stays at Totnes and Devonport. But after dining with Sir Massey Lopes, descendant of an affluent Portuguese Jewish family which had made a fortune in Jamaica and had property and influence around Devonport, Ferrand went home for Christmas.

When the new parliament assembled in February 1866 the Devonport investigations continued, and Fleming was getting worried. The Admiralty actually ordered dockyard officers to cross-examine workers who had voted Tory and served Speaker's warrants on them. Whigs were using every method to get rid of Ferrand but he put a brave face on it when writing to his brother Johnson:

> The Devonport proceedings are *very gross* if they can be brought to light. The petition is a government petition and everything was carefully planned by Brand the govt. Whip, so that the Solrs. for the petition should get into the Dockyard to fish for evidence, as they have no case against me.
>
> If the Leaders see their way to moving for a Committee stage, doings will come to light.
>
> The recognizance is bad in law as it is not dated; it is this very time being argued before the Examiner but he is giving every decision against our Party.
>
> If the petition goes on we shall convict Brassey of bribery, but the expense will be very heavy.
>
> I don't think it possible for them to unseat me and my Colleague, if he will stand his ground.

Despite the unfairness, against which Derby protested in the Lords and Pakington and Disraeli in the Commons, the investigation was going against Ferrand and Fleming; and, despite Somerset's denials and Government blaming officials, the Whigs were using the very methods for which they had harried Augustus Stafford in 1852. 'The Devonport Election Enquiry promises to be memorable in more ways than one', commented a local journal:

> It has set the Administrators by the ears as well as the Liberals and the Tories; and more especially in the matter of that unfortunate telegram which somebody from the Admiralty sent down to the Devonport Dockyard has trouble and misunderstanding been created. It now seems that the official position of Lord C. Paget is more intimately bound up in the matter than the seat of Mr. Ferrand. The whole affair, from the proceedings in the County Court at Stonehouse, down to the issue of the Admiralty message relating to the service of the writs upon the witnesses, has been one unbroken chapter of meddle, muddle and failure. The result, of course, is that every one impatiently repudiates any connection with it . . .

Having denied any bribery, Ferrand spoke on the Naval estimates, soldiers' pay and waterworks and attended debates on reservoirs, the Reform Bill (and 'Bob Lowe's great speech' in opposition), the Oaths Bill and the Oxford Test Bill, returning home at weekends, to read family prayers.

April was a busy month. Ferrand attended the magistrates' meeting and the Bradford turnpike trust's meeting before Parliament gathered. He attended the Irish Church debate, Lord Salisbury's meeting for Derby and the Reform Bill discussions, when Derby 'paid me great compliment for my services'. And he was infuriated by Reform petitions from the North – and especially from Harden, where the manufacturer Samuel Watmuff had compelled workers to sign (as he had forced them to move from Church to chapel.) Ferrand also found many names were forged. Tho right of petitioning was very important, he declared on the 24th, but it 'had been prostituted in the manufacturing districts for years'; Gladstone should help him, instead of opposing 'in the most discourteous, unjust and unfair manner'. Seconded by Salomons, he moved for a Select Committee. Despite opposition from Forster, Sir Francis Crossley, Bazley and Gladstone and advice to withdraw (notwithstanding his correctness) from Edwards, he got his Committee – though only on Harden. The local Liberal Press jovially maintained that

> The signatures can now all be authenticated; names and addresses are all ready for the Committee; and gleeful anticipations of a gratis holiday in London pervade Harden . . .

Meanwhile, the Devonport evidence was mounting and the Reform Bill was succeeding, as Ferrand returned home to give evidence in a case against Townend on the 28th. His position at this time was described not altogether unfairly and with surprising gentleness by some old local opponents. The Keighley paper (accustomed to treading warily between the Whig Devonshire and the Liberal masters) recalled Ferrand's campaigns for the workers:

> He, of all the members on the Tory side of the House, can oppose the admission of the operative classes into power and yet point back to a long series of efforts in their behalf to prove he is their sincere friend. As a country gentleman, his kindness to the poor of the neighbourhood is no less genuine for being unobtrusive, and although a strict game preserver, the indigent sick know that he is bountiful in giving what he permits no man to take.

It 'highly respected' him as a magistrate; 'when there was neither hare nor pheasant in the case, he was both sagacious and impartial'.

Furthermore, 'there was a good side even to his failings':

> His passionate intolerance of anything like a sham, and his sensitiveness in the point of personal dignity and selfrespect foreclose his judgment on the first blush of a thing touching himself, and make him appear at times unreasonable and quarrelsome. And again, his ingenuous trustfulness of disposition lays him open to be easily imposed upon by the earliest comer: he believes what he first hears, and what he once believes becomes an ineradicable prejudice, on which he acts with the whole-hearted energy of his nature.

Consequently, he continually found 'mare's nests' and tilted at 'straw men'. The latest example of 'credulity and irascibility' was his reaction to the Harden petition. The explanation seemed clear to the Liberal journalist:

> The simple fact is that good wages and short hours (and the name of Ferrand will be for ever honoured in connection with the latter) have done their work for Harden, have developed free thought and free action; and the political suzereignty of the feudal lord of the manor – one of the best of the old Tory

type, with all his faults, though he be – is broken and gone for ever. It is as extinct as the Dodo or the custom of Borough English.

And he got close to the heart of the matter by adding:

> Very significant in its symbolism is the engraved crest and intimation which arrest the pedestrian by the highway just as he enters the village. 'The soil and ground of the way leading from hence to Bingley Bridge belongs to Benjn. Ferrand Esqr. 1730', and the crest is a mailed arm, brandishing a battle axe, with the edge towards Harden. The 'soil and ground' of the public road may still belong to the Squire, but the public themselves have slipped his grip in the seat of thriving industry. He may lift the battle-axe of his wrath and of contumelious speech against the peaceful and independent hamlet; but Harden recks the battle-axe of his political displeasure as little as the battle-axe on the crumbling stone by the roadside.

The Bradford paper almost simultaneously made a similar comment:

> Over that district he rules with mild patriarchal sway, and his paternal feelings must have been harrowed to hear that, when his back was turned, his people, the Arcadians of Harden, went gadding after the strange doctrines of Watmuff and the varieties of Reform . . .

Such indications of a certain amount of sympathy cannot have displeased the family, and Johnson carefully preserved them. But the worry over Devonport remained.

IV

On May Day Ferrand briefly visited London over the Harden petition, returning home as the Devonport Committee was named. The chairman was Charles Williams Wynn, a Welsh Tory from the Principality's greatest political family. The other members were the Conservatives Adderley and Percy Herbert, the Liberal Lancashire manufacturer John Cheetham and the Whig Sir Hedworth Williamson. Counsel for the petitioners were Henry James and Lopes and for the MPs three QCs, Price, Cooke and John Karslake, the lifelong rival of Ferrand's *bête noir* John Coleridge.

From the start, matters went badly. James confessed that Brassey and Phinn did not support the petition or demand a scrutiny; but 300 voters had been paid 10s. to vote Tory. He called as witnesses shipwrights, a boilermaker, a sailor, a messenger, labourers and a ropemaker. The difficulties of Victorian election committees were exemplified in the case by George Poppleston, a labourer earning 2s.6d. daily:

> THE CHAIRMAN called upon him to swear distinctly whether he had ever stated that he had received 10s.
> WITNESS: I am turning it over in my mind.
> THE CHAIRMAN: Did you say so?
> WITNESS: Yes, I did. I cannot say from whom I received the money. It was left with my wife. I have been told to say that I received no money. I was told by Mr. Tooke that if I had not seen it I could not say I had it.

Joshua Tooke was called in and denied having said anything of the kind of Poppleston.

The Committee ultimately committed Poppleston into the custody of the sergeant-at-arms for perjury, to be dealt with as the House should direct. He was removed by the police.

Poor Poppleston might fudge the issue, but on the 7th others were more forthcoming. Price himself admitted that 10s. had been paid to 71 men; James declared the figure was 150–200. Phinn craftily prevented a question as to whether 10s. had been paid at previous elections. But the story was clear:

> Robert Barneycott, coal and potato dealer, voted for Fleming and Ferrand, and received 10s. after the election as pay for his day's work from Mr. Cudlip. Would not have voted for anyone without payment. Had two quarts of beer on the polling day at the 'Prince of Wales', for which he did not pay.

Phinn instantly pointed out that he paid nothing for lost time and had moved his committees from the pubs. Lord Clarence Paget was present but was not called, and left to take command of the Mediterranean Fleet. But various publicans stayed to press their claims for election beer. And a silly partisan, James Cudlip, manager of the local savings bank, admitted to paying between 70 and 100 men something less than £150, of which £20–30 was his own. He did not know the law, had not corrupted anyone and kept no accounts!

On the 8th Fleming stated that he authorised no payments but had given his agents £300. It transpired that his bill was £332, but he would never pay for 'lost time'; indeed his refusals led to two subsequent court cases. Ferrand insisted that he had never paid any illegal money, had warned against such expenditure and had even visited each committee room to check that no payments were made. He had no paid professional agent and in fact had spent nothing personally; after four contests, the Party had assumed the cost. This surely was the most convincing case possible. But Price's final submission that there had only been some small payments for lost time, that the MPs did not know of them and that as Cudlip did not know they were illegal it would be unfair to unseat the MPs was scarcely helpful. After consultation Wynn announced that Fleming and Ferrand were not properly elected; that 71 electors had been improperly paid 10s; that the Members did not know of the payments; that the election was null and void and that the corruption was not widespread.

The result was a hazard faced by any mid-Victorian politician, but was particularly grievous to Ferrand, the great denunciator of corruption. He was harassed by the Harden case, further examinations on the Townend affair and now his ejection from Parliament. The hectoring Admiralty telegram – a gross misuse of public facilities almost certainly instigated by the obnoxious Paget – had provoked Ferrand's downfall.

When the Committee officially reported on the 9th there was the consolation that 'Whigs and Tories declared it a most cruel case'. But Ferrand was not one to wallow in self-pity. That day he travelled to Devonport with the two new Conservative candidates, Reginald Abbot and Henry Raikes, and commenced a hard campaign for them, with much unwanted advice from Abbot's mother, Lady Colchester. They were met by 500 people at Plymouth at midnight and on the 10th he 'addressed 10,000 people at 6 o'clock from Royal Hotel: great sympathy: candidates addressed 1500 in Town Hall: splendid reception. I spoke last'. Next day the trio held a large Stonehouse meeting, with 'excellent effect'. The usual election work followed: an 'address to 3 or 4000 at Keyham Gates [with] great effect', attendance at the dockyard church, speeches in the borough and at Stonehouse and Stoke, and wide canvassing. Ferrand took only one day off, to visit Fanny at the 'very good' Green Dragon Hôtel at Hereford – 'a lovely day and scenery'.

'You may imagine my intense anxiety', wrote Lady Colchester, in her effusive way:

> ... I do hope the Govt. feel how poor their chance of success must be at Devonport, since they are forced to allow their Candidates to promise to vote against their own measure.
>
> I asked Mr. Lowe if the Conservatives would find Mr. M[ontague] Chambers a formidable opponent, but he assured me last night, that he would certainly *not* be so, as he would not even allow that he was possessed of Interest.
>
> What I dread in the Liberals is their unscrupulous Canvassing. I am sure they were all taught in their Youth that 'Honesty was the Worst Policy' and now they are old they do not depart from it. I trust there may be no violence or rioting but it is very unfortunate that Whit Monday and Whit Tuesday should be the days of Nomination and Polling.

Two days later she made further observations:

> Lord Morley, whom I met at dinner yesterday, told me he heard we should carry both seats He is a friend of Reggy's and was very kind about it, though he has hitherto belonged to the Govt. side. I sincerely hope there will be no confusion and rioting at the Nomination or at the Polling or after it is over, when the Successful Candidates will have to return thanks.
>
> I always dread the excitement produced by large Potations amongst the Crowd, even of friendly Supporters.

The Tories seemed assured of victory. Their canvassing returns gave them a majority of 60, and they won the show of hands on the 21st. 'Your most graphic report of the electioneering proceedings interested me greatly', wrote Manners,

> and I did not fail to hand on your letter to my brother, who was very much grieved at the untoward result of the Committee. Of one thing I am certain, that if the two Devonport seats are saved next Tuesday it will be owing to your energy and ability. Long it cannot be before you reappear in the House, and the cheers which will welcome you will be long and hearty.
>
> I hope tonight our amendments to the Reform Bill on going into Committee after Whitsuntide will be placed upon the paper, and that we shall have a successful division ...

But Tory hopes were dashed on 22 May, when Lord Eliot (with 1275 votes) and Chambers (with 1269) defeated Raikes (with 1216) and Abbot (with 1215). 'Gross Whig bribery', Ferrand grimly recorded and started to get up a petition. Lady Colchester was heartbroken at her only child's defeat:

> I am very much obliged to you for your kind condolences on this sad and unlooked for result in the Devonport Election. Reggy bears it manfully, and Lord Colchester tries, by concealing his own Disappointment, to lessen my vexations, but I confess it is a sad blow to all my Hopes, for when we saw Mr. Spofforth, I was led to believe that our Party was so certain of Success, with regard to *both* the Seats, that the proposal of a Compromise ought not to be entertained, and when Lord Colchester, after a little hesitation, consented under these circumstances, that Reggy should embark in this contest, I flattered myself the expence was the only thing we *could* have to regret.

Wearily, Ferrand – who knew much about elections and about indolent heirs – joined Fanny for a West-country holiday. After a few days with Thierens they took lodgings at St. Catherine's near Torquay. There was pleasant bathing in Tor Bay and Babbacombe Bay – but not in Torquay's 'miserable' public baths, from which Ferrand 'walked out'. There were enjoyable jaunts to Dartmouth, Totnes, Lord Devon's seat at Powderham Castle, to Lady Sinclair's, the Newmans at Mamhead and to Lady Julia Lockwood's 'very pretty spot'. The Ferrands interestedly watched 'the fishermen preparing their herring nets' at Teignmouth, but found 'good lodging houses not so nice as Dawlish', a favourite place. And amidst the drives, walks and decorous bathing there was the horror, in early June, of an accidental visit to a Puseyite church – Six parsons, six boys, six collectors – Sermon 'give a tenth you possess' – the outraged Ferrand recorded. And there was work to be done. On 5 June a petition was presented against the return of Eliot and Chambers.

After '19 bathes' the Ferrands moved to London on 11 June, to dine with the disappointed but grateful Colchesters. Invitations flowed in – to dinners and luncheons with du Pré, Sempill, Henry Butler-Johnstone in Montague Place, the increasingly ineffective Spofforth (with whom Ferrand had long discussions), Rashleigh, Edwards, Raikes, Rutland, Waterhouse and Blantyre. While Government was defeated on Reform (on the 18th) and sent its resignation to Balmoral next day, Fanny was inevitably 'taken very poorly with internal inflammation'. On the 29th, as Derby started to create his third and most important Ministry, the Ferrands returned home.

CHAPTER TEN

The Last Elections

It was an unusually morose Ferrand who attended the rent dinner in Bingley on the 2nd July 1866. As his friends – Lord Chelmsford, the Duke of Buckingham, Malmesbury, Disraeli, Walpole, Lord Stanley, General Peel, the Earl of Carnarvon, Pakington, Northcote, Cranborne, Manners, Lord Naas and Gathorne Hardy formed a strong Tory Cabinet under Derby, Ferrand, no longer an MP, could not even hope for a junior post. He went to London on the 4th to withdraw his Devonport petition, stayed to dine with Lord Derby, Lord Shrewsbury (from whom he bought some setters) and Sir Henry Foulis and worked on the Townend case (which was postponed on the 23rd).

Familiar faces gathered for shooting parties from August, but as his 'holydays' were short, Manners could not join them. Writing from Southampton he told Ferrand:

> The harvest hereabouts is being well got in, and the crops are heavy: no one can over estimate the importance of a good harvest this autumn, for the state of the commercial and monetary world is highly unsatisfactory. Gladstone, I hear, goes for the winter to Rome: let us hope he will remain there.

Through the late summer and autumn Ferrand busied himself with mundane local affairs: the moors, the Guardians, agricultural shows, the bench and the like. Manners tried to tempt him to Dunkeld:

> Our kind friends, the Grahams, are again at Murthley, where the new Billiard room is finished, and sundry smaller improvements made . . .

But Ferrand preferred to stay in Yorkshire, shooting over his own moors and those of William Middelton and Henry Edwards. His bag, as usual, was widely distributed.

I

The leisurely rural routine was broken in November. A day's visit to London was followed on the 5th by an appearance at Leeds to give evidence to the River Commissioners and another in Vice-Chancellor Stuart's court to prove the case against Townend on pollution. There followed three days' shooting with Duncombe. And on the 20th Ferrand returned to politics with a speech at the inaugural banquet of the Bradford Working Men's Conservative Association, of which he became president. In familiar style he told a cheering audience of 'thinking, educated working men' of Bright's and Gladstone's plan to misuse trade union power for political ends:

> The working men of England have a right to their trade societies, their organisations and their trade unions for the purpose of protecting their labour, so long as they do not deprive or deny to any man the right to sell his labour where he likes, and how he likes. But when working men combine to compel working men to be their slaves and do their bidding, then they become a curse to their country.

He strongly condemned strikes – often provoked by Gladstone and Bright: 'employers and employed [should] look upon each other as entwined like ivy on a tree'.

'Don't tell me that the working men are downtrodden!', roared Ferrand, instancing the example of Sir John Elley, a Tory MP who started life as a delver near Bradford and rose from private to general in the Army. Bright, who urged workers to 'fight for their rights', would desert them in their hour of need, for 'a greater political coward never entered the House of Commons':

> He never comes down . . . to make a speech unless it is to stir up strife and bad blood throughout the country . . . I never heard him speak a word in favour of working men in the House of Commons. You have been reminded of what his conduct was in Lancashire during the cotton famine. He took no part either in purse or person, to relieve the distress in his native county . . .

And he urged moderate workers to band together to save the Constitution from 'sedition and rebellion'.

Manners (who had sent a long message to the meeting) was delighted with the speech and with a hamper of game. He had recently permitted political assemblies in London:

> A precedent has been formally set of offering Primrose Hill for political meetings, and there is no longer any pretence for saying that the Working Men cannot obtain a free and open place wherein to air their grievances . . .

Ferrand spent most of December at Belvoir with Manners' brother, returning home for Christmas and the rent dinner.

Ferrand maintained his activities among working-class Tories in the new year. During an argument with Richard Garth, Bright hit out at the 'ruffian' Ferrand. The Press took up the issue:

> Like many other men of violent temper and abusive tongue, Mr. Bright is peculiarly thin-skinned. He cannot bear, with even a show of self-command, the shadow of retaliation . . . The only kind of fighting which seems fair to Mr. Bright is that in which John Bright is to fling dirt and stones to his heart's content, while the classic sanctity which attached of old to the tribune of the people should protect him from retaliation . . .

So said *The Standard,* and *The Globe* commented similarly:

Blinded with rage, he cared little whether he struck his assailant, or some one else who had done him no harm ...

Angered by Bright's 'gratuitous and coarse attack', Lancashire workers invited Ferrand to join them against Bright. Ferrand in reply stated his own case:

> The state of things which I foretold for both employers and employed is taking place. Foreign competition is taking away the masters' profits, and reducing by degrees English wages to the continental level.
>
> This is a question which must now be discussed, I trust with good feeling, by both employers and employed; it ought to be kept entirely apart from politics, so far as party influence and feeling are concerned. Depend upon it, were I to take part in the discussions at the present time it would give great offence to many of Lord Derby's supporters in Lancashire, and would create excitement and distrust, instead of peace and confidence.
>
> I would urge upon you, and all who discuss the wage and short-time questions, to use friendly language toward the millowners. The 'fierce competition' they have to contend against in foreign markets is a thing they did not credit during the period of the battle between protection and free trade. The people of this country adopted Manchester free trade, and it can only be modified or repudiated by the united decision of employers and employed.
>
> Above all, I would urge upon the factory operatives to avoid strikes, and not to allow people residing out of Lancashire to interfere in any disputes which unfortunately may occur between them and the manufacturers, and to discuss in the spirit of friendship with their employers all matters in dispute.
>
> I thank the operatives for their kind feeling toward me. I have spent 40 years in their service, and I am happy in the knowledge that they have not forgotten me. Were I again to appear among them publicly it would only be as a promoter of peace and harmony between factory owners and factory operatives.

While refusing to revive the old factory agitation, Ferrand kept up his work with the Conservative working men's movement. On the 23rd he spoke at the Huddersfield Association's dinner and on the 30th at Leeds again. The message remained constant: the need for unity against Bright's assaults on the Constitution; and he underlined the theme in the Press. 'Your speech was capital', wrote Manners, 'and you trounced that foul-mouthed demagogue famously.'

Ferrand visited Belvoir and London in February and anxiously watched the progress of Disraeli's Reform Bill, introduced on the 11th. He busied himself at home with a colliery disaster fund, Hugo's health, the organisation of the Bradford Tory workers and renewed trouble over the Bradford waterworks. And on the 26th he addressed a great meeting of the South Lancashire Constitutional Association in Manchester Corn Exchange. Here he demonstrated his old mastery against organised heckling by 'the dirty tools of dirtier men' who should learn that 'good manners made the man' and that 'deep down in the mire must that cause be which had to be supported by forgery'. He lashed the 1832 Reform Act for disfranchising workers, praised Derby's efforts for reform, supported Disraeli's Bill and lambasted Bright's 'revolutionary language'. The speech was an immense success and the Association sent him a highly-coloured address of thanks.

March began with a week at Belvoir. Thereafter Ferrand paid his monthly visit to Hugo, now in hospital at Wakefield, attended a meeting on Stanbury enclosures and a conference in Leeds which called for a national organisation of Working Men Conservatives, served on the Grand Jury, welcomed the second reading of Disraeli's Bill and wrote to the Press about Forster's attitudes. Much the same pattern was repeated in April – the Grand Jury, a visit to poor Hugo, estate work and a visit to Leeds to be elected president of the Yorkshire Working Men's Conservatives. But on the 25th he carried his campaign to Norwich.

A vast East Anglian throng greeted Ferrand at Norwich – 'the most gratifying spectacle [the local president, Sir Samuel Bignold] had ever witnessed'. Ferrand was in good form, as he explained the new Reform Bill:

> There can be no greater proof of the right of the working men to the restoration of the franchise than the patience and loyalty which they have shown during the last 35 years, in which they have been deprived of their rights . . .

'The Day of retribution had come at last', when workers' rights – destroyed by Whigs and Radicals in 1832 – were restored. He stressed the Tory record and contrasted it with Bright's:

> imagine any man so base, so unprincipled, that he would keep the women and children in a state of bondage and slavery too horrible to contemplate, and sacrifice them on the altar of Mammon, and stand by, watching them in their agonies, rather than vote to relieve them from this tyranny and misery because they were supported by the landowners!

He urged workers to support the Tories and avoid those 'skulking, shrinking villains, who would send, if needs be, women and children to the front, while they skulked behind in secrecy'. Ferrand 'knew . . . that the working men of England . . . would walk in the light of the Constitution, fear God and honour the Queen'.

III

Ferrand went on to London, to dine with Tyrell and attend the Tory MPs' meeting. More importantly, he had discussions with Disraeli and Corry about the Party's (and his own) prospects and an hour's talk with Derby at which he stressed the importance of the working-class vote. After a fortnight at Dawlish with Fanny – during which he wrote to Corry on dockyard corruption and the Reform League held its Hyde Park rally – he returned to town to negotiate a settlement (on 15 May) with the Bradford waterworks.

The talks were 'exceedingly friendly' and resulted in the payment of an additional £4000 to Ferrand. Although some councillors thought the sum excessive, the settlement was accepted on the 21st. Ferrand again met Corry before returning to Dawlish, for trips to Westward Ho! and Clovelly and a dinner with the Yeomanry at Barnstaple. He wrote to Derby on political opportunities and welcomed the spread of his type of Toryism with the foundation of a Pitt Club in the old Chartist bastion of Holbeck in Leeds, on the 28th. And he mourned the death of William Walker, the Bradford Tory industrialist and reformer, on the 31st.

The mixture of holiday (at Westward Ho! and Torquay) and political activity continued in June. Ferrand wrote on railway policy and on the 12th went to London on Conservative business, grimly witnessing the Reform League's breaking-up of a Tory rally on the 17th and calling on Derby, Raikes, Rutland and Blantyre. He was busy, speaking for Conservative Working Men's Associations in Reading (on the 19th), Manchester (on the 27th) and Bradford (on the 29th). At the Manchester conference of South Lancashire groups there was excitement and nostalgia. The grandees – Derby, Lord Wilton, Towneley Parker and Sir Robert Gerard – sent their apologies, as did (very naturally) the invited MPs – Wilbraham Egerton, William Hart Dyke, Admiral Duncombe, Lord Arthur Trevor, Edwards, Colonel James Hogg and Charles Turner (a colleague of Ferrand's at Bingley School). Ferrand did not trouble about a truncated platform party; he was equally at home with operatives. His friend from factory reform days, Robert Sowler, recalled that his own first speech in the Town Hall was at the foundation of the Operative Conservative Society whose demise he regretted. Ferrand briefly urged the necessity of better publicity and ward organisation; 'he would impress upon the meeting that for the future 'the working men themselves should be the chief element in working the registration'. Charles Wardell of Liverpool, a trade union agent in 1845 and member of Stockport Operative Conservatives in 1846, recalled the Ten Hours campaigns and condemned the 'Sheffield Outrages'. Other workers spoke of how they always carried the show of hands at elections in Blackburn, Ashton and Bolton (where there were 502 members of the Working Men's Church and Conservative Society). They were right. There was a special Tory strength in industrial Lancashire, where the Wigan W.M.C.A. claimed continuity from the Operative Association and where, Engels told Marx after the 1868 election, 'once again the proletariat had discredited itself terribly', returning 'practically nothing but Tories'. It was here that two Tories, W. H. Wood and Samuel Nicholson, founded the T.U.C. in 1868; and it was here that James Mawdsley, a Tory candidate in 1899, led the spinners' union. For here the classic battle between Oastlerites and the Manchester School was long remembered and its closing stage fought.

Not everything went smoothly. When Ferrand complained that Devon had appointed a known Whig as a registrar in preference to a Tory, Derby – notably careless on such matters – testily replied:

> I should be sorry that the Patronage at the disposal of any Member of the Government should be so disposed of as injuriously to affect the interests of our political friends; but knowing nothing of the circumstances of the case to which you refer, I cannot speak as to the motive which may have actuated Lord Devon; nor indeed do I clearly understand how the appointment to a Registrarship of Births and Deaths came to be at his disposal. Apart, however,

from the merits of the case, you must excuse me if I am unable to see anything 'discourteous' in the note, however short, in which Lord Devon expresses his regret that he could not meet your wishes in regard of an office which was no longer vacant.

Derby perpetuated an honourable but electorally unwise Tory habit.

After visiting the Leeds Tory workers, on 3 July Ferrand returned to London, busying himself with political trivia, and addressing a Greenwich rally. On the 10th he heard of the death of Morgan Treherne, Conservative Member for Coventry, and on the 13th was offered the candidacy. As the Liberal candidate, the barrister Henry Jackson, was already active, speed was essential. Ferrand hastened to Coventry on the 15th, addressed a large meeting, was adopted and issued an address 'to the freemen and electors', pledging firm adherence to 'the great constitutional principles which had guided him through his political life', religious freedom and sincere support of 'reform of all abuses' and regretting Coventry's depression through Free Trade.

IV

Coventry, which had returned two MPs since 1298 under a freeman franchise, had been a notoriously corrupt borough under corporation influence before 1832, until when most male residents had votes. The centre of silk and ribbon weaving and clock manufacture was new to Ferrand, and he had little time in which to learn of its problems; it had generally voted Liberal. The contest began contentiously, when Jackson's father, 'speaking from personal knowledge of the man, characterised [Ferrand] as a regular old Cannon Ball Tory, one who has all his life resisted progress and acted the part of spoliator and a robber, by robbing, or trying to rob, his fellow men of their political rights'. 'It is not only untrue', retorted Ferrand, promising a 'gentlemanly' campaign,

> but ever since the Working Men were unjustly deprived of the franchise by Lord John Russell in 1832, I have never ceased to condemn their disfranchisement and to advocate its restoration.

Ferrand absented himself on Treherne's funeral day, but on the 15th and from the 18th he was an energetic candidate. Hailed as the only living Ten Hours leader, he explained his 'cruel and dishonest' deprivation at Devonport, regretted Coventry's suffering under the French Treaty and recalled his career over factory reform, the Poor Law, Truck, allotments, industrial arbitration and the 'Working Man's Reform Bill'. He urged industrial and social peace:

> My friends, it has taken a thousand years to build up the gigantic fabric of this mighty empire. A week's revolution would crumble it in the dust.

He was well received in the watch, ribbon and silk factories, and 789 Devonport men loyally sent a 22-page address of good wishes, deep regret at 'the severance of ties' and 'great admiration of his noble and unflinching exertions on behalf of the Working Classes'.

Ferrand won the show of hands on the 22nd, backed by Dalrymple Treherne (Morgan's son). 'I am here to set your trade on its wheels again', declared Ferrand,

> to set its wheels and machinery at work, so that the employers may be once more prosperous, and the workpeople have good wages and happy homes. If you lose me tomorrow, will you get another to serve you like me? If I am defeated, you are left to the tender mercy of the Whigs.

It was all in vain. By 9 am. next day Jackson led by 662 votes to 620, by midday by 2145 to 1886 and by 4 pm. by 2429 to 2123, after a riotous contest.

The Tories instantly complained of 'Whig corruption'; the local Tory journal claimed that 200 men had been paid. 'A better candidate or a more thoroughly honest man than Mr. Ferrand never stood before the electors of Coventry', asserted one voter. But, wrote the editor,

> Money has exerted all its influence on poverty and party; and principle has been swamped in a great carnival of corruption . . .

Ferrand himself was convinced that the election was unfair. 'Had I stood before you', he declared,

> a candidate fairly and honourably defeated I would have asked for your sympathy, but I came to this City to fight your battle by fair and honourable means, and this evening I should be sorry to change places with my opponent. I was not anxious myself to stand before you . . . I was sought for and urged and told that I was the fittest man . . . My success, after that first meeting, was certain, unless there was the greatest violation of the law by our opponents . . .
>
> . . . Mr. Flower retired because he would not be guilty of treachery and bribery and violation of the law. The party then found a more supple agent; they brought down Mr. Jackson senior MP, and he has been ready with his money with a vengeance! Now listen! We are at this moment in possession of proofs — proofs that would unseat a dozen Members. A petition will be presented . . .

The petition was sent to London six days later.

As always, there was kindly commiseration from Manners. 'One word of thanks for the gallant fight you made', he wrote,

> and of sincere sympathy in its unsuccessful issue. I can't understand it, and regret it exceedingly on all grounds, public and private, personal and political.

But Ferrand was undeterred by the experience. He stopped at Leeds on party business on the way home and on the 29th went to York for a Yorkshire W.M.C. conference, with Lord Nevill and Sir George Wombell. He praised the Reform Bill, which 'would strengthen the institutions of the country, by rallying around them the heart's best blood of the working population'. And he made familiar attacks on Bright, asking him 'when he ever proved himself [the workers] friend'. One Crowther recalled the Factory Movement, under Sadler, Oastler and Ferrand, and John Holmes, the national secretary, praised 'his friend' Ferrand.

V

The Ferrands celebrated their twentieth wedding anniversary on 10 August. The shooting had scarcely started when Ferrand went to Leeds to hear a case affecting Rutland, missing a Stafford Tory dinner but attending Bingley Show. On 7 September he also missed a Stalybridge W.M.C. dinner, but he was in fine form at Halifax on the 24th. The Halifax W.M.C.A.'s inaugural banquet in the Riding School, under Captain John Rothwell, was patronised by Feversham, Nevill, Edwards, Sir George Armytage, Sir Lionel Pilkington, Walter Spencer Stanhope, John Waterhouse and other squires and clergymen. Ferrand's message was simply a thoroughgoing support of Disraeli's Bill. *The Standard* considered that it

> contains one of the most vigorous and practical vindications of the policy and principles of the Conservative party that has been uttered in reply to the numberless and unmeasured invectives of their defeated and disappointed enemies . . .

Ferrand returned home for Henry Wickham's funeral, and to find that Townend's industrial effluent had killed his fish. The problem got worse in October, when both Cullingworth and Harden becks were polluted.

Ferrand attended Tory dinners at Manchester and York, but gout made him miss one at Coventry; and Fanny was also ill. November was spoiled by recurring gout. A few December days in London for shopping and a visit to the Home Office were followed by a Christmas stay at Clifton and visits to Sir William Miles at Leigh Court, Sholto Hare and Belvoir. Ferrand returned home for just four days on 10 January 1868, before returning to Belvoir, London and Clifton. On the 22nd he addressed two large meetings at Bristol.

A Tory banquet was graced by the Duke of Beaufort, Stanley, Pakington, Hardy, Sir George Jenkinson, Miles, Nevile Grenville, Robert Holford and Sir Alexander Hood. Ferrand praised Derby and proposed the toast to the Gloucester and Somerset MPs. He next spoke to a larger audience of Tory workers in the Drill Hall. He regretted Manners' inability to attend; he had known him for 26 years, as a 'noble man – noble in nature and noble in heart', who had constantly supported improvement of working conditions. Like Ferrand, he was a Tory – and

> Toryism was political freemasonry; it united every rank and every class in one common bond of amity, cementing the whole in mutual interests; and it was on account of Toryism working that principle and that action throughout the country that he was a Tory.

He looked over the Tory record and, in Disraelian style, regretted that those 'who had for centuries been the natural leaders of the working population' should be attacked as enemies.

Again, Ferrand demonstrated his versatility. At Beaufort's grand banquet he was with the grandees – Lord Tredegar, Lord Northwick, Sir Lawrence Palk, Sir Massey Lopes, Sir Edmund Lechmere, Sir John Neeld, Earl Bathurst – and a host of MPs. In the Drill Hall, with Raikes and Fowler, he faced 5000 men, including numerous hecklers: Raikes was shouted down; but Ferrand lashed their 'blubber and noise':

> Let them roar, he had a good pair of bellows. Those who made the uproar were the men who boasted of the liberty of their political principles . . .

It was the old Ferrand, easily dealing with the yellers. Thanking him for his 'far too kind and complimentary allusions . . . to me in your great speech', Manners commented:

> It is wonderful to me how in your enfeebled state of health you could go through such fatigue, and face for so long a time the outrageous interruptions you had to encounter. But 'pluck has it' in the long run, and I don't doubt that more good will result from those scandalous interruptions than would have followed a perfectly harmonious meeting . . .

And the Bristol men wrote of

> their grateful acknowledgment of his patriotism, as evinced by his life's devotion in defence of our glorious Constitution, his great regard for the general welfare of the Working Classes . . . and his kindness in accepting the invitations . . .

As the retiring president of the Bradford W.M.C.A., Ferrand attended the annual meeting in St. George's Hall on 3 February, to deliver a long speech for Disraeli's Bill, social reform, peaceful industrial relations and the movement which he had largely created. His spleen was vented on Beales, Forster, Gladstone and Republicanism. There followed a large, multi-coloured parchment address for Ferrand's bulging collection, regretting his resignation, praising his Parliamentary record, his 'doings and example as a Country Gentleman' and his 'frank and cordial intercourse and fellowship, matured advice and free converse with our Association': he was 'the Working Man's true Friend'. Furthermore,

> We hope, nay, we believe, the Working Men of England will, on the earliest opportunity, prove themselves worthy of the enlarged Franchise, by returning you to Parliament, as one of the lion-hearted, sound-minded, and honest-principled Men whom the Country shall so much require, when she first enters on the practical experience of the greatest experiment to which she has ever submitted.

This document took time to prepare, and Ferrand left on the 4th for a long stay at Belvoir – now almost his second home.

The delights of Leicestershire were broken for two days only, when Ferrand visited London on the Townend case and next day (the 19th) again spoke to the Bristol W.M.C.A. He briefly went home for three days and on his return to the Castle (on the 25th) was greeted by the news that Derby had resigned and Disraeli was Prime Minister.

The Townend case finally came before Lord Cairns, after twenty-five months, on 2 March, when Sir Roundell Palmer led for Ferrand in the first case in the Lord

Justice's Court. It was by now a complicated affair, basically emanating from Ferrand's attempts to prevent Townend's Cullingworth Mills from pouring filth and soap suds into Ferrand's trout streams, where hundreds of fish had died. Ferrand again proved his case, gained his costs but had little satisfaction. Better news followed: the Coventry election committee met on the 12th, unseated Jackson on the 14th and reported to the House on the 16th. From Clifton Ferrand went to Disraeli's reception in London, dined with Tyrell and went home to discuss Haworth springs with Bradford waterworks. Naturally, he watched events at Huddersfield and Coventry by-elections.

Government defeats started in April, as Whigs, Liberals and Radicals reunited against Toryism, though Ferrand rejoiced at a Conservative victory at Bristol. But non-party matters currently concerned him. Hugo's condition worsened and he had to be taken to London for treatment. Pleasure at Johnson's appointment as a Riding magistrate was rather marred by Liberal complaints of his own absences from the Keighley bench while away on political affairs. And the Bradford water business would not die. Seemingly settled in London on 7 May, it arose again on the 9th, when Ferrand left Torquay to prevent further breaking of the agreement by the Corporation; he attended a Committee on the council's 'Waterworks and Improvement Bill' and reached a new agreement on the 14th. He visited old Party friends in Devonport and reached London on Derby Day.

VI

By June Ferrand was happily busy at St. Ives, overseeing the farms and watching the reservoirs. There was sadness in the death of his friend Lord Shrewsbury, Talbot and Waterford, head of an old, largely Roman Catholic, family whose genealogy was a catalogue of British history, and in the unseating of John Miles at Bristol. But there was the charming experience of sitting with Fanny in the drawing room at St. Ives on a warm Saturday afternoon, when eight Bradford Tory workmen presented and read their address and Ferrand, much moved, formally replied that, if elected,

> I shall again place myself under the leadership of Mr. Disraeli, whose government, I solemnly believe, now stands between our Protestant constitution and a sectarian revolution. Let me therefore urge you and every working man to remember that Mr. Gladstone has suddenly become the subservient leader of all those who have united to secure the downfall of the poor man's Church. Its sworn defender, he has sunk into its vindictive foe – resolved to tread upon its ruins on his road back to the Treasury bench . . .

The delegation stayed for dinner and further conversation.

Yet another chance of contesting Devonport was approaching, and after his rent dinner on 1 July Ferrand became increasingly busy, with regular London visits to settle details and to dine with the Duke of Buckingham. He did not neglect local business, addressing Leeds Tories on the 7th and chairing Keighley bench on the 6th and 8th. Two cases came up on the second day, both examples of Ferrand's instant justice. Seven boys caught stealing gooseberries were admonished:

> A system of robbing gardens . . . is now going on to a most alarming extent by young lads who are turned out of their house on an evening by their parents, without either thought or care, and unless something was done to put a stop to it there was no telling where it would end, nor what would become of the lads.

Thefts from a working man's allotment were worse than theft from a rich man. The boys were fined between 2s.6d. and 15s, with costs, and 'if any more boys were brought up for robbing gardens they would be sent to prison', for 'there was but a very short margin between robbing gardens and houses'. In those pre-sociological days, this was a generally effective cure for juvenile delinquency. After many complaints about drunkards, Ferrand turned on the publicans:

> We have no objection to a man going and getting a pint of beer on an evening, but we have a decided objection to an innkeeper filling a man with beer or spirits until he is beastly drunk.

Amid administering justice, Ferrand penned an Address for Devonport and sadly shot his horse.

In London Ferrand 'resumed friendship' with Fleming (whose laxity had lost them the two Devonport seats in 1866 and whose bills remained embarrassingly unpaid) and returned home on the 30th, to be summoned back next day as 'Fleming [had] bolted', and a new candidate must be found. Ferrand issued his own Address on 1 August, warning of dangers in Ireland, created by Gladstone's party ('who were anxious to stamp out Protestantism in Ireland as the prelude to the overthrow of the Established Church of England'). He hoped for his return to 'cancel the wrong' of 1866 and warmly welcomed the Reform Act. As Yorkshire Tories met in the Queen's Hotel, Leeds, under the whip Rowland Winn of Nostell Priory, to select their champions, on 3 August, Ferrand was absorbed in Devonport's affairs. He would, however, not have objected to the Eastern West Riding candidates proposed by Lane Fox – Joshua Fielden and Charles Beckett Denison, representatives of the Radical Fieldens and Tory Becketts.

Ferrand talked with Disraeli, spoke in Devonport, Stonehouse and Keyham five times, bitterly condemning the means by which he had been unseated, went home to shoot and visit Keighley Show and Leeds Exhibition and examined business. 'I am truly glad to hear so satisfactory a report of your prospects at Devonport', wrote Manners. 'Altogether, I think the prospect not discouraging.' He would help Ferrand's proposal of some reward for his constituency chairman, Thierens. The Colonial Secretary, Buckingham, wrote that

> I . . . will take care that Mr. Thierens' name is noted as a candidate for the Provost-Marshal's Place in Jamaica. I do not, however, yet know the particulars of the place or the qualifications required, or even whether the selection is with the Secretary of State or the local Government. I trust you may prosper at Devonport.

Ferrand always did his best to aid friends seeking positions, but neither he nor the Party cared to emulate Whig methods; indeed, Tory reluctance to appoint supporters to (even unpaid) official positions often irked partisans, who knew that no such sentiments inhibited their opponents.

One potential row was stilled when Ferrand told Chambers that he never claimed that he would withdraw. But there was considerable controversy. Sir Robert Collier hotly denied making illegal payments at Plymouth, but Ferrand insisted that all the party agents in the dockyard towns had paid the traditional cash for 'lost work'. Manners wrote anxiously:

> I don't understand what you say about Devonport: if Major Palliser is the 2nd Conservative Candidate, who is the 1st? You, I hope.

Ferrand and Palliser were adopted.

At home there was considerable work to be done. Ferrand's long campaign against pollution of the Aire was now backed by another squire, the Whig W.R.C. Stansfield, who gained an injunction against Bradford Corporation. At the Brewster Sessions on 2 September Ferrand again complained of local drunks, and met a deputation of Temperance advocates. The *Alliance Weekly News* wrongly reported that he had refused a meeting, and the issue was taken up by the *Western Morning News*:

> If Mr. Ferrand treats this great public question in such a manner at Bingley what hope is there that he will deign to consider it at Westminster? We have many grounds for deprecating Mr. Ferrand's election. We do not like egotism, his political bigotry, his violence towards his opponents; but all these are small objections compared with his tyrannical disregard and contemptuous treatment of the seventy-one ratepayers of his own town. It is unfortunate for Bingley that he is a magistrate. It would be unfortunate for England if he were a member of Parliament.

This 'stupid and vicious election canard' disgusted the equally Liberal *Keighley News*. Ferrand 'chiefly shone' as a magistrate:

> His diligence, his quick insight into the equity of a matter and the veracity of a witness, his humane feeling especially towards juvenile offenders, his sharp handling of liquor sellers who encourage drunkenness and vice, and his anxiety to keep down litigation and put prevention before punishment are acknowledged by all in the locality – by his enemies as fully and even cheerfully as by his friends . . .

On the 6th Ferrand went to Devonport, spent two days in Plymouth and started his election campaign, with a Stonehouse speech. He revealed that only he had dissuaded Plymouth Tories from petitioning against Collier and Walter Morrison. He praised the Royal dockyards, welcomed further factory legislation, urged legislation on river pollution and condemned the 'revolutionary' attack on the Irish Church. He praised the Reform Act in familiar terms and condemned what he regarded as a Popish-dissenting plot against the Church. In order to overcome Liberal distortions, the speeches were published as a pamphlet. Ferrand then spent a fortnight canvassing, returning home on 12 October.

'Bother politics!' Manners had written in September, but he was now heavily involved himself. 'I do sincerely rejoice in your good prospect of success', he wrote:

> There seems to me to be a heartiness and confidence among our voters which has not been shown since 1841, and which ought to produce great results. Stirling Maxwell was here on Saturday: he is threatened with an opposition by an unknown Mr. Parker; but I can hardly believe it will be serious . . .

Tory hopes were too high: the 'unknown Mr. Parker' (in reality Charles Parker, the biographer of Peel) actually won Perthshire, one of the few Tory bastions in Scotland. And in Devonport Ferrand faced unemployment in the dockyards, due to Liberals giving tenders to expensive private firms.

The election was still weeks away, but most candidates (including Manners, despite his painful shingles) had started canvassing; Denison and Fielden were at Bingley on the 30th, supported by Ferrand. Conservatives fought strongly in defence of the Church, raising harrowing pictures of plots against it. Inevitably Ferrand spiced the scene, with references to the Reformation, Ridley, Latimer, the Armada, James II, Irish atrocities and ultramontanism. And he condemned the Liberal cry for 'competition':

Abolition of all Government Manufactures! is their cry!! Supported by a new Conservative journal – to whom he was 'an honest and independent veteran' – Ferrand worked ceaselessly from 2 November, speaking at Devonport three times and at Stonehouse, Stoke, Tamar and St. Aubyns and canvassing daily.

The nomination on the 17th gave little indication of what was to come. Next day the Tories were soundly defeated. The Liberals, John Lewis and Chambers, had 1541 and 1519 votes respectively, to Ferrand's 1370 and Palliser's 1365. Manners read the 'sad and unexpected news' on his way to vote in Derby:

> I cannot tell you how grieved I am at it – how grieved we all are. Nothing shall persuade me that it was the deliberate and unbiassed decision of the people: but, arrived at as it may have been, the result is most mortifying and distressing. You will be able to think that if Devonport was not won, it was not owing to any want of care, labour or courage on your part.

Ferrand was naturally sad. 'Both parties expected us to win by a large majority – 200 was our safe return', he told Johnson;

> There was not a man in our party, and only those in the secret of the other, who doubted the result at the opening of the Poll, but we were defeated by wholesale bribery during the last 18 hours. The money was found at headquarters, not only for Devonport but in many more small Boroughs – Falmouth was only saved by employing scores of watchmen placed at the poor voters' doors.
>
> Helston and Windsor are to be disfranchised, and no doubt others – perhaps Devonport. I have done with the ungrateful scamps, but there is frightful suffering among them on account of the wholesale discharge of the Dockyard men by our Admiralty.

You see there is not a single workingman returned, and a House less approaching to them than the last . . .

Johnson thought that Ferrand would retire and devote himself to country sports, as the family had long urged. But it was not so simple.

VI

In London Ferrand met Devon and Buckingham, before returning home to share in Denison's and Fielden's triumph in the Riding on the 30th. In early December he was busy forming a Bingley Tory Association. And then he rested for a week at Morecambe and a week at Belvoir, returning home for Christmas. He was never again to sit in Parliament; but politics still fascinated him.

Rural life dominated much of January 1869: the rent dinner in the White Horse and sport during three visits to Belvoir, with Rutland, Frederic Grant, George Norman, Henry Manners, the Powletts, Edward Fitzwilliams, Welby, Forbes, Walter Gilmour, Sir Henry James and other friends. But he returned North to speak at the Holbeck Pitt Club's anniversary banquet with William Wheelhouse, newly-elected at Leeds, and a militant Anglican priest, J.H.F. Kendall, in downtown Holbeck. Kendall had founded the club in May 1867, with 13 Tory workmen; it now had 140 members, a 4s. 4d. subscription (to the W.M.C.A.'s 1s.), a newsroom and a long lecture programme. Ferrand gave what even he thought was a 'very good speech' on Pitt, Reform, Peel, Ireland and the need for a return to the enthusiasm of 1841. He also regretted that borough nominations were now largely decided by London headquarters; he condemned the adoption of wealthy carpetbaggers who did not know a division. 'The candidate who is selected now in the majority of boroughs is weighed by his purse, and not by his brains or his social position', he complained; they must break London control.

Certainly, such central organisers as Beresford, Forbes Mackenzie, Philip Rose and Markham Spofforth had not only favoured wealthy men but had not been averse to certain corrupt practices, of which Disraeli and Gorst disapproved. Nothing that the importance of Kendall's work in Radical Holbeck was demonstrated by the presence of Ferrand, 'one of the most respected members of the Conservative party', the local Tory journal asserted that he had delivered 'one of the ablest [speeches] which even that veteran orator had ever uttered'. It was especially important in drawing attention to the lack of Tory effort in the boroughs.

Ferrand's life continued in much the same pattern: sport, largely at Belvoir, and politics – where he was the authentic voice of provincial Toryism and its working-class supporters. When, on 12 February, Ferrand went to 2500 Bolton Conservatives' dinner, he stayed at Smithhills Hall with the former Radical Peter Ainsworth, who was to die in 1870. But (unknown to Johnson) Manners wrote hoping that Ferrand and Cochrane would soon get seats and noting that 'Bright appeared to have lost his head at the Fishmongers'. Ferrand, nearly 60, was still riding energetically with Rutland, Lord Scarborough and Charles Stuart-Wortley.

On reaching St. Ives on 2 March, Ferrand received a 'telegram from Mr. Brydie.

Hugo very ill', and next day anxiously hurried to London with Fanny. For a week they consulted numerous doctors and by the 8th Hugo had recovered sufficiently to dine with them – 'quite well and calm. Mr. Rowe agreed to take him as Pupil at £200 a year'. While Hugo and his attendant went home and Fanny to Leamington, Ferrand was back at Belvoir, with the Manners, Normans and their circle.

Estate matters dominated April, as Ferrand pruned trees, fished, sowed oats and clover, set potatoes and planted rhododendrons. He formally opened the Volunteers' drill shed and 'handed my Father's Vol: Colours to them', attended Wakefield Sessions and presided over a tea-meeting in the People's Park and a Harden cemetery meeting. And he went to London to discuss another Bradford Waterworks Bill, returning on 2 May for several days before the Committee, noting Gott's perjury, rejecting a 'worthless clause' and allying with Keighley's representatives. He visited Hugo in King Henry's Road (and gave the wretched youth 2s. 6d.), ate with Rutland, Cochrane and Laird (to meet Sir John Burgoyne) and went home to examine the reservoirs, mark and transplant trees, sow swedes, fish and work on the bench.

VII

One great local event demanded Ferrand's attendance. Ever since Oastler's death in 1861, factory reformers had hoped to erect at least one monument to him. Eventually, they resolved to site it in Bradford. The Committee (of which Ferrand was a founding member, with Edwards, Walker and his son, Akroyd, Balme and Sam and Thomas Fielden) had difficulty in raising funds, as the principal organisers, the ever-loyal Balme and John Rawson knew: Lancashire could spare little during the cotton famine, and although the Manchester fine spinners contributed £100, such craft unions as the Liberal – inclined Amalgamated Society of Engineers simply thought that a note that Oastler was 'a great friend to the working classes, and laboured hard . . . on their behalf' sufficed. But a mixture of 'great' men (headed by the Archbishop) and individual workers subscribed £1500, of which £1000 was spent on the statue (height 10 ft. 6 ins., with a boy of 6 ft. 6 ins. and a girl of 5 ft. 6 ins., using three tons of bronze, with a total height of 22 ft. 7 ins. and weight of 30 tons, as meticulous Victorians recorded).

On 15 May the statue was 'inaugurated' by Shaftesbury and a huge crowd of perhaps 100,000. Banners to Oastler, Shaftesbury, Fielden, Sadler, Wood, Ellesmere, Feversham, the Bishop of Oxford, Manners, Walker, Newdegate, Ferrand, Bull, Brotherton, Rand and Hindley led a long procession of children, operatives, overlookers, ancillary workers, Trade Unions and friendly societies, clergy and 'notables'. Shaftesbury praised Oastler's 'force of talent, vigour of mind and earnestness of heart'; Forster noted his 'earnestness, patriotism and sincerity'; and Ferrand gave the speech of the day on one of his 'most intimate friends'. Oastler

> had done more for the welfare of the working population of this part of England than any other man, living or dead . . . a more noble-minded philanthropist or a purer Christian never walked on British soil. He spent

his life in fighting the battle of the poor. It is true he was persecuted, oppressed, imprisoned; but the factory operatives set him free . . . He taught you through his career that labour has its duties as well as property and if there was one circumstance connected with the whole of his public life that should be noticed, it was his anxiety to inculcate in the breasts of employers and employed friendship and good will . . . Long may his memory live in your hearts, and in the hearts of your children and your children's children.

Edward Miall, who spoke next, was shouted down, as an old enemy of Oastler.

That night, after Ferrand had gone home, Shaftesbury agreed with Forster in deprecating some of Oastler's more violent outbursts, but, in his list of old campaigners, praised 'as true a man as ever laboured in this great cause – Mr. Ferrand'. The nostalgia of old campaigns and old friends and the personal charisma of 'the Factory King' seized the memories and imagination of Bradford's teeming population – though all too briefly.

CHAPTER ELEVEN

The End of Politics

At 60 Ferrand was a portly, energetic sporting squire, with a vast range of friends from dockers to dukes, labourers to lairds. He was a crack shot, a renowned rider and a successful fisher. He was undoubtedly an esteemed J.P; and, though out of Parliament, he was prominent in the councils of Disraeli's new Conservative Party's national organisation. He had a reasonable and growing income, which allowed him to live in style at St. Ives and to play his favourite role of the generous paternalist. And, like his ancestors, he was fiercely proud of his acres and determined to preserve them, especially against desecrators and thieves (whether poaching gangs or municipal corporations). Only in his family life – with a hypochondriac wife, a mentally defective son and an estranged daughter – was there sadness and regret.

I

As he moved into his seventh decade Ferrand still had time and energy for local politics. In the summer of 1869 he broke off from a holiday in Somerset to join in the widespread national protests against Gladstone's proposal to disestablish the Church of Ireland. On 10 June he took the chair at a great Protestant meeting in St George's Hall, Bradford before an audience which he estimated as five thousand. Sharing his Bradford platform with the M.P. for Salford William Charley, Fielden, Stanhope, Powell and many clergymen, Ferrand bitterly attacked the 'popish revolution' against the Irish Church and the 'renegade and apostate ministry's' secret negotiations with Sir John Gray and the ultramontanes. He excitedly declared that

> if one shot were fired in Ireland at the Protestants, the last shot would not have been fired in the dire contest till every Roman Catholic church, chapel and convent had been levelled in the dust, until the battle of the Boyne had again been fought, and their civil and religious liberties again secured.

Such hyperbole was pale stuff compared with the outrageous William Murphy, an Ulster Protestant lecturer whose detestation of Fenian murderers led to thunderous denunciations (with titillating stories of confessions and nunneries) of Roman Catholicism. But it was enough to anger a large crowd of Liberals outside the Hall, who had to be cleared by a force of police.

Through his secretary, William Gurdon, Gladstone denied any plot; and he denounced the 'miserable little counter-meeting to the great demonstration'. Ferrand retorted that Gladstone 'Jesuitically intimated that the sense of the great community of [Bradford] was entirely in favour of [his] Church Spoliation Bill' and challenged him specifically to deny that the measure despoiled the Church of Ireland and that he regularly met Gray, who promised Gladstone's support to Irish ultramontanes. The Conservative *Yorkshire Post* thought that 'the Premier would not be able to answer without confirming in the main what Mr. Ferrand stated'. Gladstone, however, who had made the Irish Disestablishment issue the keynote of his general election campaign and had a Liberal majority of over a hundred in the House of Commons, was not to be stopped by rhetoric from Bradford Tories. The same month, in the intervals of bathing, driving and walking in Devonshire, Ferrand gloomily noted the Lords' passing of the 'Irish Church Plunder Bill' by 179 votes to 146.

He had a better chance of influencing events in the more circumscribed field of his interminable feud with the Bradford Water Works. In July he appeared before a House of Lords Committee on a new bill. Lord Methuen presided over an impressive committee, composed of the Duke of Grafton, the Earl of Dartmouth and Lords Fitzwalter and de Vesci. Counsel were equally high-powered: James Hope-Scott, Edmund Beckett Denison and George Venables for Bradford, Henry Cripps and Messrs. Rodwell and Bidder for Ferrand, and Granville Somerset for Halifax Corporation. Such *dramatis personae* guaranteed an expensive and contentious battle.

Basically, Ferrand wanted power to examine local reservoirs. Denison argued that Ferrand had already receive £6000 for nominal damage and now wanted more:

> He had extorted money from them on every possible occasion. He was claiming to have power which he could make noxious, and which he would probably sell next week, as he had done before.

Gott (the Corporation Surveyor) claimed that Ferrand was always wanting money and had sold a moor for Stubden reservoir for £3000. When Rodwell defended Ferrand's rights as the landowner, Lord Methuen was sympathetic. Ferrand and George Venables for Bradford, Henry Cripps and Messrs. Rodwell and Bidder had 4000 acres in the Hewenden valley, of which 1800 would be flooded; surely he had a right to protect his land. Their lordships could scarcely disagree; and Denison had chosen the wrong man to attack, in his usual bullying way.

When Ferrand was called, he bitterly recalled his experiences with the Corporation, who had stolen water, broken promises and given no protection. The Committee accepted his case and amended clauses in his favour. 'My dear Brother', he wrote to Johnson,

> I have got 2 clauses giving me full protection against the new water works of the Bradford Corporation. Hope Scott and Dension used the most vulgar and ruffian language against me, but I gave the Corporation in return a dressing they will never recover from.

Law and West, past and present mayors, were disbelieved, and

> Counsel made repeated efforts to induce the Committee to alter the 2 clauses, but they would not, and their scheme which was to spread destruction over my property in time of floods cannot be carried out.

> I believe no Corporation was ever before so overwhelmed with disgrace, and they skulked out of the room hanging their heads.
>
> I formally applied for costs, but they are never given – a great shame.

It was a notable victory.

Nevertheless, for all this activity there were signs that his once great physical powers were beginning to fail. When on his west-country holiday earlier in the year he had suffered a severe attack of deafness which he attributed to a cold. It proved in fact to be the precursor of a growing infirmity.

For the rest of the year, however, he continued to intersperse his customary sporting activities and country-house visiting with an occasional public appearance. In September, at the invitation of the local rector he addressed a dinner of local allotment-holders at Methley near Wakefield and gave them practical advice on growing vegetables. In December an even more congenial occasion presented itself when he and Lord John Manners addressed 2,000 Tory workmen at the inaugural meeting of the Leicester Working Men's Conservative Association.

Leicester Temperance Hall was crowded. The platform party, under Charles Brook of Enderby Hall (with whom Ferrand stayed the night), included the local MPs, Samuel Clowes of Woodham Eaves, Lord Curzon and the sturdy farmer Albert Pell. In what Ferrand considered 'a great speech', Manners praised Derby (who had died on 23 October) for his benevolence; rejoiced that workers and gentry were again allied, as they had been against frame rents in the hosiery district; recalled Bentinck's forecast that workers would rise against Free Trade; welcomed support for Imperial and home institutions; and condemned Irish murders and secular education.

Ferrand recalled that Tory meetings were broken up by Liberals until Tory workers were recruited to keep the peace. And he reviewed the Tory record in his own lifetime, recalling that Oastler, Sadler, Wood, the chairman, Disraeli, Manners and himself had fought for factory reform, against Bright's bitter opposition. He praised Walter, Eldon and the Bishop of Exeter for fighting the New Poor Law. Conservatives had also fought Truck, advocated (through Manners) 'recreation and holidays for the hard-worked classes' and started allotment schemes (through Disraeli, Manners and himself). And now Lord Derby, Disraeli, Manners and their Party had restored a working-class franchise:

> Let them remember who had been their friends upon all these occasions during the last 40 years. Deeds, not words, had been the watchword of the Conservative party. They had promised, and they had performed.

The *Standard* enthused over both speeches and the remarkable progress of the Working Men's Conservative Associations.

All reporting and comment was not equally acceptable. Manners found *The Times* 'refreshingly accurate after the dreadful nonsense of the local journal'. But

> why is your sterling speech omitted? I think I can guess. Because the contrast it suggested between the past and present line of the Times is too marked and discreditable to the present management. I hear the Manchester and other

local papers have fair reports. If you ever attend another Leicester Meeting we will take care to have a London reporter present, and you may be sure of a most enthusiastic reception. The Times leader is much more fair and civil than has been its wont; and I assume from it that the Times don't like the look of the Irish and Free Import questions.

Lord John added that the Duke of Rutland had been 'very unwell' but had improved and that 'he hopes you will look upon the Castle as your home whenever you like to make it so'. A loyal friend himself, Ferrand had generous and true friends. As Christmas approached and Manners looked forward to New Year hunting, Ferrand could relish a *Globe* article:

Devonport, after it ceased to be called Plymouth Dock, and after it obtained two representatives for itself, was for a time largely under Admiralty influence. By no means entirely, however. It is but seven years ago since the First Sea Lord, a Grey to boot, was defeated by the redoubtable Mr. Ferrand. He, after being six times a candidate and four times unsuccessful, has finally shaken off the dust of his feet against the borough.

There were interesting political opportunities to come; but Ferrand, immersed in work on Bingley Grammar School, Keighley magistrates, Bradford reservoirs and Harden shooting, now had to face the problem of his growing deafness. A public career was a diminishing possibility.

II

Meanwhile his loyal friend Manners continued to hearten him with regular news. After attending another gathering in the Tower Hamlets constituency, for example, he reported to Ferrand in February 1870 that

About 130 working men dined, and were very hearty in their expressions and applause. Their spokesman, a bookbinder, spoke well. The general statement was that the working men are rapidly becoming Conservatives; and I quite believe it.

He continued with more political gossip:

You never saw such a lot of cripples as the leading statesmen are. Bright quite disabled, Gladstone looking fearfully ill, Clarendon just escaping gout in the stomach, Granville hardly able to crawl, or speak, Disraeli looking like a ghost. The man who is halest and strongest is Cairns! – and he goes back to Mentone next week. Nothing is yet absolutely settled about our leadership in the Lords, but it is generally believed Lord Derby will be the man.

The question of the party leadership in the Lords was exercising Manners. Malmesbury had resigned from that office in 1868 and the anti-Disraeli faction had wanted Lord Salisbury to succeed him. In the event Cairns was elected but he in turn resigned towards the end of 1869. Derby was chosen to replace him but refused and in the end the Duke of Richmond was elected to the post, beating Lord Salisbury. Manners was not amused. 'Between ourselves', he wrote in March,

> I am a little astonished at the choice of leader by the Conservative Lords – though of the Duke's capacity for business and administrative ability I am well aware. Disraeli is still far from well . . .

Constantly he hoped for Ferrand's re-election:

> You *must* return to us: and before next Session I confidently expect to see you and Cochrane sitting side by side on the old seat.

Early the following year in fact Ferrand was offered the Tory candidature in a by-election at Stalybridge; but he declined because of the steady progress of his deafness. It must have been heartbreaking for a still active sportsman to give up all his parliamentary aspirations for such a reason. Manners, however, still kept up his regular budgets of news and comment. The Franco-Prussian War which broke out in July 1870 induced in him, as in many other English observers, mixed feelings:

> What an awful Christmas prospect it is for Europe! I still believe that France will pull through, and that Prussia will regret the march to Paris . . .

And in early December he reported that 'The French news is so exciting that I can think of hardly anything else'. Defeated France was divided: republican Paris might fall to murderous Communards, but France as a whole was monarchist. The problem was the choice between Henri V, Comte de Chambord and Duc de Bordeaux, grandson of Charles X; the Orléanist Louis Philippe, Comte de Paris, grandson of King Louis Philippe I; and the Emperor. Manners undoubtedly favoured the legitimist Chambord. But France drifted into an inglorious Third Republic.

In the spring of 1871 he was commenting on the government's budget proposals, the most notable and unusual feature of which was a tax on matches. This was greeted with violent disfavour by the public and ultimately abandoned:

> What a budget! The fiery Cross is sent out . . . and I hope we shall be able to defeat its worst features. Governments are more unpopular than they yet have been, and find great difficulty in getting on with their measures.

And in August:

> The 'Times' has become weary or shy of reporting the Army Bill debates, and if you want a full report you must now read the 'Standard'! No business makes any progress to speak of and at the rate we are going the Session will last till Xmas. Gladstone has lost all hold over the House and his colleagues do nothing but blunder. Lord Halifax told Hardy yesterday that he felt Goschen's and Bruce's great bills were so certain to collapse that he had not even looked at them! I don't think that a Dissolution can be deferred beyond 1872. Our party are well together, not one of them voting last night with Government . . .

The End of Politics 175

Goschen's bill was one to reform local rating; Bruce's to stiffen the law on licensing public houses. Understandably neither was popular with the British public and in fact the parliamentary session, of which (according to Gladstone) 150 hours had been spent after midnight, did not end until 21 August, a phenomenally late date.

Manners never tired of passing on even the smallest item of news which might prove a source of some consolation to Ferrand in his exile from Westminster. In November, when Ferrand was unable to attend a mass rally at Bristol of the local Working Men's Conservative Association, Manners asked Mrs. Ferrand to

> ... Tell Ferrand that he was greatly missed, and that he would have thoroughly enjoyed the Working Men's meeting: 3000 of them packed as close as herrings in a barrel, most orderly, yet enthusiastic ...

A more peaceful and domestic topic had been touched on the previous month:

> We are all wild here about garden-golf, which has entirely superseded croquet; it occupies more ground and affords more exercise and variety. You could have a capital ground in front of the Drawing room at St. Ives.

But there were other features of Victorian country-house life that were less attractive. In the summer of 1872 Manners was writing that

> It is satisfactory to have discovered the cause of the ill savour we perceived the last day of our delightful stay at St. Ives. A report on the drainage at Belvoir has been made to my brother, which shows an alarming state of things here. Every house ought, I believe, to have its drains thoroughly examined every year.

Both Manners and Ferrand had a certain obsession with hygiene. Since only a decade earlier the husband of the Queen of England had died of typhoid fever, it was an understandable concern. In fact, earlier that same year, when Ferrand went for a week's holiday on the south coast, Manners made the comment that

> I am very glad to hear of your selection of Worthing; so far as my experience goes it is the only seaside place in England properly drained.

In 1872 there were echoes of old controversies. In that session a Short Time Bill (for a working day of 9 hours) was introduced by A. J. Mundella, the liberal manufacturer and M.P. for Sheffield, at the instance of the Lancashire cotton operatives. 'I have had some talk with Fielden about the new Short time movement', wrote Lord John, of the 9-hours campaign:

> He says he and his firm were kept in ignorance about it, but that he is favourable to it, and believes it to be inevitable. There is little chance of Mundella's bill being seriously discussed this Session, and Bruce [The Home Secretary] expressed himself the other day hostile to it.
> ... The Government appear getting weaker and weaker every week ...

The thought of the half-Italian radical industrialist Mundella taking over his cause must have irked Ferrand, who was consequently ambivalently cautious on the issue. But Manners was enthusiastic:

> Don't be afraid of my committing myself on the 9 hours question. When the French Government raise, as they probably will, the duties on English manufacturers next year, we shall arrive at an important epoch in commercial and manufacturing legislation.

Like the 10 Hours Act in the 1840s, Mundella's bill was ostensibly to limit the hours of women and children only and on those grounds gained the support not only of Trade Union champions like Thomas Hughes but humanitarians like Lord Shaftesbury and Samuel Morley. In reality it was intended to effect, as a practical and inevitable consequence, a shorter day for male workers also. In the then climate of opinion it would have been impossible to obtain a statutory limitation specifically on the working day of adult males. Even so, the bill was strongly resisted and the government lent it no assistance. Though reintroduced in 1873, it made no progress and eventually the question was shelved in time-honoured fashion by referring the whole question of the working of the Factory Acts to a Royal Commission.

Joseph Arch's attempt to organise agricultural workers – bitterly opposed by farmers but initially sympathetically treated by some squires and clergymen – was another matter touched on by Manners in the spring of 1872:

> The Agricultural movement does not seem to make much way here [Belvoir]. Two of Hornsby's men went to Bottesford, and a regular discussion lasting 2½ hours, with F. Norman in the chair, took place. They were obliged to admit that the Bottesford labourers were much better off than they were, and it became apparent that they wanted to bring the former into their Union for the purpose of strengthening their own position. Still, a certain number of labourers have joined.

In a letter of 3rd April he optimistically reported that

> The Agricultural wages question is simmering in all the neighbouring villages; but a little kindness and firmness on the part of the farmers will soon terminate it in our part of the world.

Joseph Arch's crusade had started in Warwickshire in February 1872 and spread rapidly in the midland counties. Though not especially linked with orthodox Trade Unionism, it was inevitable that it should be regarded with some suspicion as forming part of the general movement for organising workers which was a feature of the 1870s. The demand of Arch's Agricultural Union for a rise in their average weekly wage of 12/- (in Dorset it was as low as 8/-) was strongly supported by Liberal M.P.s like Mundella and in general by the Nonconformist churches. The Anglican clergy, though there were some notable exceptions, were less friendly; as inevitably were, as a class, landlords and farmers. The general refusal of the latter to pay the 16/- a week demanded by the Union helped to speed the drift from the land to the towns and colonies which in the end proved a more efficacious weapon than strikes. It also helped to fuel the growing Liberal campaign headed by such M.P.s as George Trevelyan, W.E. Forster and ultimately Gladstone, for giving the rural labourers the parliamentary franchise. In the short term, however, the farmers were victorious. In the late autumn Manners was able to write from Scotland that 'the [agricultural] labour question appears to be dying away in most parts of England; how is it with you? Here it has never been raised'.

In contrast Manners still retained a decided sympathy for the factory workers. On April 18 he had written that

> Mundella has brought in his 9 Hours' Factory Bill: from what I hear I believe that Masters on our side of the House, Herman, Fielden, Tipping, etc . . . will support it; but all the names on the back of it are Radical. I am on the Truck Act Committee. One of the main questions before us is making short payment of wages – i.e. either weekly or fortnightly – compulsory by law; another is applying the Act to Agriculture. What are your opinions on these points? Politically, the march of events is rapid, and the disintegration of the Whig-Radical party is nearly complete . . . A Dissolution is highly probable this summer.

It was with the Hermans and Tippings and Cohens that the immediate future of the Party lay; and Ferrand had already expressed his disapproval. But soon the agricultural depression induced by prairie corn and refrigerated meat was to drive many of his rural friends from Westminster and sometimes from their often ancient estates.

In November Manners was able to send news of their party chief:

> Our last visit was to Hughenden, from which we returned yesterday.
>
> Lady Beaconsfield has made a surprising rally, considering her age; but it was clear that Disraeli regarded her condition as most critical, and my wife was the only lady of the party: the other guests were, for the first 2 nights, Lord Rosebery – for the second, Lord Ronald Gower and Vernon Harcourt. Disraeli is a charming host, and our visit, in spite of atrocious weather, was interesting and pleasant; and I am in hopes that it cheered up a little both host and hostess.

Sending Christmas and New Year greetings, Manners wrote in December of a splendid visit to Oldham:

> The Standard report was very poor. I sent you a local paper which had a really good and faithful report of the speeches: from it you will see that I did not omit all reference to the French Treaty and I wish you had been present to witness the Lancashire heartiness of the people. Sergeant Spinks actually wept on the stage! So far as I know the Times gave no report at all.
>
> I went over several of the principal works in the place, among them Platt's Machine Works, which are gigantic, employing 7000 men and boys. The Chairman of our meeting showed me a new spinning shed he had erected, which covered all but 2 acres.

Lord John had now assumed the mantle of Oastler and Ferrand as a Tory apostle to industrial workers, finding a worthy new paternalistic 'feudalism' among some great manufacturers. It was he who had reported on Disraeli's triumph at Edinburgh in 1867 and the great Crystal Palace gathering which followed, when 'the Working Men spoke out, literally and metaphorically, every seat was filled and nothing occurred to mar the success'. Poor deaf Ferrand missed such fruits of his long labours.

III

In August 1873 Ferrand visited Edinburgh and Erskine, returning home on the 11th to open the shooting season next day. But the ritualistic pleasure ended on the 26th: 'my last day, attacked with Bronchitis and only survived after a long illness'. The tough, resilient, athletic frame was at last weakening.

Through the late summer of 1873 Ferrand hovered between life and death at St. Ives and, when he recovered, a long convalescence abroad seemed advisable to restore his strength. His 'affectionate and joyful Friend' Manners wrote from Sandbeck in October:

> The sight of your handwriting, even in pencil, was indeed a delight and gratification to us. Most thankful are we to know from such good authority that you are on the highway to recovery, and are daily regaining strength. Thank God we do for this great mercy. I am greatly relieved to hear that Monaco is substituted for Palermo, which sounds a very far off place. A winter on the shore of the Mediterraean will, I hope and believe, complete your cure, and you will come back to enjoy life in discharging its duties.

He wondered whether to visit Ferrand, after staying at Raby, and added:

> Everyone here rejoices to hear of your recovery, and Lady John (please, dear Mrs. Ferrand, don't read this) sends you her love, and her command that you obey your doctor and your wife in all that appertains to your health.

But Ferrand only ventured downstairs on the 19th and outside on the 23rd. Manners regretted not seeing him: 'Goodbye, my dear friend, and may all prosper and go well with you and yours!' On the 24th the Ferrands went to London, on the 28th to Boulogne, on the 29th to Paris and on the 31st to Marseilles. Still travelling slowly, they reached Nice on 3 November, Monaco on the 5th, San Remo on the 7th, Nice again on the 8th and finally hired a villa at Nice on the 22nd. The worried Manners noted the 'hardships and annoyances' of house-hunting and rejoiced that 'you have borne them well and are at last comfortably established', cheerily noting among his own news a good dinner at Ipswich, where the first Tory mayor and a Roman Catholic priest attended.

A long exile in Nice, away from shooting, hunting and farming, was not a pleasing prospect to Ferrand. But Manners sympathetically counselled that

> This winter abroad will, under God's blessing, probably result in your being in a better permanent state of health than you have known for a long time and purge your system of gout . . .

In November Disraeli had gone up to Glasgow to be formally inaugurated as Lord Rector of the University, an office to which he had been elected two years earlier. In a crowded week of festivities he had taken the opportunity to vindicate a full-blooded (and much criticised) attack he had made, in a letter to the Conservative candidate at a by-election at Bath in October, on the Gladstone administration's record of 'plundering and blundering'. The Conservative Party had been pleased by his various Glasgow speeches and Disraeli himself thought it had been 'a great week'. Manners reported on their chief soon after his return to London:

> I saw Disraeli at the Carlton: he looks 10 years younger than he did in the summer, and was in high feather, as well he might be, about his Scottish campaign. One direct fruit of it is Stirling Maxwell's candidature for Perthshire – another my reconciliation with John Blackwood who, under the influence of those marvellous speeches, wrote me a letter which could well be taken as an apology for the unjustifiable portion of the attack on Lothair which I had resented. I asked Disraeli what had struck him most during his week at Glasgow: he at once answered the torchlight procession of the students: 700 lads in scarlet gowns waving torches through the streets.

Ferrand, however, remained seriously ill.

'I do not hear much of difficulties between farmers and labourers in these parts', Manners wrote in a New Year's greeting for 1874, 'and am disposed to think that Mr. Arch is losing his influence but the relations between labour and capital generally are certainly assuming a dangerous character.' Later he reported that he was to speak in Manchester Free Trade Hall, staying with Romaine Callendar, a leading manufacturer and Tory convert, at Mouldeth Hall:

> I dread the Trades Union questions which may crop up there. Callendar himself is in favour of the Nine Hours' Bill and Trades' Unions: methinks it will require wary walking.

Manners need not have fretted. Disraeli had refused to form a minority Ministry, was preparing to challenge Gladstone (now Chancellor as well as Premier) to fight his Greenwich seat and was amazed to read on 24 January that Gladstone had dissolved Parliament and promised to abolish income tax. Another General Election battle now loomed with the prospects for the Conservatives better than they had been for over thirty years.

For most of February Ferrand was ill in bed 800 miles away from the political battlefield. But Manners sent him cheering news, between campaigning and voting (at Marylebone, South Derbyshire and the City). By the 4th there were 18 clear gains, though Hare had lost by 210 (from 8500) votes at Bristol. Hare was 'much cut up about Bristol', but Pakington was not surprised to lose Droitwich. 'The vindication of our Reform Bill is now complete', wrote Lord John: 'every class of Constituency has pronounced in our favour'. By the 17th he could write:

> Well – all is over – a clear majority of 50 against Government has induced Gladstone to resign (at least so says the Times this morning) and I suppose

Disraeli will at once be sent for. He has just got into a good house in Whitehall Gardens belonging to the Dowager Duchess of Northumberland, and is ready for all emergencies.

I have not the least idea what he thinks of doing with me, and shall not add to his troubles by expressing the faintest wish on the subject. An incoming Prime Minister is the most miserable of men. You, with your usual kindness, rate my services to the party far too high; but I do look back with pleasure to the work which you and I and others have been able to do outside St. Stephens.

The Working Men, in whom we always believed, have this time come to the front – and even Scotland has shared in the reaction. The discomfiture of the Government in Ireland is a signal act of retributive justice, culminating in Chichester Fortescue's defeat.

Backed by the first Conservative majority since 1841, Disraeli formed a strong Government, with Lord Cairns, the Duke of Richmond, the Marquess of Salisbury (India), the Earls of Malmesbury, Derby (Foreign), and Carnarvon (Colonies), Richard Cross (Home), Gathorne Hardy (War), Sir Stafford Northcote (Chancellor), Ward Hunt (Admiralty) and Manners (Postmaster-General).

By May Ferrand was sufficiently recovered to plan a slow return home. Manners wrote while awaiting a Cabinet meeting in Downing Street:

I am under orders to be in attendance on the Queen at Balmoral on the 25th – but am to be relieved on the 30th by Malmesbury. Politically things are quiet. You will have read with interest the debate on Mundella's Bill. Our compromise of 56 hours is generally accepted, and will, I doubt not, be carried.

I shall chance this to Cannes. My advice is don't come to England till the weather is warmer . . .

But Ferrand was restless, spending two days in Marseilles and finally leaving Nice on the 12th. He travelled by easy stages, only reaching Paris on the 30th where he was again overtaken by illness. He left for Boulogne only on 16 June, arriving in London two days later. After visiting the Local Government Board, he reached St. Ives on the 27th. Still weak, he missed the rent dinner, but on 15 July he could not resist speaking at a Bingley and Morton Tory banquet in the Mechanics' Institute. He recalled Stuart-Wortley's 1835 campaign, the visit of Disraeli and Manners, the Poor Law and Factory campaigns and his part in Derby's Reform Act. But, against wide dissent, he declared it was time to retire. His speech, wrote Manners, was 'vigorous and racy as of old'.

There were echoes of old days in April 1875. On the 3rd, Manners, Ferrand and Joshua Fielden met, amidst heavy rain, at Todmorden, to unveil a monument to John Fielden and attend a memorial banquet. Sam Kydd, the Chartist and Oastlerite veteran, reported:

It was gratifying to see Mr. Ferrand once more in public life, and to hear his voice proclaim, not his own services, but those of others who contributed towards the legislative protection of children and women in factories . . .

Ferrand praised 'that worthy patriot', recalling a pathetic march of Manchester workers, headed by crippled children, in 1832. He rejoiced at having lived to see 'such a glorious day' and declared:

> This, my friends, will probably be the last time I shall appear in public. I am worn-out and nearly done. But may the blessing of Heaven be sent down upon all residing in the valley of Todmorden; may you all remain united and happy, united to your employers – factory operatives and employers pulling together heart and soul; and may the name of Fielden ever be honoured in the vale of Todmorden . . .

But memories lingered long. 'Todmorden quite did for me and ended in a fit of gout', wrote Manners:

> I tried to persuade Joshua Fielden to let me say something handsome of Shaftesbury, but found, if I did, he would break out in abuse; so thought it best to maintain a strict silence.

Later in the year bronchitis struck Ferrand again, and in November he was 'dangerously ill for some time'. When the news came of the Dowager Lady Blantyre's death, Ferrand could not leave his sick bed, but he subsequently erected a little monument on the estate in which he recorded among other things that

> In 1857 St. Ives was altered and enlarged from plans entirely drawn by herself, and her daughter, the Hon[ble] Mrs. Ferrand. The Terrace and its flower gardens were also designed by them.

Manners sent condolences and wrote of 'anxious times'. Ferrand's life was quieter now: selecting a new butler or hearing from Manners was a major event. Politics itself was unexciting. 'Political life at present is very still and dull', wrote Lord John during the 1876 session:

> even the thanks to the Ashantee Force last night in our House was decorously lugubrious; and the division on Sir W. Lawson's motion to reduce the Army by 10,000 men, showed how completely, for the present, the Radical party is cowed.
>
> I say for the present, for experience teaches me that such depression is not likely to be lasting . . . I expect in a year or two to see party fights recommenced on a vigorous and exciting scale.
>
> Finance seems to me the rock ahead for us. Science points one way: the predilections of the Party, including myself, another – and I fear the result will not be satisfactory . . .

But Ferrand could still occasionally be stirred into action. In February 1877 Lord Coleridge sent two Walworth poachers to 6 weeks' hard labour, but refused prosecution costs with the banal remark that

> The law ought undoubtedly to be enforced, but, as the law protected the amusements of rich people, they must pay for its enforcement.

This was a monstrous doctrine, coming from a Lord Chief Justice, and an infuriated Ferrand instantly exploded into print, over the signature of *Fiat Justitia*. 'Sir', he wrote to the *Yorkshire Post*,

> There is no wonder that gamekeepers and policemen are murdered when Chief Justice Coleridge only punishes ruffians armed with bludgeons who commit midnight robbery on game preserves by the lenient sentence of six weeks imprisonment, and then refuses the prosecution's costs because he is 'rich', under the plea that he 'was only following the dicta of eminent judges'.
>
> I am on the verge of three score years and ten, and don't remember any such 'dictum' by any judge except that of his lordship's father whose public announcement as Northern circuit judge was always followed in the game season by desperate night attacks on game preserves and murderous assaults on gamekeepers when resisted, the ruffians looking upon him as their patron judge, who sympathised with them and would let them off easily if they were tried by him.
>
> One of these cases occurred at Templenewsam, when the head keeper was killed. The prisoners were tried at York by the late Judge Coleridge and were found guilty. Mr. Meynell-Ingram was bound over by the magistrates to prosecute, and on his counsel applying for costs, Lord Chief Justice Coleridge's father refused them with the 'dictum', 'If Mr. Meynell-Ingram chooses to preserve game, he must pay for it'.
>
> The 'dictum' was celebrated by a pothouse song, called 'The Poacher's Judge', the chorus to which was:
>
>> Damn Meynell-Ingram and his keepers,
>> From them we will not budge;
>> And here's a health to Lord Coleridge,
>> For he's the poacher's judge.
>
> Not long after Mr. Justice Coleridge's 'dictum', a midnight attack was made on Lord Harewood's game preserves, with another murderous attack on the keepers; some of the gang were caught, tried at York Assizes and found guilty. On counsel applying to the judge for the costs of prosecution, he said 'I think it right to inform your lordship that Mr. Justice Coleridge refused Mr. Meynell-Ingram's costs in a similar prosecution'. On this occasion the judge's 'dictum' was, 'Of course Lord Harewood will have his costs; Lord Harewood has as much right to have justice in this court as the poorest subject in Her Majesty's realms'. Such was the 'dictum' of an impartial judge.
>
> I do not know who the prosecutor is in the case tried at the Durham Assizes, before Lord Chief Justice Coleridge, on Friday last; but this I know – he has been deprived of his 'right to have justice' by that judge, because he is 'rich': and were I in his place I would require my representative in Parliament to call the attention of the Home Secretary to the 'dictum' of this eminent judge, and ask if he approves of a 'rich' prosecutor being deprived of his 'right to justice' and fined in the costs of the prosecution because 'the law protected the amusements of rich people'.

It was a brilliantly withering argument.

Sir Charles Legard and Lord Middleton raised the matter in Parliament, when Cross was reduced to quoting a letter from Coleridge bluntly declaring that he was not accountable to the Commons. *The Times* asserted that Parliament must have some control and, more correctly, stressed the need for equal justice.

In June of that year Hugo was again ill. Ferrand hurried to London and stayed with his poor, demented son until his death on the 24th. His only child by Fanny, since 1865 the ostensible but clearly incompetent heir to St. Ives, had spent most of his 29 years in assorted asylums. The death of their rarely-seen child, whom both parents dearly loved, must have been heartbreaking; Ferrand was now left with only a permanently estranged daughter. He saw his last hope of perpetuating an ancient line lost. Johnson and his son meanwhile bought some land at Bingley, in anticipation of Ferrand's fifth will (dated 29 August).

IV

In 1879 Fanny was seriously ill and 'made herself worse by staying out of bed for her prayers'. An economic depression was gathering, at least in the countryside, and the Ferrands subscribed to a local distress fund; Ferrand bluntly ascribed it to Free Trade. Signing himself '*Pro Bono Publico*', he thundered in the *Yorkshire Post* against 'this one-sided, take-all and give-nothing trade', for 'instead of England "dragging the world in her wake", the world was dragging England through her bankruptcy courts'. He demanded an official inquiry.

Ferrand was too concerned about Fanny during February to notice much else, but in the end she recovered sufficiently to let Ferrand fish in Scotland from March. '70 years old!', he wrote on 26 April. 'Thank God for all His mercies through the ages of man.'

In February 1880 Lilla, having broken with her husband, very contritely asked Manners to try to effect a reconciliation. Lord John gently and emotionally put the matter to Ferrand, excusing himself as a 'true and attached friend'. In reply, Ferrand appreciated the 'beautifully expressed letter': no-one but Manners 'could write such feeling language, and no-one could influence him under the circumstances like [Manners]'. He would not 'oppress [him] with a long history of domestic misery', but recalled warning Lilla and that 'she would not even speak to me'. He 'was not surprised at the present state of affairs, for her temper was dreadful':

> Now, since the time she extinguished my authority over her, and affection for her, I have not borne her the slightest unkind feeling and I am sorry for her sufferings, as I should be for any person under similar painful circumstances.
>
> She caused constant misery in her Father's house before she left it, and now that she is suffering the same in that of her own selection, I have too vivid a remembrance of the past, and am too old willingly to allow her to make my happy, peaceful home wretched again.
>
> If it is any consolation to her to know that her Father forgives her conduct

towards him, I do so thoroughly, but all approach on my part must there cease, nor be allowed on hers.

I thank you most heartily for your kind expressions of regard for me. Your Friendship has been one of the chief sources of my happiness for nearly 40 years, and not to yield to your wishes is most painful to me.

When Johnson went to Kelso in March, Ferrand stayed at home to prepare a codicil to his will and to vote in the election called by Disraeli, lulled into optimism by Edward Clarke's surprising gain at Southwark in February. Ferrand supported Denison and Lascelles at Bingley and Lord Frederick Cavendish and 'Sam Lister' at Allerton. Only the ill-fated Cavendish (Ferrand's first Whig choice) succeeded, in the North West Riding. And Gladstone was swept into power once more.

CHAPTER TWELVE

The Close of an Era

At 71 Ferrand was much weakened, very deaf and sadly divorced from his long involvement in public life. He retained his obsessional determination to protect his inheritance from all assaults. He was fortunate enough to have the resources of physical stamina and personal finance to continue a sporting life, though the white-bearded septuagenarian could now rarely follow the hounds. As a man delighting in his ancestry – and, indeed, sharing James Fox-Lane's eighteenth-century pride in belonging to 'one of the very few old English families, a commoner (not a trader) of high birth and fortune' and reputedly refusing a title himself – Ferrand was bitterly disappointed over his own progeny. His old charisma on so many platforms was gradually forgotten, as friends and enemies died and new controversies arose under a harassed Gladstone Ministry. A new society of millionaire plutocrats and sometimes Tory-supported socialists, of Liberals who actually cared about social reforms and of growing decline among squires, of *fin de siècle* 'new morality' and a brief, classless, Imperialist enthusiasm and stirrings of a class-obsessed form of trade unionism marked the death-pangs of that bucolic and hierarchic system which Ferrand had always enjoyed and defended. Economically pressed by cheap prairie grain and Antipodean and Argentinian meat, the families who had formed Ferrand's House of Commons deserted politics, reduced their paternalistic rôles and eventually were often obliged to sell their beloved manors and acres. Ferrand, situated between Bradford, Bingley and Keighley, was fighting a rearguard action which he could not win against a form of capitalist society which he could only dislike.

I

As if Ferrand had not enough to bear already, in 1880 came a new and painful affliction. At Longshaw in September 1880 there was tragedy: 'keepers ready but I was not right in water works'. There followed days of agony and Ferrand went home, doped with opium, for a gradual recovery under Dr Spencer, who sat with him day and night and refused his offer of £300. Gout and cholera followed, but he was able to look after estate matters, leased water supplies to Bradford at £900 *per annum* for 999 years and followed a gathering row between Bingley and Bradford over water supplies, in which he occasionally participated.

As Ferrand suffered renewed bladder trouble (described in horrific detail in his diary), Busfeild recalled his and Ferrand's attempts to stock the Aire with grayling from 1831 and their losing battle against Keighley and Bingley sewage. *The Field* (then subtitled *The Country Gentleman's Newspaper*) observed:

> in justice to Mr. Ferrand it may be fairly said, with regard to this river and its tributaries in the neighbourhood of Bingley and Keighley, that pollution has had no sterner or more determined foe to fight; nor has sport in all its branches, with the hounds, the gun, or the rod, had any more ardent votary. And the heat and burden of seventy-one summers appear to have had no appreciable effect in cooling his ardour, since during the present season we heard of him being on Malham Tarn, deftly whipping for trout, by 3 o'clock in the morning for 3 days in succession. That his patience was only rewarded by the capture of one trout . . . does not detract from his pertinacity.

Busfeild retorted that Ferrand never started before 9 am and caught six trout! Shooting became increasingly uncomfortable for Ferrand. The Bingley water problem continued as did Ferrand's urinary problem.

II

Still painfully ill with 'rheumatic gout in bladder', Ferrand attended the rent dinner on New Year's Day 1881 and delightedly noted 2000 people skating in frozen Bingley, but left Johnson to negotiate an end to the long battle over water supplies. Eventually, a compromise was arranged, by which Bradford yielded the St. Ives springs to Bingley. Thus Ferrand's old control over supplies was ended and the town authorities assumed responsibility. There were further sadnesses during the year. Disraeli died in April, 'Emmie' Busfeild (after giving birth to a baby) and Lilla's 16-year-old son, the paralysed Wilfrid Hailstone in July, and Walker Busfeild of Northfield in December. Emma's husband William was to become the Ferrand heir: he already had one son William, aged 8, and now the baby Guy.

Ferrand mourned 'Dizzy', 'thanked God for all his mercies on his 72nd birthday', fished at Morland and bought horses at Penrith. Back at home in August he was again in pain until passing a stone. He added a codicil to his will and acted as godfather to the baby Guy Busfeild. That Christmas he distributed many gifts and gave a local tea-party. 'Thank God for all his mercies,' he wrote on 31 December. 'Spared over another year.' He was to be spared several more, battling against a variety of recurrent complaints but never giving up for very long his sport (now mainly shooting and fishing), his social life, and holidays with Fanny in various parts of England, Scotland and Wales. Inevitably old friends and relatives died around him in steady procession. One great loss was Johnson Busfeild, his brother, who died of angina in 1882. Apart from their temporary coolness over Lilla, Johnson had been a lifelong companion. Solicitor, treasurer of the old Bradford Court of Requests and of the county court, he had supported and recorded Ferrand's career and produced the family hagiography.

At the end of 1883 Ferrand once more took Fanny to France, though he himself returned in January 1884. Manners had urged him to winter in Pau:

> Where can you be better? To come back now into our fogs and rain and cold would be bad for you, and the journey contemplated by dear Mrs. Ferrand appals me.

The Close of an Era

> I am rather inclined to think with you that the Egyptian muddle may afford Gladstone a not unwelcome excuse for postponing Reform.

But Ferrand energetically sought salmon – and even hunted at Bingham.

As Ferrand's health further deteriorated, Manners advised him 'to be very prudent as to shooting and fishing and not over-exert yourself'. Later he confided that

> We shall, no doubt, have a hard and disagreeable time of it until the next election, but I think Gladstone's star is no longer in the ascendant, and his failures are too numerous and patent to be hid even in the cloud of his oratory.

But politics were now far away from Ferrand's life. He took no notice of the Third Reform Act in 1885, giving the vote to the rural workers, or of the general election. His relative W.E. Surtees, the only other surviving grandson of John Ferrand, wrote to him that

> Both Disraeli's and Gladstone's lowerings of the franchise have been dangerous. I question whether Gladstone (notwithstanding his cunning) is now in his right mind.

'Gladstone preserves his fluency and his cunning: but I think his mind is now, and has been latterly, off its balance', insisted the old Tory, 'and he has become the most dangerous man to every established interest of the country.'

In 1887, though he had ignored the conflict within the Liberal Party over Home Rule and the victory of the Conservative Party under Lord Salisbury the previous year, Ferrand led the celebration in Bingley of the Queen's Jubilee. In March the following year came the death of the Duke of Rutland. He had been one of Ferrand's dearest friends and a generous host at Belvoir and his other country houses. He left Ferrand 'the large screen in the Smoking Room' and Lord John Manners now succeeded as 7th Duke of Rutland. By the autumn Ferrand was too frail to shoot regularly. Then, in March 1889 when he was hoping to travel on to Scotland, he was taken seriously ill while at Morland, the little property in Westmorland belonging to his nephew and heir William Busfeild, and insisted on returning to St Ives. There, amid his memories and mementoes, surrounded by his beloved acres, he died at 5.30 am. on Sunday, 31 March, a month short of his 80th birthday and four days after his old opponent, John Bright.

III

The passing of the deaf old squire, sincerely mourned by a still wide circle of friends from dukes to labourers, marked the end of an era in the Aire valley. Rutland told William Busfeild that 'he has left his mark for good on the social legislation of the century'. But beyond Airedale Ferrand was scarcely remembered by journalists recording the life of Bright. And obituaries tended to be written from partisan political viewpoints. Thus Tory journals would recall 'Young England' days and the battles for factory legislation, against Truck and the New Poor Law and for a range of social reforms. And Liberals would recount tales of 'Madcap Ferrand's' 'friendlessness' at Westminster over the Mott affair or the 'Tory Conybeare' angered by Members emptying the House as he attacked Milner Gibson; he was 'the greatest bore in the House . . . a violent Protectionist and the hero of some stormy scenes with Sir Robert Peel, Sir James Graham and Mr. Cobden'. *The Times* merely carried a two-line death notice.

Local commentators were similarly divided. Keighley Liberals thought that Ferrand belonged 'to the Miocene and Pliocene formations of English political life', that he was a feudalistic reactionary hankering after 'condescending patronage on the one hand and respectful subservience on the other'. 'And yet', they grudgingly admitted,

> with all his strength of will bordering on obstinacy, his love of litigation, his stern upholding of the Game Laws and his reluctance to allow the public a share in the beauties with which nature had endowed his seat, Mr. Ferrand has some claim to be remembered by the working classes for his efforts to protect children from the unnatural labour to which they used to be sent while in the years of mere infancy.

They talked of 'the party of inaction', while local Tories recalled 'the Tory and country party's' work for the Ten Hours Act – 'the most beneficent act of legislation that ever adorned our statute book'. Ferrand 'was the last survivor of the noble band of true philanthropists who headed that movement'. And 'if he had been living now as he was in his prime, what a tower of strength he would have been to the Fair Traders of the present day'. He had lived to see the Bradford worsted masters lose faith in free trade.

Stories of Ferrand were legion. To Liberals his vigilance against local authorities and conservation of water, the Druids' Altar and Goit Stock earned 'a respect that had no kinship with affection'; on the bench he was 'just rather than merciful'; he had offered his former poaching partner Jack Clayton the choice of 'listing for a soldier' or imprisonment. Certainly, he had abolished Truck, but 'the Bull of Bashan' went in for heated invective; he could turn a fine phrase, but was a 'rough old Tyke'. He was 'a survival of an old order of things', a tactless 'champion of the yeoman class'; and one Swire Smith claimed that he had confessed that 'Mr. Bright was right, and we were wrong' over Free Trade – an unlikely tale. Yet even opponents grudgingly acknowledged 'his stalwart frame, his resonant voice and his dauntless courage'. Indeed, 'his qualities were all of a warlike order. He was bold, tenacious and unyielding in strife, and he never asked for, and he seldom gave, any quarter'. He had cost Bradford waterworks many thousands and scarcely had 'a consuming desire to live in peace and friendship with his neighbour'.

Tories recalled his work for factory children, handworkers, paupers and agriculture, his allotments and preservation of the countryside (at considerable financial loss) and his numerous charitable acts. They remembered happy days in George Slicer's Old Queen's Head inn and Ferrand leaving the Commons in 1844, 'remarking cheerfully that he didn't care to sit there when such men were in it'. The Keighley and Bingley benches praised his long service and Fanny replied to Bingley Board that he had always been devoted to the town and regretted that he could not help very much as an old man. He was buried with his ancestors in Bingley church on 4 April. And among the floral tributes was a cross of lilies, ferns and forget-me-nots 'in loving memory of my dear father, from his only child, S. H. Lilla Hailstone'.

Lilla went unrewarded. As was expected, Ferrand left the estate, allegedly producing over £10,000 a year, to William Busfeild of Morland (who took the name of Ferrand); Fanny was to receive £1500 *per annum* and Rutland was left £1000 (which led him to decline to help prove the will). The land was again strictly entailed. All this was very disagreeable to Mrs. Hailstone, who soon entered a *caveat* against the will, already knowing that her husband (who died in March 1890) had cut her out of his £33,000 will.

Fanny erected a little monument in the heather:

> In Bingley cemetery rests William Ferrand of St. Ives . . . In early life he took an active part in support of the ten hours Factory Bill and after seventeen years of ceaseless effort he assisted as M.P. for Knaresborough in carrying it before the House of Commons. He brought under notice the iniquities of the truck system and stringent laws were passed to compel the payment of wages in the current coin of the realm. He vigorously exposed the clauses of the new Poor Law until they were removed from the Statute Book, and he was a firm denouncer of corruption amongst public men.

And then she left, to live in southern France: she died, aged 80, at Cannes on 18 December 1896, living on her £500 capital and £1500 annuity left by Ferrand, together with money intended for Hugo and sums guaranteed under the marriage settlement.

The gross value of personalty was sworn at £11,450, with residuary personal estate held upon trust. St. Ives estate and Bingley Moor passed to William Busfeild, with the proviso that he and his son William Harris were to drop the name of Busfeild and assume that of Ferrand. The family plate and Margaret Ferrand's diamonds were to devolve as heirlooms. Ferrand's other provisions were typical. His 'faithful agent' Walter Middleton received £100, his 'friend and doctor' Herbert Spencer £200, Mary Stuart ('the loving and lovely' daughter of Charles, Lord Blantyre) £100 and the Master of Blantyre £100. His niece Emily received an annuity of £100 while a spinster; his nephew Currer Busfeild had an annuity of £100 and Colonel Busfeild of Upwood received £1000. Every labourer, keeper, watcher and servant was to have £20.

The awful Mrs. Hailstone – whose estranged husband was now dying at Walton Hall – and her ghastly (and also estranged) daughter, Mrs. Etheldreda Carter, opposed probate in the Probate, Divorce and Admiralty Division in March 1890. Lilla argued that Ferrand was of unsound mind when making his will of January 1882 and codicils of April 1882 and January 1887. Mrs. Carter intervened, pleading 'undue influence'. Busfeild was put to great expense, hiring two QCs to conduct the case. Even in death, Ferrand could raise a controversy. But this one was thoroughly unpleasant.

The Busfeild counsel acknowledged that property which 'if capitalised, would perhaps realise about a quarter of million sterling' was at stake: the land paid about £8000 a year. Ferrand was 'a shrewd and clear-headed but very obstinate man', who for 36 years had determined that Lilla 'should not have a shilling of his property'. Before she left his house, he had intended to give her an interest, though he always wished the estate to go to a man – 'he had been heard to say that he did not see what women wanted with money'. The whole wretched story of the family feud was recounted. In every will and codicil from 1853 Ferrand had omitted any mention of his erring daughter. A 'very long statement' obtained from Fanny at Nice in December 1889 was read out, stressing Ferrand's dread of the return of the 'regular firebrand'. Under cross-examination she had described her step-daughter's vain, egoistic hopes, sexual unattractiveness, personal nastiness and silly suicidal threats. Rutland sadly talked of his friend and quoted their correspondence of 1880 about Lilla. 'Was not [Ferrand] rather a bully in his manner', he was asked. 'You will not get that from me', answered John Manners:

> His manner was vigorous, his voice was loud, and his language was strong.
> You may draw your own conclusion from that answer.

William Busfeild's case ended with evidence of Ferrand's 'perfect mental capacity ... throughout his life'.

Johnson's distraught letters of February 1853 were read out, clearly proving that Lilla of her own free will had chosen to leave Harden Grange. The President of the court thought this evidence conclusive, peremptorily dismissed Mrs. Carter's case and declared that cutting a daughter from a will was certainly no sign of madness. He pointed out that Mrs. Hailstone had quarrelled not only with her father, but also with Fanny, her grandmother, her uncle Johnson, her husband, her daughter, her son-in-law and her friends. The special jury agreed: the will and codicils had been duly executed, the testator was of sound mind and no undue influence had been exercised. Busfeild generously waived his costs.

It was a sad business. As one journalist commented, 'there was little or no excuse for raking up the less amiable eccentricities of William Ferrand'. But a jaded *fin de siècle* Press, soon to report in meretricious detail sordid cases of upper-class decadence and scandal, found little to say about the Ferrand affair. The consensus was that so little evidence had been produced that it was 'a little strange that it should have been brought before the Court at all'.

IV

Between the first and second World Wars the great St Ives estate went the way of countless other Victorian landed properties. Its lifeblood had dramatically declined during the great agricultural depression at the end of the nineteenth century. Wool, once selling at up to 9d, fetched 3½d in 1904; mutton had fallen from 10d or 1s. a 1b. to 7½d; and beef from 12s. to about 8s. a stone. And there were many disputes after Ferrand's death with Improvement Commissioners and radical Urban District Councils, which though long and bitter could have only one outcome. Piece by piece the estate was gradually sold off. When Ferrand's heir William died in 1927, only a rump remained and that soon went in 1928. Finally the manor house and park followed and Bingley was left without a resident Ferrand family.

Old Ferrand would have been dismayed by the rapid disintegration and ultimate demise of the estate. That the mansion lovingly planned by Fanny and her mother might become a hydropathic establishment and end as a café, flats and a turf research institution, that the park should become a golf course, that the allotments where Disraeli and John Manners once played should fall to a co-operative company and that the public – the new proprietors – should (until 1936) be charged 2d. or 3d. for sightseeing would have been beyond his comprehension. Yet the 'romance and mystery of St. Ives' and Harden Grange lingered on.

For a time the old squire's memory also remained. Lord Lamington recalled the astonishing performance at Westminster in 1842. And locally there were many recollections. 'Bill o'th' Hoylus End' could recall hearing Ferrand, Oastler and Joe Firth speak on Ten Hours in days when Keighley folk were known as 'th' crooked legged 'uns' after factory accidents. Old Bill remembered an Addingham case, where an outraged father assaulted a caretaker and took his children from a night-working mill; despite Oastler's support, he was fined,

> but Captain Ferrand, who had been disgusted with factory oppression, assisted in taking the case further. The upshot was that the manufacturer was fined. Captain Ferrand's interest in the relief of the poor was deep and abiding, and he did a great and mighty work in connection with the factory laws.

Bill discounted Radical claims that Ferrand's 'work was dominated by political expediency rather than by pure humane feelings':

> The captain was a stern disciplinarian but, under a rough exterior, Bill was sure there beat a warm heart for the weal of the poor, and especially of pity for those confined so long in factories.

As a boy of 8 during the 1841 Riding election, Bill first saw Ferrand riding through Hoylus End; the squire noted his blue favours amidst a sea of 'Whig' children and threw him 'a big handful of coppers'. And 'from that day, I can say, I have been a Tory'. He considered Ferrand

> a typical English squire . . . He sprang from an aristocratic family, who had ever been loyal to monarchy and country . . . He was a soldier, a civil administrator, an ardent and exceedingly able politician – Tory of course, to the backbone . . . As an agriculturalist he was an enthusiast, and all who had tenancy of land found all well so long as they observed strictly the conditions of their tenancy, but woe to them and to all concerned if they infringed in the slightest degree the iron rule of discipline set down by Mr. Ferrand. In every capacity of life, he was a disciplinarian who could not brook any breach of rule. Poaching and every offence that interfered with the rights of preserve on his estate, called forth prosecution for the offence . . .

He admired Ferrand's courage against 'the roughs' during the Keighley riot of 1852. This had arisen from an incident when a poaching gang beat and tied up Ferrand's keeper Daniel Johnson one Sunday in October. When some men were charged at Keighley a mob collected, Ferrand and Johnson were besieged in a shop, the Riot Act was read and 140 troops of the 21st Regiment arrived from Bradford. 'It was', said a local account, 'a case of one brave man and a mob.'

Halliwell Sutcliffe was equally perceptive about Ferrand's personal bravery during the Chartist troubles of 1848. 'The bonniest highway in the Dales, some say, is the road that runs from Harden down to Bingley', he wrote,

> a road that is noteworthy also for two houses that lie scarce a stone's throw from each other on either hand the way. St. Ives, hidden among the trees that crown the hill-crest yonder, recalls instinctively the old-world sportsman who lived and died there – that bluff, hard-hitting Squire of Bingley whose memory, green amongst us yet, takes us backward to the days when sport was the one vital interest of the parish, and to hunt the fox was accounted a merrier game than weaving fleeces into cloth ...

He recalled 'many pithy tales' of Ferrand's sporting exploits – of his hounds, misled by an old dog, rampaging through a butcher's shop and of 'the mighty hunt' which

> started a fox at Bingley, a mile down the valley, and chased him hell-for-leathers up the Vale of Aire and brought him to a reckoning in the middle of Skipton town – ten miles as the crow flies, but somewhat further as the fox-brush trails.

He deliciously recollected the Chartist alarm in Bingley church in 1848:

> the old Squire, for all his robust qualities, had an eye for spectacular effect, and he grasped the occasion promptly as affording just one of those romantic backgrounds which his friend D'Israeli delighted in. Leaning impressively over the pew-front, the Squire looked down on the devout yeomen who were seated underneath. 'To arms, my men! To arms!', he cried, with magnificent effect.

Sutcliffe fairly 'summed up' that

> Staunch in his hatreds, kindly and keen in friendship, straight-running whether friend or foe were to be met, 'the old Squire' stands yet as a type of the true Yorkshire landowner. They knew him well in Haworth parish, and if you ask the moor folk what they thought of him, they'll answer guardedly, 'He war a staunch 'un! Ay, he war a staunch 'un'. And that means more in moorland parlance than one could get into a page of print.

It was no bad obituary.

Lord Cranbrook reminisced about Ferrand's turbulent election campaigns 'in those stormy times [when] all was thought fair in the war of politics'. And one Jabal Barrett recalled (in 1908) that some forty years previously he and other boys used to swim in Coppice Pool before St. Ives awoke and while the family was at church. One Sunday Ferrand missed church and found the lads in his pond. Ferrand angrily ordered them out and when they refused sent 'old Haigh' out in a boat for them. The lads overturned the boat:

> Mr. Ferrand, who was always ready to forgive almost anything but cowardice, at once burst into a hearty laugh, and calling to the boys to come out, he promised to forgive them. On their coming to the shore their clothes, which had been hidden by Haigh, were restored to them, and Mr. Ferrand gave each of them a shilling on their promising not to repeat the offence.

There was much nostalgic affection in local people's memories. Later writers were inclined to be less sympathetic – and much less knowledgeable.

V

Ferrand had fought valiantly for his beliefs, from youth to old age. His work for the ten hours day in the textile industries, against Truck and the 1834 Poor Law, for workers' compensation and against the dreaded cotton-dust disease, byssinosis, were important. For a man who served in Parliament for only nine years his achievement was considerable. His work outside Parliament was also highly successful, in the Factory Movement, for Oastler's liberation, in latter-day Protectionist agitations and in helping to create the new Conservative Party. He had courage and astounding stamina, and in sheer invective he could hold his own against any opponent in or out of the Commons. Certainly, he made enemies. When he attacked Cobden, George Byng told the victim:

> Don't trouble yourself about him. I have been in the House for 50 years, and no such ruffian has been here before in my time.

Or so Bright (who 'did not trouble himself with what Mr. Ferrand might say') told Garth in 1867. And Liberals alleged 'corruption and debauchery' at the 1865 Devonport election – which was considered in Stonehouse county court, Exchequer Chamber and the Commons. At his last contest Ferrand was chosen by the modern method – a selection committee reporting back to the democratic constituency council.

At home Ferrand was a stern but just magistrate. An obstinate drunkard in the Busfeild Arms at Morton was fined 10s, a swearing policeman £1, a Keighley drunkard who broke windows £1.5s, with £3.15.10 costs, other drunks 5s. or 2s.6d, and innkeepers were regularly cautioned. A fraudulent beggar went to prison for ten days, as did two Keighley prostitutes; a wife-beater was sentenced to four months' hard labour and another to six months; a man who stole a coat received a two-month sentence. Being asleep in charge of a cart brought a 5s. fine, trespass a total (fine, damages and costs) of £4.14s. As Ferrand asserted,

> Three-fourths of the crime in this land arises from the consequences of getting too much beer, and it is a fearful thing for men to get a livelihood and get money by supplying them with too much beer.

But he also dealt with poachers, assault, 'unnatural crime', blocking a sewer and assaults on the police.

Throughout his life the squire was on easy terms with working people – agricultural labourers, northern factory operatives and Devonport dockyardmen alike. When 2559 dock workers presented him with 'an elegant silver Grecian vase' in 1860, it was 'as a token of their high esteem for his untiring exertions to promote the welfare of the working classes generally'. He was 'ever in the van when a patriotic duty was to be discharged', observed the *Intelligencer* in 1861, noting 'with pleasure' his 'very excellent dinner' for the Keighley Volunteers:

> Nothing is better calculated to maintain the *esprit de corps* than for volunteers, officers and men, to mingle together on such occasions . . . Such unions bring them into closer connection with each other and kindle those feelings of emulous companionship which form so great a mainstay to the movement.

From the celebrated allotment dinner of 1844 onwards Ferrand enjoyed and provided such repasts.

Ferrand was undoubtedly litigious. He could not bear to be cheated, nor could he endure Whig corruption and bullying, such as Somerset employed after the Totnes election of 1863, when he evicted Tory tenants. Over game and manorial rights he was adamant, and when the two issues arose together he was prepared to brave much Liberal hostility to maintain his claim.

Ferrand undoubtedly hated the Manchester School, with its sedulous pursuit of wealth. The 'Cobden treaty' of 1860 with France was anathema, and the proposal of 1861, to 'grow cotton for the British and French cotton spinners with Chinese slaves and Manchester money' in Algeria, he bitterly condemned from Paris, quoting mainly French sources and *The Times*. 'Cotton' was indeed 'The Soul of Slavery' – white, black and yellow – and even in his later years, when he preached reconciliation, Ferrand could never forgive or forget the horrific industrial conditions which he had helped to expose. It is increasingly fashionable to deny their existence; but they were real enough to some generations of factory operatives. The argument that the squires passed the Factory Act in 1847 in revenge for the repeal of the Corn Laws in 1846 or simply to harm brash entrepreneurial rivals is simplistic nonsense. Men do not spend a lifetime advocating causes in which they do not honestly believe. Some backwoods squire may have cast his vote on 'class' grounds – though the tradition of paternalism undoubtedly affected many – but a Ferrand, an Oastler, a Manners, who toiled and sacrificed for no gain to themselves for what they believed to be morally right, was no self-seeking party hack. *Noblesse oblige* is an easily derided concept; but in the fight against the Poor Law it was a valid and honourable attitude. 'Young England' and the Factory Movement, the anti-Poor Law agitation and agricultural Protection, hostility to colonial expansion and to 'exploitation' of workers at home or abroad, a reverence for the past and a desire to improve the present, an intense loyalty to Crown, Church and country, an addiction to traditional ways – social, political and sporting – and a sense of community, as opposed to atomistic Liberal individualism or Benthamite social structuralism, an intense love of the land and an acceptance of the divinely-ordained seasons were the reasonable and intuitive doctrines of the squirearchy. Against the wordy architects of social planning or Peelite administrative efficiency they could express little but apoplectic bluster. Ferrand and his friends were no philosophers. But politics arises from the heart as well as the head; instinct may be more important than transient rationalism. Whether or not Ferrand ever read Burke's *Reflections* of 1790, he acted on Burke's principles.

There were many controversies during Ferrand's stormy career. Sometimes he was unfairly condemned, as in Parliament in 1844, when one sympathiser commented that

> Never was man so pertinaceously persecuted as he has been; never has man found the advocacy of the rights of the poor such up-hill work as he. Belied out of the House, and 'baited' in it, no wonder his words are not precisely the scented articles that are drawled forth amidst the vapid sentimentalities of a drawing-room.

He was occasionally egregiously wrong, despite considerable supporting evidence, through making hasty decisions. At times, he did not fully appreciate the entire background to an issue but Ferrand was generally well briefed, as he showed in his long war with Bradford waterworks. And he was often right, as in the Westbury scandal, and the accusations against Bright and Cobden, and over Mott. Charges that he deliberately sought trouble were unfair, though he certainly knew how to defend himself; a politician unable to rout hecklers would be a poor creature. Devonport politics remained boisterous long after Ferrand had departed. When, in 1888, the Conservative MPs Captain George Price and Sir John Puleston addressed their constituents and blamed incompetent bureaucrats and 'obsolete admirals' at the Admiralty for recent dockyard dismissals,

> the meeting became so uproarious that the two members and their supporters hurriedly left, and the opposition passed a vote of no confidence in the hon. gentlemen.

Ferrand would have held his ground.

At one of his late political appearances, Bingley Conservatives' inaugural banquet of 1874, Ferrand looked back on 48 years' Party work and praised Powell's expertise on

> the great question of the day – sanitary reform – so necessary to be carried out to secure health and prolonged years for all, especially for those living in towns . . .

Fresh from his sick-bed, he recalled the long fight from 1832 to win the Riding, Peel's triumph in 1841, with

> one of the most talented and able Conservative Ministries that ever held the reins of office in this country . . .

and 'Young England's' visit to Bingley, when Disraeli had 'fore-shadowed the political principles which he had adhered to from that day to this'. He praised Disraelian Toryism's attitudes to allotments, Truck, the Poor Law, factory reform and the extension of the franchise – in which he claimed a modest part, following his interview with Derby. But, he insisted,

> it was high time for him to retire from public life. He had had a severe ordeal to pass through during the last twelve months. He had had a most active life as a public man – perhaps few men in England more so. It had pleased God to restore him to health, with the exception of his former strength, which he believed was returning steadily. He was glad to appear that night in his own native town, for he felt proud of old Bingley. When they commenced the battle in 1834 Lord Morpeth stated, at Keighley, that he had travelled through the West Riding and there was not a Tory who dared to show his face. He wished some of the Liberals who in those days, and for a long time since, had ridiculed the idea of the Conservative reaction were in that room that night. He was convinced that Conservative principles were sinking into the hearts of the people of this country. They had had a great deal of sham Liberalism for a number of years – great professions with very little practice – but he believed they had now got into power and office men who had the real interests of their country at heart, who did not wish to hold office from selfish motives, but who were anxious to see all ranks and all classes in this country cemented and united in the bonds of peace, friendship and harmony.

Before this swansong Ferrand had often faced abrasive and grossly unfair treatment. For instance, at Devonport in February 1863, he reasonably complained that, while he had 'never . . . offensively alluded to his honourable and gallant opponent' (Grey) he had been personally 'assailed . . . by foul calumnies and deliberate false-hoods'. Trouble certainly dogged his political peregrinations, but he did not really seek it, while certainly never fearing it.

Ferrand was brought up as a loyal Churchman and remained a staunch Anglican throughout his life. He was content with the plain order and dignity of Cranmer's prayer books, as loved and cherished by three centuries of his forefathers. Neither Evangelical 'enthusiasm' nor the Tractarian ritual espoused by Manners and Gladstone held any charm for him. Religion inevitably impinged upon politics during Ferrand's career; but it never affected his friendship with the Roman Catholic Talbots or with local dissenting preachers. Defence of the Church led him also to protect corporations associated with it, such as endowed schools and charities, often anciently-established with abstruse legal provisions encrusted with the accretions of centuries. Erastian radicals sought to destroy or 'reform' such time-honoured institutions. The issues – as Trollope showed – were complex. But Ferrand saw spoliation of property – particularly the desecration of Church-connected property, English or Irish – as a thoroughly odious proceeding to be fought to the end.

Ferrand had a keen eye for a pretty girl throughout his life. He always included in electoral effusions some cheery reference to the ladies – whether inhabitants of downtown Devonport or matriarchs of bourgeois villas. He might condemn Somerset, but he long remained friendly with his Duchess – that lovely Lady Seymour who had been the 'Queen of Beauty' at the Eglinton Tournament. After his marriage to the equally beautiful Fanny there was no hint of sexual scandal, in days when such affairs were notorious among even the most prominent politicians.

Sport was Ferrand's fetish. Hunting – for the sheer exhilaration of the chase – shooting and fishing (strictly for the pots of his friends and himself) were increasingly obsessional recreations. He did not approve of those massive and pointless slaughters in which Prince Albert indulged and which so shocked Tory sportsmen. The *battue*, with its senseless killing of huge numbers of birds and animals for some strange bloodlust, was anathema to the squires – and to the Press and public. He was a splendid shot, a renowned rider and a patient fisher. He was proud of his moorland achievements, but never approved of wholesale carnage. For he was, in his way, a pioneer preserver and ecologist. And he was a stickler for the game and fishing laws and traditions. His hunting prowess was widely acknowledged – with Bingley harriers, the Bramham Moor, the North Craven and the Belvoir.

Ferrand was not the dour, semi-literate lout of Radical slander. He owned some fine paintings, a respectable (subsequently broken-up) library and a cherished assortment of family memorabilia. He was never a betting man (apart from small stakes on country-house card games) and rarely visited races. He travelled widely throughout the United Kingdom and western Europe. His education was desultory, through sheer lack of funds; but he was accepted as a dear friend by Etonians and dukes. His accent was undoubtedly Northern; but that obviously mattered less (except to Whigs) in his day than subsequently. He enjoyed society. As an inveterate early-riser, he seems to have gone to bed soon after dinner. The sheer tedium of country-house life after nightfall might briefly be relieved by the circulation of the port decanter, a game of cards or guessing the answers to topical riddles. What survives of his collection of this curious Victorian pastime is hardly likely to arouse much hilarity today. It is not surprising that Victorian squires retired early.

Ferrand's life witnessed the first three Reform Acts, the development of gas lighting, the telegraph and the penny post, a huge industrial expansion, agriculture's golden years and depression, the reformation of education, the largely-accidental but increasingly-determined creation of the Empire upon which 'the sun never set', the creation of a massive railway network, the real start of socialism, the growth of arrogant quasi-'democratic' local authorities and at long last the demise of the Whigs. 'The Working Man's Friend' remained to the end a thoroughgoing Tory. The most-travelled Ferrand since Hugo Ferrant, the founder of the family fortunes, took part in the twelfth-century Crusades to the Holy Land, he kept his deepest love for his cherished acres.

Note on Sources

It does not appear that Professor Ward compiled a Bibliography for his life of J.B. Ferrand. Nevertheless, the set of footnotes and references he assembled for each chapter provides a comprehensive survey of the sources he used. Indeed, even allowing for the larger scale of the work he planned, his annotations were unusually full. They occupy 130 pages of typescript, comprising over 2,300 separate footnotes, most of which cite more than one source. Many of these footnotes take the form of brief biographies of the persons mentioned in the text. Even if these were omitted, however, what is left would still be out of proportion to the present shortened version of the text. Any process of selection or compression offered serious editorial difficulties and in any case it was doubtful whether such an elaborate scholarly apparatus would be required by the majority of readers. A more radical solution seemed preferable: namely, to deposit the original text, together with the accompanying footnotes and references, in the library of Strathclyde University where they will be available to students and researchers; and to provide here only a general indication of Ward's range of sources.

What gave his book its special flavour and originality was his intensive use of two particular categories of historical information. The first comprises various collections of Ferrand family papers, including the diaries of W.B. Ferrand. The other is the accounts of Ferrand's activities given in local newspapers and to a lesser extent in the national press. The variety of these periodicals attests to the extraordinary thoroughness of Ward's research as well as to the wealth of provincial newspapers available in this period.

A. THE FERRAND PAPERS

(Names and abbreviations appearing in brackets are those used by Ward in his footnotes).

(a) *J.A. Busfield, Fragments relating to the History of Bingley Parish* (privately printed, Bradford, 1875). Johnson Atkinson Busfeild, a younger brother of W.B. Ferrand, was the family historian. The original MS is in the possession of Mr D.F. Ferrand.

(b) *Ferrand MSS (C.M.M.)*. Formerly in the Cartwright Memorial Museum, Bradford. Now in the possession of the West Yorkshire Archive Service, Bradford.

(c) *Ferrand MSS (Y.A.S.)*. In the possession of the Yorkshire Archaeological Society, Leeds. They include W.B. Ferrand's diaries for 1843 and 1847–89. The whole collection is described by Sylvia Thomas in her *Guide to the Archive Collections of the Yorkshire Archaeological Society, 1931–83*. A catalogue is available on application to the Society.

(d) Ferrand MSS (Milnathort). Formerly in the possession of the late Mr and Mrs Ferrand of Tillywhally, Milnathort, Kinross.
(e) Ferrand MSS (Oving). Formerly in the possession of the late Col. G. Ferrand of Oving Manor, Sussex.

Grateful acknowledgement is made on behalf of the late Professor J.T. Ward by the editor and publisher to the owners of all these papers for allowing them to be used.

B. NEWSPAPERS AND PERIODICALS

(a) *Provincial*
Bingley Chronicle
Bingley Herold
Bingley Telephone
Blackburn Standard
Bolton Chronicle
Bradford Chronicle
Bradford Courier
Bradford Herald
Bradford Observer
Bucks Herald
Coventry Standard
Coventry Times
Devonport Independent
Devonport Telegraph
Doncaster Chronicle
Halifax Guardian
Huddersfield Chronicle
Huddersfield Examiner
Huddersfield Weekly News
Keighley Herald
Keighley News

Leeds Intelligancer
Leeds Marcury
Leeds Patriot
Leeds Times
Liverpool Mail
Liverpool Mercury
Liverpool Standard
Manchester Chronicl
Manchester Courier
Manchester Guardian
Nottingham Guardian
Plymouth Mail
Preston Chronicle
Sheffield Independent
Stockport Advertiser
Wakefield Journal
Western Morning News
Western Weekly
York Gazette
Yorkshire Post

(b) *London and Scotland*
The Age
Bell's Life
Bell's Weekly Messenger
Courier
Dundee Advertiser
Edinburgh Advertiser
Edinburgh Evening Courant
Glasgow Saturday Post
Globe
Illustrated London News
John Bull

Morning Chronicle
Morning Herald
Morning Post
Northern Star
Punch
St James's Chronicle
Scotsman
Standard
Sun
The Times

The above lists, while not exhaustive, represent the bulk of the newspaper sources on which Ward drew.

(c) It is not possible to list the general and local histories, monographs, biographies, pamphlets, articles in learned journals, and standard reference works such as Hansard's *Parliamentary Debates*, which Ward as a matter of course also used. These are mentioned in their appropriate places in his footntes and references.

Index

Abbott, Reginald, 152, 153
Aberdeen, Lord, 116
Accidents Act, 136, 139
A'Court, Edward, 82
Addingham, 44, 47, 191
Admiralty Order 1861, 128
Agricultural Protection Society, 92
Agricultural Union, 176
agriculture *see also* Corn Laws : 1851 depression, 9; employment protection, 3; organisation of workers, 176; protection, 5; wages, 4, 176; WBF support for, 30, 94
Ainsworth, Peter, 167
Airedale, 15, 71; Volunteer Rifle Corps, 125
Albert, Prince, 98, 99, 175, 197
alcohol, electioneering, 19
Aldham, William, 62
Alexander, Robert, 113
Allbutt, Thomas, 56
Allotment Bill, 45–47, 48, 50
Almack, John, 35
Alresford, 90
Amalgamated Society of Engineers, 168
American Civil War, 127, 129
Andover, workhouses, 85, 87
Anglicans *see* Church of England
Anti-Corn Law League, Bingley factory masters, 25; complicity in coal strikes, 40, 41; growing strength, 79; objectives, 3; opening of mail, 75; opposition to WBF, 44; petitions, 82; Ten Hours Movement, 62, 78; Tory dislike, 3; WBF attacks on, 33, 34, 35, 54
Arch, Joseph, 176
aristocratic supremacy, 3, 49
Armagh Orangemen, 50
armed forces, 3; flogging, 20, 22
Armytage, Sir George, 41, 50

Ashbourne, 41
Ashley, Lord, 33; 1841 campaign, 28; 1844 Factory Act, 68; character, 12; Dorset conditions, 62; Oastler Liberation Movement, 53; support, 3; Ten Hours Movement, 2, 12, 63, 84; WBF attacks on, 99; Westbury affair, 146
Ashton, 44, 47
Ashworth, Edmund, 30, 43, 44
Atkinson, Dr, 12, 13, 14
Attwood, Mathias, 42, 53
Attwood, Thomas, 42
Augusta of Cambridge, Princess, 55
Auty, Squire, 47, 59, 61, 64; Labour League, 113, 115
Aylesbury, 48, 50; contest, 105–107
Aysey, John, 15

Bailey, Frederick, 38, 41
Bailey, R. S., 55
Baillie, Henry, 49
Baillie-Cochrane, Alexander, 32, 49, 50
Baines, Edward, 63, 146
Baird, Sir David, 93
Baker, Robert, 81
Ball, Edward, 100
Balme, Matthew, 21, 61, 63, 84, 168
Bankes, George, 81, 83, 84; Ten Hours Movement, 87
Banks, George, 21
Bannister, Anthony, 100
Baptists, 7, 17
Baring, Rev. Frederick, 101
Barnard Castle, 13
Barneycott, Robert, 151
Barnsley, 47
Barrett, Jabal, 192
Bateman, Josiah, 86
Bathhurst, Earl, 161
Baxter, George Wythen, 45

Baxter, W.E, 128
Beaufort, Duke of, 116, 161
Beaumont, Sir George, 53
Beckett, Sir John, 22
Beckett, William, 28, 32, 39, 42, 51, 56; Corn Laws, 82; Ten Hours Movement, 62
Beckett-Denison, Charles, 164
Beckett-Denison, Edmund, 26, 28, 94, 171; Factory Movement, 84; opposition to Poor Law, 39
Beckwith, John, 56, 74
Beer, John, 147
Belper workhouses, 44, 73
Belvoir, 49, 122, 155, 167, 187
Belvoir Hunt, 117, 124, 128
Bentham, Jeremy, 4
Bentick, Lord George, 81, 83, 84, 87, 172
Benyon, Richard, 48
Beresford, William, 83
Berkeley, Sir George, 117
Berkeley, Captain Grantley, 66
Bernal, Ralph, 68, 87
Bethell, Richard, 142, 143, 144
Bethell, Sir Richard, Lord Westbury, 106, 107; corruption, 141–145; motion of censure, 146; resignation, 146
Bevor, Henry, 100
Bingley, 14, 15, 16; charitable trustees, 25, 111; Chartists, 91; cricket club, 70; factory masters, 25; grammar school, 24; Rifles, 125; strikes, 104; waterworks, 186
'Bingley Bull,' 140
Bingley Operative Conservative Association, 16
Bingley Tory Association, 167
Birmingham operatives, 36
Birstal, 47
Blackburn, 47
Blackstone, William, 65
Blantyre, Lady, 88, 181
Blantyre, Lord, 53, 88
Boase scandal, 134
Boddington, John, 21
boilers, 136, 139
Bolland, William, 74
Bolton, 47
Book of Bastilles, 45

Borthwick, Peter, 50, 65, 83
Bournemouth, 116
Bovill, William, 142
Bowling Green Inn, 19
Bowring, John, 33, 38, 42; *Great Mott Case,* 87; opposition to WBF, 44, 83, 93
Bradford, 17; 1837 election, 18–22; operatives, 33; Poor Law enforcement, 45; riots, 92; Short Time Committee, 25; waterworks, 135, 138, 141, 195
Bradford Conservative Association, 16, 18
Bradford Corporation Waterworks, 112, 163
Bradford Coursing Club, 50
Bradford Operatives Conservatives, 25, 47
Bradford Waterworks Bill, 168, 171
Bradford Waterworks Company, 25, 133
Bradford Working Men Conservative Association, 154
Bramham Park, 50
bribery, Devonport election, 147, 148, 150–151, 153; elections, 144
Briggs, William, 45
Bright, John, 3, 41, 55, 62; attacks on WBF, 123, 155; Charity Board, 137; death, 187; opposition to Ten Hour Movement, Hours Movement, 68, 82–83, 84, 87, 172; WBF attacks on, 98, 100, 101, 155, 160, 167
Brontë, Charlotte, 103
Brooks, John, 53, 54, 55, 100
Brotherton, Joseph, 35, 62, 84, 100, 168
Brougham, Lord, 96
Brown Cow Inn, 16
Brown, George, 101
Bruce, Henry, 137
Buckingham, Duke of, 33, 105, 163
Buller, Charles, 62, 68, 135
Buller, Sir Arthur, 120, 144
Bunsen, Chevalier, 37
Burdett, Sir Francis, 48
Burroughs, William, 113
Busfeild, Benjamin, 24, 48
Busfeild, Caroline, 75
Busfeild, Currer, 23, 69, 110
Busfeild, Currer Fothergill, 12, 13, 14, 18, 124
Busfeild, Dr, 22, 50
Busfeild, Elizabeth, 12, 124

Index

Busfeild, Emma, 186
Busfeild family, 12, 13, 75, 124
Busfeild, Johnson, 14, 17, 19, 22, 48, 50; coal strikes, 41; death, 186; go-between, 110; relations with WBF, 124; support to WBF, 24, 42
Busfeild, Walker, 186
Busfeild, William, 13, 14, 17; 1841 election, 26; Anti-Corn Law League, 25; Bingley grammar school, 24; Bradford election, 19, 22
Butler-Johnstone, Henry, 153
by-elections, corruption, 147; Coventry, 159–160; Devonport, 127, 144; new protectionist party, 81; Plymouth, 126–127; Stalybridge, 174; West Riding, 15, 79, 80
Byng, George, 193

Caird, James, 97, 132
Cairns, Lord, 173, 180
Callendar, Romaine, 179
Calvert, Frederick, 105, 106
Cameron of Lochiel, Donald, 50
Campbell, Holland, 41
Cape, Lady Caroline, 53
Cardwell, Edward, 84
Carlos, Don, 49
Carlyle, Thomas, 4
Carnavon, Lord, 180
Carr, Lady, 53
Carrington, Lord, 106
Carter, Etheldreda, 189
cartoonists, 67
Castlefields cotton mill, 13
Catholics, 7; 1829 emancipation, 1, 6, 38; anti-catholic feelings, 7; early 19th century policies, 6; idolatry, 61; Ireland, 6–7; Irish immigrants, 7; Maynooth College, 7, 75, 76; Peel's policy, 76; spreading influence, 57; WBF opposition to, 28, 170
Caulke Abbey, 41
Cavendish, Lord Frederick, 184
Cayley, Edward, 53, 93
Cecil, Lord Robert, 143
Central Agricultural Protection Society, 78
Chain and Cables Bill, 132
Chambers, Montague, 152, 153, 166

Champion, Henry, 100
Chandos-Poles family, 41
Charity Board, 136–138
Charity Commission, corruption, 136
Charley, William, 170
Chartists, 1841 election, 28; 1848 violence, 90, 91; attitude to Corn Laws, 34; colliery strikes, 40, 41; co-operation with WBF, 8; demonstrations, 9; Keighley, 28; Labour League, 114; leader, 7; opening of mail, 75; policies, 9; support for WBF, 80; Tory Chartists, 90–91; WBF's attitude to, 9
Chatsworth, 41
Cheetham, John, 150
Chellingworth, Henry, 104
children see factory children
Church of England, 1845 Irish policy, 7; Agricultural Union, 176; attacks on, 3; education, 6, 57; Factory Movement, 84, 86; gentry's attitude to, 5–6; need for reform, 6; Oxford Movement, 7; plots against, 165, 166; rates, 16–17, 26; WBF support, 18, 20, 196
Church of Ireland, appropriation of funds, 15; disestablishment, 170, 171; reform, 6; WBF support, 16
Clarendon, Lord, 104, 147, 173
Clarke, Edward, 184
Clay, Sir William, 119
Clayton, Jack, 188
Clements, Charles, 39, 44, 45
Clerk, Sir George, 82
Cleveland, 2nd Duke of, 53, 93
coal miners, 40, 43
Cobbett, Richard, 53
Cobbett, William, 4
Cobden, Richard, 3, 30, 33, 34; children's night work, 35; employees, 55; Factory Movement, 84; free trade, 44; opposition to WBF, 36, 39, 42; Peel's attacks on, 83; repeal of Corn Laws, 78; treaty with France, 194; Truck system, 73; WBF attacks on, 92, 93, 95, 98
Colborne, Hon. Robert, 27
Colchester, 50
Colchester, Lady, 152, 153
Coleridge, John, 150, 182
Coleridge, Lord, 181

Collier, Sir Robert, 165
Colquhoun, John, 76, 84
Colville, Charles, 41, 48, 50, 51, 56
competition, 5, 156, 166
Complete Suffrage Union, 56
Congregationalists, 7
Conservative Party, 1841 divisions, 5; 1845 Irish policy, 7; 1866 administration, 154; Anti-Poor Law Tories, 5; boroughs, 8; Derby and Disraeli eras, 8; religious attitudes, 6; social concern, 43; Toryism, 161; working men, 8, 16, 47, 125, 156; Young England movement, 5
Constitutional Association, 17
Cooke, Frederick, 103
Copeland, William, 53
Corn Laws *see also* Anti-Corn Law League : 1842 Act, 5, 33; 1846 Corn and Customs Bill, 78–86; campaign for repeal, 25, 26; Canadian corn, 5; Chartist attitude to, 34; Parliamentary motions, 34; repeal, 1, 44, 78–84; WBF support, 20, 34–35, 38–39; Whig policy, 5
corruption, 133; by-elections, 147; Charity Commission, 136; Coventry by-election, 160; Devonport 1865 election, 151; dockyards, 157; Leeds Registry, 142–145; politics, 167; Westbury affair, 141–142
Coryton, Colonel Augustus, 147
Cottingley Bridge, 13, 71
cotton industry, child workers, 11; cotton famine, 128, 129, 168; employment legislation, 2; exports, 3; Indian cotton, 132; Manchester, 33–34; reduction of duties, 38; WBF dislike, 194
cotton lords, 30, 98, 106, 122
cotton-spinners unions, 2, 57
Courtenay, Lord, 85
Coventry by-election, 159–160
Crabtree, Mark, 86
Cranborne, Lord, 145, 146
Cranbrook, Lord, 192
Crawford, Sharman, 30, 32, 39, 42; Factory Movement, 84, 87; Poor Law migration, 44
Crewe, Sir John, 41
Creyke, Ralph, 93

cricket, 70, 71
Crimean War, 116
Cripps, Henry, 171
Cripps, William, 82
Crispin, Commander, 75
Croker, John Wilson, 40, 41
Crompton, Joshua, 93
Cromwell, Richard, 16, 41
Cross, Richard, 180
Cudlip, James, 151
Cullingworth Mills, 163
Cumberland, Duke of, 19
Cunliffe-Lister, William, 18, 21, 26, 28

Dartmouth, Earl of, 171
Dawson, George, 118, 120
De Vesci, Lord, 171
demography, Malthus, 4
Derby, Lord, 8, 108, 158, 173; death, 172; Devonport bribery, 148; dissolution of Parliament, 117; patronage, 158–159
Derby workhouses, 44
Devon, Lord, 158
Devonport, Admiralty influence, 173; bribery, 147, 148, 150–151; campaigning, 152; elections, 117–121, 127–128, 144, 152–153, 164–167; meetings, 132, 139, 144; nullification of election, 151; politics, 195
Devonshire, Duke of, 22, 27, 41, 116, 138, 149
Dewes, Richard, 44
Dick, Quentin, 50, 107
Digby, Kenneth, 49
Disraeli, Benjamin, 1874 government, 180; allotment dinner, 71, 72; anti-Corn Law motions, 34; at Hughenden, 177; cartoon, 67; Chancellor, 109, 117; commiseration to WBF, 107; *Coningsby*, 72; death, 186; Devonport bribery, 148; electoral support, 8; game from WBF, 111; *Great Mott Case*, 65, 66, 69, 87; illness, 173, 174, 179; love of Fanny Ferrand, 116; opposition to Peel on free trade, 81; protectionism, 82, 83, 84, 87; rector of Glasgow University, 179; Reform Bill, 156, 157, 161; religious policies, 76; support for Factory Act, 172; support for WBF, 83, 108; *Sybil*, 5,

72; *The New Generation,* 72; *The Two Nations,* 72; triumph in Edinburgh, 178; WBF association with, 49; WBF support for, 100, 162, 163; WBF wedding, 90; Westbury affair, 146; witticisms, 78; Young England movement, 5, 195

Dissenters, Agricultural Union, 176; Bingley grammar school, 24; church levy, 17; discrimination against, 6; education, 6, 57; entrepreneurs, 21; Whig policy, 6

dockyards, 134, 136; corruption, 157; Devonport, 165; unemployment, 166; wages, 141

Doherty, John, 44
Downshire, Lord, 100, 101, 102
Drummond, Edward, 41, 43, 55, 57
Dublin, 47
Dublin Protestant Operative and Reformation Society, 61
Dudley, 47
Dukinfield, 44
Duncombe, Admiral, 158
Duncombe, Arthur, 48, 100, 104
Duncombe, Octavius, 48
Duncombe, Thomas Slingsby, 28, 39, 65, 75; 1844 Factory Act, 69; opening of mail, 75
duties, 5, 81 *see also* Corn Laws; free trade

East Lothian, 92
Easton, Henry, 48
Ebrington, Viscount, 87
economic depressions, 9, 183; 1837-1841, 2, 4
Edinburgh, 47, 178
Edinburgh Review, 3
Edmunds, Leonard, 141, 142
education, Anglican attitudes, 6; Church of England provision, 57; Dissenters, 24, 57; paupers, 6; reform, 26; state assistance, 6
Edwards, Henry, 56, 102, 158, 168
Egerton, Lord Francis, 62
Egerton, Wilbraham, 158
Eglinton, Lord, 83
Eldon, Earl, 53
elections, 1837, 18–22; 1841, 26–29; 1852, 109–110; 1865, 146–147;

borough politics, 8; bribery, 144, 148, 153; Devonport, 117–119, 152–153, 164–167; electioneering, 19; Liskeard, 133; nullification of Devonport election, 151; WBF campaigns, 192–193

Eliot, Lord, 153
Elley, Sir John, 155
embezzlement, 141–142
emigration, 131
employment legislation *see also* Factory Acts; factory children : 1844 Master and Servant Bill, 69; attitudes, 2; cotton industry, 2; debates, 3; distrust, 3
enclosures, 157
Engels, Friedrich, 158
England's Trust, 49
English, James, 113
Escott, Bickham, 38, 42, 82, 84
Etwall, Ralph, 85
Evangelicals, 7
Evans, General, 22

Faber, Frederick, 49, 155
Factory Acts, 1833 Act, 2, 12, 15, 16; 1843 Bill, 57; 1844 Act, 2, 68–69; 1847 Act, 1, 20, 87; debates, 3; earlier legislation, 2; Royal Commission, 14, 15
factory children, 1833 Act, 15; early legislation, 2, 11; education, 128; northern mills, 43; prohibition, 129; textile industry, 11; WBF's championship of, 11, 16
factory inspectors, 2
Factory Movement *see* Ten Hours Movement
Factory Reformation Society, 15
factory women, 2, 43, 129
Farquhar, Sir Walter, 53
Fawkes, Francis, 22
Ferrand Arms, 51
Ferrand, Edward, 12, 13, 14, 18
Ferrand family, 13
Ferrand, Fanny, *née* Stuart, 88, 90; death, 189; Disraeli's fondness, 116; illness, 90, 108, 124, 153, 161, 183; marriage, 90; pregnancy, 90; relations with stepdaughter, 90, 110
Ferrand, Hugo, 90; death, 183; illnesses, 124, 133, 157, 163, 168

Ferrand, Lilla, Mrs Hailstone, 10, 88, 108; attempts at reconciliation, 183–184; character, 110, 190; departure from home, 110; disinheritance, 189; marriage, 110; relations with father, 124; relations with step-mother, 110
Ferrand, Margaret, 23, 50
Ferrand, Mrs Walker, 21, 48
Ferrand, Sarah (WBF's mother), 12, 13, 18, 48, 124; death, 110
Ferrand, Walker, 13, 14, 29, 50, 110
Ferrand, William (son of WBF), 24, 109; death, 124
Ferrand, William Busfeild, 1844 Leeds speech, 64; accent, 197; aged 50, 121; aged 56, 140; aged 60, 170; aged 71, 185; Anglicanism, 18, 88, 121, 196; assumption of Ferrand name, 24; attitude to women, 196–197; Aunt Margaret, 79, 83; background, 1, 7; brand of Toryism, 8, 12, 161; break with Peel, 40, 63–64, 74; burial, 189; character, 9, 12, 66, 100, 121, 130, 135, 149, 188, 197; children, 10, 75, 84; coal strikes, 41; culture, 197; deafness, 172, 173; death, 187; death of first wife, 10; description, 102; ecologist, 197; economic views, 9; education, 1, 197; ejection from Parliament, 151; establishment, 110, 122; failing health, 172, 178; family origins, 12; friends, 173; gout, 147, 161; hunting, 15; illness, 23, 85, 124, 178, 179, 181, 185; inheritance, 189; investments, 24; Irish loyalism, 50; lack of respectability, 8; litigiosity, 9, 194; magistrate, 23, 163, 164, 188, 193; monument, 189; mother's death, 110; obituaries, 187–188; open-air rallies, 14–15, 118–119; pamphlets, 25; Parliamentary bore, 188; Parliamentary career, 8; Parliamentary motions, 37, 38, 133; Parliamentary speeches, 30–31, 33, 82, 128, 129, 131; paternalism, 140, 149–150, 170; philosophy, 25–26; polical consistency, 82; political achievement, 193; political rows, 42; political views, 9, 20, 78, 79; popularity, 68; private Bill, 45–47; private life, 9, 10, 88; property, 1, 10, 110, 170; publicity, 34; recollections of, 191–193; return to Parliament, 128; royalism, 79; second marriage, 88, 90, 121–122; sport, 197; squabbles, 24–25; supporters, 56; sympathy for suffering people, 47; Tory opinions of, 38; travels abroad, 108, 110, 124, 178; unpopularity, 37–38; Volunteer Corps, 125; Wakefield Deputy Lieutenancy, 86; West Country holiday, 153; widowhood, 75; will challenge, 189–190; wills, 124, 183, 184, 186, 189, 190; withdrawal from Knaresborough, 90; Wool League, 92–107; working man's friend, 162, 194
Feversham, Lord, 48, 51, 56, 59, 168
Fielden, John, 39, 51, 53, 56; Poor Law rallies, 74; statue, 122; Ten Hours Movement, 62, 64, 84, 86
Fielden, Joshua, 164, 180, 181
Fielden, Sam, 124, 168
Fielden, Thomas, 53, 56, 168
Firth, Joe, 191
fishing, 197
Fitzherbert, Sir Henry, 41, 53
Fitzwalter, Lord, 171
Fitzwilliams, Edward, 167
flax, 104
Fleet Papers, 29, 36
Fleming, John, 139, 144, 145, 151, 164
flogging, 20, 22
Follett, Sir William, 61
Forster, W.E., 168, 176
Fortescue, Chichester, 180
Foster, T. Barham, 138
Fountayne Wilson, Richard, 53
Fox, W.J., 100
France, 124, 174, 178–180, 186
franchise, agricultural workers, 176, 187; extension, 196; petitions, 148–149; Reform Act 1832, 1, 156, 159; Reform Act 1867, 8; Reform Act 1885, 187; Reform Bill, 156, 157, 161; universal suffrage, 20, 21, 34, 114; working men, 157, 159, 162, 172
Franco-Prussian War, 174
fraud, Charity Commissioners, 134; industrial frauds, 37
free trade *see also* Corn Laws : attacks on, 115; cause of depression, 183; concept,

3; East Lothian, 92; effect, 95; in religion, 6; Ireland, 105; motions, 43; Peel's policy, 5, 80–81; petitions, 33; principle, 3; rebellion of workers, 172; WBF opposition, 44, 128, 129; worsted industry, 188
French, Fitzstephen, 65, 67

game laws, 3
Garth, Richard, 155
Gascoigne, Misses, 50
Geneva, 49
gentry, 5, 38
Gerard, Sir Robert, 158
Giant's Causeway, 50
Gibson, Milner, 62
Gifford, Dr Stanley, 59
Giggleswick School, 14
Gilmour, Walter, 167
Gilstead, 14, 50
Gladstone, W. E., 33, 75, 120, 137, 173; 1865 administration, 147; disestablishment of Church of Ireland, 170, 171; dissolution of Parliament, 179; franchise to agricultural workers, 176, 187; on Whigs, 141; return to power, 184; WBF attacks on, 155, 162, 174, 187; Westbury affair, 146
Glasgow, 47; spinners' union, 57
Grafton, Duke of, 171
Graham, Sir James, 5, 31, 32, 33, 37; allocation of waste lands, 46; cartoon, 67; character, 70; coal strikes, 40; Corn Laws, 82, 84; Factory Movement, 57, 62, 63, 68, 84; *Great Mott case*, 63–68, 69, 85; opening of private mail, 75; Poor Law, 39, 40, 44; religious policy, 77; separation of poor families, 53, 60; WBF's attacks on, 63, 64, 65, 99; workhouses, 45
Grange Farm, 111
Grant, Frederick, 167
Grant, Isaac Ironside Philip, 56
Granville, Lord, 173
Gray, Sir John, 170
Great Exhibition, 98
Greenwich, 48
Greg, Robert Hyde, 30, 43, 44
Gregg, Dr, 61, 68, 75, 88

Gregg, Tresham, 59
Gregory XVI, Pope, 25
Grenville, Neville, 161
Greville, Charles, 62, 76, 80–81; character, 86; protectionist debates, 81
Grey, Earl, 20, 60
Grey, Ralph, 133
Grey, Sir George, 62, 86, 93, 139
Grimsditch, Thomas, 42, 44
Grimshaw, Mortimer, 113
Grocott, William, 113
Grogan, Edward, 88
Gurdon, William, 170

Haddon, 49
Hadfield, George, 18, 138
Hailstone, Edward, 110
Hailstone, Lilla *see* Ferrand, Lilla
Hailstone, Wilfrid, 186
Halifax, 22; *Great Mott Case*, 67; Oastler Liberation Movement, 53; Poor Law enforcement, 45; treadmills, 73
Halifax, Lord, 174
Hall, Robert, 46, 126
Hall, Sir John, of Dunglass, 92
Hammer, Sir John, 42
Hanson, John, 56
Harden Grange, 1, 13, 22, 24, 111; conditions, 149–150; decline, 191
Harden Manor, 29
Harding, Rev. George, 144
Hardy, Gathorne, 180
Hardy, John, 18, 19, 22, 26, 161; attacks by Liberals, 21; defection to Tories, 16; Oastler Liberation Movement, 53; son, 73; support for WBF, 42; Ten Hours Movement, 62
Harewood, Lord, 8, 79, 89, 182
Harney, Julian, 28, 63
Harris, Charles, 19
Harrison, John, 41
Hart Dyke, William, 158
Hawes, Benjamin, 68
Haworth, 22
Haworth, L., 61
Hay, Sir John, 128
Hearne, Fr Daniel, 64
Heaton, James, 113
Herbert, Percy, 150

Herbert, Sydney, 82, 94, 99
Hey family, 63
Heygate, William, 143
Heywood, Abel, 55
Hill, William, 56
Hindley, Charles, 39, 42, 62, 168
Hoare family, 88
Hobhouse, John Cam, 12
Hobson, Joshua, 27, 53, 56, 57, 63
Hogg, James, 63, 65, 67, 68, 158
Holder, Reuben, 19
Holford, Robert, 161
Holland, Dr George, 45
Holmes, John, 160
Hood, Alexander, 53, 161
Hook, Walter, 56, 63, 86
Hope, Henry, 49, 50
Hope-Scott, James, 171
Hornby, John, 53
Horsfall, John, 113
hounds, 116
House of Lords, 18
Houston, Sir George, 92
Houstoun, Admiral Wallace, 122
Howard Vyse, Richard, 88
Howick, Lord, 42, 43, 61, 66, 68
Howley, Dr, 37
Huddersfield, 17, 18, 22; Oastler Liberation Movement, 51; Operative Conservative group, 47
Hughes, Thomas, 176
Hull, 47
Hull, John, 113
Hume, Joseph, 38, 50, 63, 64; Factory Movement, 84, 87
Hunt, Ward, 146, 180
hunting, 15, 116, 117, 133, 197
Hutt, William, 37
hygiene, 175

Ibbetson, Sir Charles, 16, 22
Illustrated London News, 37
import duties, 5
Improvement Commissioners, 190
income tax, 1842 re-introduction, 5, 73; abolition, 179; Disraeli budget, 109
industrial frauds, 37
Ingestre, Lord, 66
Inglis, Sir Robert, 62, 75, 76, 84, 87

Ingram, Herbert, 37
Ireland, Catholic emancipation, 6; Coercion Bill, 83; flax, 104; free trade, 105; immigrants, 7, 9; O'Connell campaigns, 6; Repeal Movement, 6, 7; Tory policy, 84; WBF contacts, 75; WBF visit, 50; WBF's views, 50, 61–62; Young Ireland, 83

Jackson, Henry, 159, 160, 163
Jacobites, 49
James, Henry, 150, 167
James, Sir Walter, 42
Jermyn Street, 43
Jocelyn, Viscount, 28
John Bull, 31
Johnson, Daniel, 192
Jones, Ernest, 113
Jowett, Benjamin, 63
justice, 182
justices of the peace, 25, 32

Karslake, John, 150
Keighley, 17, 18, 22; Chartists, 28; paupers, 30; Poor Law enforcement, 39, 40, 85; Poor Law Guardians, 25; riots, 191; speeches, 27; waste lands, 45
Keighley Union, 39, 69
Kelly, Fitzroy, 59
Kendall, J.H.F., 167
Kenyon, Lord, 56
Kirby Hall, 93
Kirklees Park, 41
Knaresborough, 8; Anti-Corn Law League, 59, 78; borough, 27; election, 27–29; electors, 45; Operative Conservative group, 47; WBF withdrawal, 90
Knight, Frederick, 48
Knight, Henry, 68
Kydd, Samuel, 113, 114, 115, 124, 129

Labouchère, Henry, 68
Labour League, 112–113; cure for strikes, 114; disappearance, 115; objectives, 114–115
Labour Test Order, 39
Laird, John, 132
laissez-faire, 3
Lancashire, American Civil War, 129;

campaign, 53–56; colliers' petition, 43; cotton famine, 168; cotton operatives, 175; textile industry, 97, 130; Tory strength, 158; tour, 49; wage cuts, 40, 156; workers, 156
Lancashire Relief Bill, 131
landowners, attitude to Poor Law, 4; attitude to 1842 Corn Law, 5; Cobden policy, 92; poaching, 9; WBF support, 34
Lane Fox, George, 50, 80, 86, 164
Langdale, Charles, 27
Lascelles, Arthur, 48
Lascelles, Edwin, 28, 48, 79, 80, 82, 90
Lawrence, Miss, 80
Lawson, Andrew, 27, 28, 39
Lawson, Sir W., 181
Leach, James, 53
Leachman, John, 19
Lechmere, Sir Edmund, 161
Leech, John, 56
Leeds, Operative Conservative group, 47
Leeds Registry, 142–145
Legard, James, 93
Legard, Sir Charles, 183
Leicester, working men, 48, 172
Leith Hay, Sir Andrew, 87
Lewin, Sir Gregory, 26
Lewis, George, 85, 86
Lewis, John, 166
liberty, 3
Liddell, Henry, 68
Lindsay, Hugh, 48
Lister, Sam, 184
Liverpool, 47; *Great Mott Case*, 67
Lockwood, Lady Julia, 153
Lopes, Sir Massey, 147, 150, 161
Low Moor, 21, 86
Lowe, Robert, 133, 137, 152
Lullington Hall, 41

Macaulay, Lord, 68, 84
machinocracy, 47
Mackenzie, Forbes, 105, 167
mail, 75
Malins, Richard, 133, 137, 143
Malmesbury, Lord, 81, 83, 109, 173, 180
Malthus, Rev. Thomas Robert, 4
Manchester, cotton spinners, 33–34; *Great Mott Case*, 67; industrialists, 30; Labour League, 112–113; Operative Conservative group, 47; paupers, 30; rallies, 53, 64; statue of Peel, 114
Manchester School, 3, 5, 9, 194; WBF opposition to, 122, 140
Manners, Henry, 167
Manners, Lord John, 50; 7th Duke of Rutland, 187; allotment dinner, 71, 72; commiseration to WBF, 106–107, 160; condolences to WBF, 83–84; congratulations to WBF, 146–147; Devonport bribery, 147; Factory Movement, 84; fall of Russell, 108; First Commissioner of Works, 117; *Great Mott Case*, 66, 67; letters to WBF, 154, 173, 174, 175, 177, 178, 180; Lilla Ferrand, 183–184, 190; London political assemblies, 155; Oastler Liberation Movement, 53; organisation of agricultural workers, 176, 177; postmaster-general, 180; praise for WBF, 162; shooting, 103; Short Time Bill, 175, 176; Ten Hours Movement, 62, 69, 87, 172; WBF wedding, 90; WBF's friend, 46, 49; Westbury affair, 146; wife's death, 115; Young England, 5
Manners-Sutton, John, 68
Marley Hall, 29, 43
Marsland, Henry, 87
Martineau, Harriet, 3
Marx, Karl, 131, 158
Maule, Fox, 38, 42
Maxwell of Pollock, John, 53
Maynooth College, 7, 75, 76
Mazzini, Giuseppe, 75
McCulloch, 3
McDouall, John, 113
McGeachy, Forster, 68
McHale, Archbishop, 76
McNaughten, Daniel, 41, 57
Mecklenberg-Strelitz, Grand Duke of, 55
Melbourne, Lord, 6, 26, 28
Methodists, 7
Methuen, Lord, 171
Meynell-Ingram, Hugo, 116, 182
Miall, Edward, 169
Micklewaithe, Thomas, 56
Middleton, Lord, 183

Middleton, Walter, 189
Miles, John, 163
Miles, Philip, 81
Miles, William, 82, 83, 161
Miller, James, 90
Milligan, Robert, 48, 70, 71
millocracy, 31, 47
Millocrat, 31
Mills, James, 56
Milner Field, 14
Milner Gibson, Thomas, 44
Milnes Gaskell, James, 22, 28, 50, 61; 1844 Factory Act, 68; waterworks, 112; WBF visits, 73, 86
Milnes, Pemberton, 93
Milton, Viscount, 26, 28
Mitchell, James, 56
Moore, G.H., 113
Morley, Lord, 152
Morley, Samuel, 176
Morpeth, Lord, 16, 22, 26, 196; attacks by WBF, 83; election, 80; Factory Movement, 84; free trade, 79, 80; West Riding by-election, 15
Morrison, Walter, 165
Morton, 27
Mott, Charles, 39, 44; *Great Mott Case*, 39, 44, 63–68, 69, 70, 85, 87
Mulgrave, Lord, 16
Mullineaux, Joseph, 84
Mundella, A.J., 175, 177, 180
Mundy, Edward, 41
Municipal Corporations Act 1835, 1
Muntz, George, 62, 68, 87
Murphy, William, 170
Murray, William, 143
Myers, John, 113
Myrtle Grove, 14, 24

Napoleon, Louis, 118, 120, 124
Navigation Laws, 1
Navy, 128
Neeld, Sir John, 161
nepotism, 133, 141
Nevill, Lord, 160
Newcastle, Duke of, 11
Newdigate, Charles, 53, 83, 87, 168
Newport, Viscount, 49
Nicholson, Samuel, 158

nine-hours campaign, 175, 177, 180
Norman, George, 167
Northcote, Sir Stafford, 180
Northern Star, 27, 31
Northland, Lord, 82
Northwick, Lord, 53, 161
Norton, John, 103
Norwich, 157
Nottingham, 48
Nunns, Thomas, 63
Nuttall, Edward, 54

Oakworth, 59, 69
Oastler, Richard, 4; 1841 campaign, 28; 1842 Corn Law, 33; 1844 Factory Act, 68; 1846, 84, 86; 1849, 92; career, 12; Chartist support, 90; coal strikes, 40; Conservative administration, 32; death, 124; debtors' prison, 25, 27, 51; debts, 59; defeat at Huddersfield, 22; description, 15; Factory Reformation Society, 15; influence on WBF, 11, 86; Labour League, 113; liberation, 59–60; liberation movement, 51–53, 59; meeting with John Wood, 11; opposition to Poor Law, 17, 18, 44; praise of WBF, 30, 32, 35, 44; protectionism, 45, 46; royalism, 19; splitting of movement, 16; statue, 168; Ten Hours campaign, 62, 63, 64; Wakefield riot, 22; WBF friendship, 103; WBF's prison visits, 29, 48; WBF's support, 15, 50
O'Brien, Augustus Stafford, 49
O'Brien, Bronterre, 28
O'Brien, Smith, 83
O'Brien, Stafford, 82, 83, 88
O'Connell, Daniel, 6, 7, 16; arrest, 60; opening of mail, 75; Ten Hours Movement, 63; treatment of, 73; WBF opposition to, 20, 25, 33
O'Connor, Feargus, 122; demagogue, 7; megalomaniac, 26; outrageous, 57; popularity, 27; prison, 28; treatment of, 73; use of 'Tory Chartists,' 90
O'Hara, Charles, 50
Oldham, 47
O'Neill, Viscount, 50
Opium War, 73

Orsini Conspiracy, 117
Osborne, Bernal, 135, 137
Owen, Robert, 15, 28
Oxford Movement, 7

Paget, Lord Clarence, 128, 135; Devonport Enquiry, 148, 151; responsibility in WBF's downfall, 151; WBF defeat to, 132
Pakington, Sir James, 119, 128, 142, 148, 161
Palk, Sir Lawrence, 161
Palliser, Major, 165, 166
Palmer, Sir Roundell, 143, 162
Palmerston, Lord, 8, 96; Charity Board, 137; death, 147; foreign policy, 139; parliamentary triumph, 101; Prime Minister, 116; WBF attacks on, 139; Westbury affair, 146
Paris, 79, 109, 124
Parker, Charles, 166
Parker, Towneley, 158
Parlington Park, 50
patronage, 158–159
Peel, Archibald, 117, 118, 127
Peel, Jonathan, 117
Peel, Sir Robert, 65; 1841 government, 32–33; 1844 Factory Act, 68; break with WBF, 40, 44, 63–64, 74; Corn Laws, 5, 78, 84; death, 101; economic policy, 5; employment legislation, 2; free trade, 80, 81; Irish policy, 6–7, 75; opposition to Disraeli, 49; Poor Law, 39; reform of Church of Ireland, 6; religious policy, 5–7, 77; resignation, 84; statue, 114; Ten Hours Movement, 62, 73, 84; WBF opposition, 76, 78; WBF support, 79; Young England movement, 5
pension list, 20
Perceval, John, 60
Perring, Robert, 26
Perry, Sir Thomas, 117, 119, 120
Philips, Mark, 44, 87
Phinn, Thomas, 146, 150, 151
Pitkeithley, Lawrence, 56
Pitt, Thomas, 56
Pitt, William, 16, 44
Plea for National Holidays, 50
Plug Plot, 55, 100

poaching, 9, 48, 181, 182, 191, 192
Pollard, George, 45
Pollard, Joshua, 21, 56, 124
Pollington, Lord, 28–29, 39, 42, 68
pollution, 154, 161, 163, 186
Pontefract, 48
Poor Law *see also* workhouses : effect, 4; Keighley, 39, 40; Labour Test Order, 39; landmark, 1; local enforcement, 112; migration, 44; opponents, 4–5; political progress, 85; Russell scheme, 87; Tory opposition, 39; WBF opposition, 15, 17, 18, 19, 20, 25, 40, 194; WBF petitions, 45; WBF speeches, 44, 51, 52, 73
Poor Law unions, 17, 30, 41
Poppleston, George, 150, 151
Post office, 75
Potter, Edmund, 128, 131
Powell, Francis, 127, 133, 137
Power, Alfred, 39
Presbyterians, 7
Preston, 47
Price, Captain George, 195
Priestley, Sarah, 14
primogeniture, 3
property rights, 9
Protection Society, 81
protectionism, 43, 44 *see also* Corn Laws; Protectionist Party, 8, 81, 83, 87, 97; WBF convictions, 45, 54, 140
Protestantism, 28, 78, 79, 89
Public Health Act 1848, 1
Pudsey, 47
Puleston, Sir John, 195
Pusey, Sir Philip, 95

Quakers, 100

Radbourne Hall, 41
Raikes, Henry, 152, 153, 162
railways, 158
Rand, John, 21, 168
Rashleigh, William, 49, 51, 56, 59, 86, 88
Rawson, John, 168
Reform Acts *see* franchise
Reform League, 157, 158
religion, 5–7 *see also* particular churches
republicanism, 162
reservoirs, 135, 137–138, 141, 163, 171

Rich, Henry, 27
Richards, John, 27
Richmond, Duke of, 78, 174, 180
riots, Bradford, 92; causes, 44; Keighley, 191; rioters' mail, 75; Wakefield, 22
Rippon, 47
River Commissioners, 154
Robinson, George, 113
Robinson, Admiral Robert, 134
Rodney, Dowager Lady, 90
Roebuck, John, attacks on WBF, 43, 82; cartoon, 67; *Great Mott Case,* 64, 65, 66, 67; opposition to Factory Acts, 68, 83, 84, 87
Roman Catholic Church *see* Catholics
Rose, Philip, 167
Rotch, Benjamin, 27
Rothschild, Baron Mayer de, 106
Rothwell, Captain John, 161
Ruse, James, 113
Russell, Lady Frankland, 106
Russell, Lord John, 5, 6, 25, 65; 1832 Reform Act, 159; 1844 Factory Act, 68; attacks by WBF, 29; fall of administration, 108; new party, 81; Poor Law scheme, 87; repeal of Corn Laws, 78; succession to Palmerston, 147; Ten Hours Movement, 62, 63, 84, 87
Rutland, Duke of, 167, 173, 187
Rutson, William, 93
Ryshworth, 110

Sadler, Michael, 11, 168, 172; 1832 defeat, 12; 1832 *Report,* 12; character, 12; death, 12; influence on WBF, 51, 86; toryism, 12
Salford, 47
Salisbury, Lord, 8, 173, 174, 180; Conservative victory, 187
Sandon, Viscount, 62
Savile, Philip, 71
Schwann, Frederick, 80
Scoresby, Dr William, 64, 75
Scotland, 86, 90
Scott, Sir Walter, 94
self-sufficiency, 101–102
Senior, Nassau William, 3
Seymour, Admiral Sir Michael, 120, 127
Shaftesbury, Lord, 168, 169, 176

Sharp, Francis, 63
Shaw, Frederick, 68
Sheffield, 47
Sheil, R.L., 96
Shipley, 16
Shipley Hall, 41
shooting, 138, 197
Short Time Bill 1872, 175
Short Time Committees, 2, 11, 14, 25
Shrewsbury, Lord, 163
Sibthorp, Colonel, 42, 67, 81, 96
silk weavers, 113
Simons, John, 137
Simpson, James, 90
Sinclair, Lady, 153
Sinclair, Sir John, 51
Skipton, 22, 27
Skirrow, Stephen, 17
slavery, 16
Sleigh, William, 45, 56
Slingsby family, 27, 116
Smith, Adam, 3
Smith, John Abel, 106, 137
Smith, Nicholas, 57
Smith, Samuel, 63
Smythe, George, 5, 49, 50, 66, 103
Snelston Hall, 41
social change, 1828–1852, 1; *nouveaux riches,* 26
socialism, 28, 140
Society for Promotion of National Regeneration, 15
Society for Protection of British Industry, 45
Somerset, Duchess of, 196
Somerset, Duke of, 129, 134, 148, 194
Somerset, Granville, 171
South Lancashire Conservative Association, 156
Sowler, Robert, 53, 56, 158
Spencer, Herbert, 189
Spencer-Stanhope, John, 53
Spofforth, Markham, 142, 153, 167
sport, 197
squirearchy, 38, 41, 68, 77, 191
St Ives, 13, 18, 24; death of WBF's mother, 110; decline, 190; demise, 191; Grange Farm, 111; move to, 111; new mansion, 111; trout stream, 25

Index

Stafford, Augustus, 134, 148
Stalybridge, 44, 174
Stanhope, James, 103
Stanhope, Lord, 45, 53, 96, 102
Stanley, Edward, 33, 65, 78, 161;
  protectionist, 83; WBF attacks on, 66
Starkie, Nicholas Le Gendre, 113, 114
Staveley, Thomas, 50
steamocracy, 47
Stephens, Joseph Rayner, 27, 45, 53, 56, 57, 90
Stockport, 47
Stockport Operative Conservatives, 158
Stocks, William, 56
Stockton, 13
Strathmore, Dowager Countess of, 37
Strickland, 22, 87
strikes, 40, 155, 156
Stuart, Catherine, 49, 88
Stuart, Fiona see Ferrand, Fiona
Stuart, Mary, 189
Stuart-Wortley, James, 21, 22
Stuart-Wortley, John, 15, 18, 26, 28, 33;
  2nd Baron Wharncliffe, 79; 1844 Factory Act, 68; desertion of cause, 94; electoral defeat, 22; opposition to Poor Law, 39; political views, 21; support for WBF, 42
Sturge, Joseph, 56
Sturgeon, Charles, 28
Surtees, W.E, 187
Sutcliffe, Halliwell, 192
Swallow, Luke, 113
Sykes, Sir Tatton, 100
Symonds, Admiral Thomas, 134

Talbot, Earl, 102, 163
Tamsworth, 47
tariffs, 5, 81 see also Corn Laws; free trade
Tempest, John Plumbe, 48
Ten Hours Movement, 1844 campaign, 62–69; 1845–1847, 84–88; creation, 11; leadership, 2, 12; men involved, 21; revival, 16; WBF's conversion to, 11; WBF's dedication to, 126, 194
Tennant, Robert, 100
Test and Corporation Act, 1, 6
Thackrash, Charles, 63
Thierens, John, 122, 139, 153, 164

Thompson, Harry, 93
Thompson, Matthew, 16, 41
Thomson, Poulett, 16
Thornhill, Thomas, 25, 59
Tissington Hall, 41
Todmorden, 18, 55, 181
Tolpuddle Martyrs, 15, 20
Tooke, Joshua, 151
Tories see Conservative Party
Townend case, 154, 161, 162–163
Tractarian Movement, 7, 196
trade unions, 155; 1844 Master and Servant Bill, 69; Short Time Committee, 11; WBF's views, 9
Tredegar, Lord, 161
Treherne, Morgan, 159
Trelawney, Sir John, 84, 133
Trevelyan, George, 176
Trevelyan, Sir John, 53, 87
Trevor, Lord Arthur, 158
Trollope, Anthony, 128, 196
Truck System, 47, 73, 172, 188
T.U.C., 158
Turner, Charles, 158

universal suffrage, 20, 21, 34, 114
Upwood, 22

Venables, George, 171
Verner, Colonel, 50
Victoria, Queen, 19
Villiers, Charles, 43; anti-Corn Laws motions, 34; attacks on WBF, 38, 42; Lancashire Relief Bill, 131; opposition to Corn Laws, 44, 48
Volunteer Movement, 125; volunteers, 125
Volunteer Rifle Corps, 9

wages, agricultural workers, 4, 176; dockers, 141; reduction, 79, 104, 156
Wakefield, Deputy Lieutenancy, 86; Operative Conservative group, 47; riot, 22
Wakley, Thomas, 39
Walker, Sir Baldwin, 134, 135
Walker, Charles, 56, 63
Walker, James, 56
Walker, William, 21, 56, 64, 124; alliance with WBF, 129; death, 158; subsidies to WBF, 63

Walker-Drummond, Sir James, of Hawthornden, 92
Walsall, 47
Walsham, Sir John, 39, 70, 85
Walter, John, 50, 51; Nottingham seat, 48; Poor Law opponent, 44, 74; Ten Hours Movement, 64
Ward, Henry, 42, 64, 68, 84
Wardell, Charles, 158
Warrington, 47
waste lands, 195; Allotment Bill, 45–47, 48, 50
Waterford, Lord, 163
waterworks, 138; Bill, 112; Bingley, 186; Bradford, 135, 138, 141, 163; Bradford Corporation Waterworks, 112; Bradford Waterworks Bill, 168, 171; Committee, 143; mania, 112, 195; safety, 136
Watnuff, Samuel, 148
Weatherhead, David, 56
Wellington, First Duke of, 5, 6, 64
West Bromwich, 47
Westbury, Lord *see* Bethell, Sir Richard
Weymouth, 116
Wharfedale, 15
Wharfedale Agricultural Society, 25
Wharncliffe, Lord, 18, 33, 79
Wheelhouse, William, 167
Whigs, 1830–1841, 5; corn law policy, 5; last government, 5; religious attitudes, 6; religious policies, 6
Whitaker, Charles, 113
White Lion, 19
White, Sir Thomas, 100
Wibsey Moor, 14
Wickham, Henry, 161
widows and orphans, 75
Wigan, 47
Wilde, Henry Sedgwick, 143
Wildman, Abraham, 56
William IV, 18
Williamson, Sir Edworth, 150

Wilson, George, 54, 100
Wilson, James, 117
Wilson, Rev. Richard, 63
Wilton, Lord, 158
Winchilsea, Lord, 76–77
Winn, Roland, 164
Wolverhampton, 47
Wombell, Sir George, 160
Wood, Charles, 83, 87, 134
Wood, John, 11, 63, 168, 172
Wood, Mary, 50
Wood, W.H., 158
wool industry, 104; child workers, 11
Wool League, 9, 98, 99, 100, 101
Wooller Charity, 74
workhouses, 4, 18, 26; Andover, 85, 87; Belper, 44, 73; Derby, 44; separation of mothers and children, 53, 60; treadmills, 45, 73
working men, conservatives, 8, 16, 156; conservatives associations, 125; franchise, 159, 162, 172; WBF popularity with, 47, 194
working time *see* Factory Acts
Worsley, Lord, 46, 50
worsted industry, 16, 21, 188
Wray, Cecil, 56, 64
Wyndham, Charles, 46, 53
Wynn, Charles Williams, 150

Yarde-Buller, 102
Yorke, Henry, 42
Yorke, Richard, 113
Yorkshire, short-time delegates, 33; Toryism, 73, 79; WBF patriotism, 28
Yorkshire Society, 48
Yorkshire Working Men's Conservatives, 157
Young England movement, 5, 187, 194; allotment dinner, 71; cartoon, 67; creation, 49
Young, George, 101